D1266468

# Diversifying Diversity

## Your Guide to Being an Active Ally of Inclusion in the Workplace

Poornima Luthra

*This book is dedicated to*
*my sons Rohan and Tejas,*
*with the hope that the workplaces they will*
*work in will be truly inclusive for all.*

**Diversifying Diversity:**
Your Guide to Being an Active Ally of Inclusion in the Workplace

1st edition, April 2021
Copyright © Poornima Luthra

Author: Poornima Luthra
Book coach: Malene Bendtsen (www.malenebendtsen.com)
Editor: Dina Honour (www.dinahonour.com)
Illustrations: Julie Jahant (www.beyondjuliesart.com)
Book layout: Diren Yardimli
Cover design: Diren Yardimli

While the author has made every effort to provide accurate internet addresses at the time of publication, the author is not responsible for errors or changes that occur after publication. Furthermore, the author does not have any control over and does not assume responsibility for third-party websites or their content.

ISBN Paperback: 979-87-015733-7-4
ISBN Hardback: 978-87-972903-0-9

To continue your journey as an active ally of inclusion, please visit:
diversifyingdiversity.com
talented.dk

# Contents

**Author's Note** 13
**Introduction** 19

**The 12 Dimensions of Diversity** 31
Making the Case for Diversification 33
Intersectionality of Diversity 35
The Benefits of Diversity 39
Improved Financial Performance 40
Improved Talent Management 42
Better Innovation and Team Performance 43
Improved Customer Representation 46
Strengthened Environmental, Social, and Governance (ESG) Performance 52
The Human Barrier to Inclusion 53
Conscious and Unconscious Bias 56
Microaggressions: Subtle Unconscious Biases 63
Systemic Biases 66
Quotas: Positive Discrimination vs Positive Action 66
The Issue of Privilege 72
Managing Bias 75
▶ MAERSK TANKERS 78

**Active Ally of Inclusion (AAI) Model** ........ 85
Being an Active Ally of Inclusion ........ 91
Knowledge ........ 92
Attitude ........ 94
Behaviour ........ 98
▶ Carlsberg Group ........ 105

**Physical & Physiological Dimensions of Diversity** ........ 111
Gender ........ 113
The Socialisation of Gender Biases ........ 120
Gender Biases at Work ........ 124
Diversifying Gender ........ 137
Impact of Gender Bias ........ 141
▶ Ikea Retail (Ingka Group) ........ 149
Sexual Orientation ........ 155
What Has Been Done ........ 159
The Business Case ........ 164
Sexual Orientation Biases at Work ........ 168
The Impact of Sexual Orientation Biases ........ 173
Looking Ahead ........ 176
▶ Telia Company ........ 179
Age ........ 185
Ageism: Is it a Real Thing? ........ 189
Ageism's Power ........ 192
Generational Intelligence (GQ) ........ 193
Generations and Micro-generations ........ 195
Are Generations Really that Different? ........ 206
Physical Abilities and Appearances ........ 209
Ableism ........ 213
The -isms of Appearance ........ 225
Lookism: Beauty and Dressing Bias ........ 226
Weightism: Weight Bias ........ 229
Heightism: Height Bias ........ 232
Hairism: Hair Bias ........ 233
▶ Be My Eyes ........ 235

**Cognitive Dimensions of Diversity** .......... 241
Education .......... 243
"We Only Hire From the Ivy League" .......... 247
Expanding the Pool .......... 250
▶ PROJECT ACCESS INTERNATIONAL .......... 253
Experiences & Skills .......... 259
Hiring for Similarity .......... 262
Hiring an Ex-convict: Would You Do It? .......... 267
Personality & Ways of Working .......... 273
Personality Bias .......... 278
Ways of Thinking and Learning .......... 283
The Power of Neurodiversity .......... 285
Fighting the Neurotypical Bias .......... 288
▶ STACK RECRUITMENT .......... 292

**Social and Lifestyle Dimensions of Diversity** .......... 297
Ethnicity & Culture .......... 299
The History of Racism .......... 303
Racism and Intersectionality .......... 306
Ethnic Diversity at Work .......... 309
Ethnic Biases at Work .......... 313
Your Cultural Thumbprint™ .......... 331
Beliefs and Practices .......... 343
The Hijab, Turban and Bindi .......... 346
What I Eat & Drink Somehow Matters? .......... 349
Marital & Parenthood Choices .......... 357
The Maternal Wall .......... 360
Support for Mothers .......... 361
Breaking Down the Wall .......... 365
▶ KROMANN REUMERT .......... 368
Socio-economic Background .......... 375
The Ubiquity of Classism .......... 377
Classism at Work .......... 381

**Active Allyship in Action**......385
Active Ally of All Genders......390
Active Ally of All Sexual Orientations......395
Active Ally of All Generations......399
Active Ally of All Physical Abilities and Appearances......402
Active Ally of Cognitive Diversity......408
Active Ally of All Ethnicities and Cultures......413
Active Ally of Beliefs and Practices......419
Active Ally of Marital and Parenthood Choices......423
Active Ally of Socio-Economic Backgrounds......427

**Final Thoughts**......433
**Thank You**......437
**About the Author**......439
**Endnotes**......441

# Author's Note

*"We cannot change what we are not aware of,*
*and once we are aware, we cannot help but change."*

SHERYL SANDBERG, *Chief Operating Officer of Facebook*

If you had asked a futurist in the early 1900s - a time when women were fighting for the right to vote - to predict what equality would look like in the year 2020, it is likely they would have predicted absolute equality for all. Yet today, a century later, inequality remains pervasive in both society and in our workplaces.

How is it that women are still struggling to sit at senior leadership tables and fighting for equal pay? Gender inequality at the top is so lopsided that there are more male CEOs named Peter than female CEOs on the FTSE 100; more CEOs named John than female CEOs on the Fortune 500; and more Thomases than women on executive boards in Germany.

How is it that decades after Mahatma Gandhi and Martin Luther King fought for racial justice, minority races continue to battle discrimination and prejudice in workplaces and in wider society?

Inequality is certainly not limited to gender and race, and the issue is not new – it is age old, with roots deeply steeped in history. There are numerous root causes of discrimination, privilege, and ideas of supremacy that include, but are not limited to, colonisation and slavery.

There has been effort, and progress. We have seen gradual increases in gender and racial representation in our workplaces as Diversity and Inclusion (D&I) has become a cornerstone of many organisations' human resource (HR) strategy. The #MeToo and Black Lives Matter movements have forced organisations to make concrete efforts towards addressing gender and racial inequalities in their workplaces, including strategy, structures, practices and even in their product lines. We have seen companies pull skin-whitening products off the shelves. We have seen brands remove or rebrand products which emphasized racial stereotypes, like Aunt Jemima's syrup and Uncle Ben's rice. We have seen brands like Crayola expand their crayon colour range to include diverse skin tones.

These are all steps in the right direction, but this progress is not nearly enough. Vast inequalities remain: we only need look at the dismal representation of women in corporate boardrooms, the low representation of women in STEM (Science-Technology-Engineering-Math) industries, police brutality against the Black community in America, as well as homophobic or Islamophobic sentiments in parts of the world.

When we look at our own workplaces, can we truly say they are diverse? Are we hiring employees who are physically challenged, or part of the neurodiverse community? Do we have an environment where our colleagues from the LGBTQ+ community feel comfortable to openly be themselves? Do we make efforts to embrace the breadth of people's educational backgrounds, skills, perspectives, beliefs, values, ways of working and parenthood choices? You may be shaking your head.

There is widespread agreement that inclusion is (1) the right thing to do and (2) necessary to embrace the diversity that drives employee engagement and innovation. So why have we not been able to achieve the inclusive workplaces we desire? While the answer to that question may be extremely complex, what we really need is a different way of looking at the concept of diversity itself. In my work, I have noticed two gaps. First, our view of diversity has been too narrow. We need to embrace the true range of diversity in the workforce, or *talent,* in our workplaces. Second, there are many of us who feel we lack the knowledge, vocabulary and confidence to be an ally; afraid of being shamed and attacked by the very groups of colleagues we seek to support. These two gaps are holding us back from making greater progress towards truly diverse and inclusive workplaces.

We need a way forward. A way that embraces the true breadth of diversity. A way that includes all and is about not just some, but all of us. For too long, the focus has been too narrow, placing blame on the majority while supporting the minority. This has not helped us move forward as fast or as far as we would have liked. Instead, we are left with colleagues who may be scared to openly support and be active allies. Some colleagues may feel D&I does not concern them directly, that it is someone else's problem. Some are unsure of what to do. We have colleagues who themselves come from minority groups which are overlooked, who experience biases and discrimination, and feel unincluded.

I wrote this book with the hope that it will motivate us to look at diversity more broadly. I will delve into twelve dimensions of diversity, making the case for why each is worthy of being an integral part of an ambitious D&I strategy in your organisation, and why having diverse talent will benefit that organisation. I will also make the case from the viewpoint of the talent within our workplaces, shedding light on the biases experienced by the minority in each dimension. I will discuss the causes, as well as the impact, of these biases on individuals, teams and organisations. Most importantly, I wrote this book to help you become an active ally for all rather than just a few - in your organisation and beyond.

Perhaps you work in an organisation that is diverse or is seeking to be more diverse. Perhaps you want to improve your personal interactions with your diverse colleagues and are looking for concrete ways to be an ally of inclusion. Or perhaps you are someone seeking to gain a broader understanding about diversity itself. Maybe you manage a diverse team. Or perhaps you are a CEO, CHRO, VP or Chief Diversity Officer. You may be part of the senior leadership team of a large corporation, or small-medium enterprise, or the founder of a start-up. This book has been written both about you and for you.

I believe the topic of D&I is not just a rational one, but an emotive one. Yes, organisations need a business case for D&I. At the same time, it should also be about doing the right thing for fellow human beings.

In my D&I training sessions, university lectures and keynote speeches, I bring together relevant research and data, interweaving them with company case studies, stories, and anecdotes. I have found this effective in convincing employees, managers and leaders of the need for diversity and the benefits of inclusion.

This book has been written in the same vein, to empower you to become an active ally of inclusion by:

- helping you empathise with a deeper understanding of topics you may not have fully understood before
- providing you with a global perspective of D&I
- giving you the vocabulary and knowledge needed to stimulate courageous, honest and open dialogue
- making you question your own biases and those of others
- enabling you to take action to make your workplace inclusive for all
- providing inspiration from companies who are taking concrete steps to make their workplaces, products and services more inclusive to their diverse talent and customers

Along the way, you can expect to get uncomfortable and you may wriggle in your seat. We need to get uncomfortable to move forward. I invite you to keep an open mind. Go on, turn the page…

*Poornima*

# Introduction

*"When a flower doesn't bloom,*
*you fix the environment in which it grows,*
*not the flower."*

Alexander Den Heijer,
Dutch inspirational speaker, trainer, and consultant

# Embracing the Diversity of Humans

We are a planet of over 190 countries and close to 8 billion people. Imagine the differences - and the resulting biases - amongst us. *Diversifying Diversity* starts with recognising that diversity comprises many dimensions.

What would you say if I asked you to describe yourself? You may mention your gender and maybe your ethnicity or race but it's likely there is more about yourself you would share. You may share your age, background, culture, sexual identification; whether you are married or in a relationship; you may talk about your children, or your profession. You may share your struggle with your weight or the fact that you are dyslexic or autistic. There are so many aspects that make us uniquely diverse; some visible; others invisible. The dimensions of diversity are much like a thumbprint; unique to each of us.

We tend to notice the visible dimensions of diversity first. Our brain categorises - and judges - others based on gender, ethnicity, skin colour and age. However, it requires an active and conscious effort to grasp the complex weave of intersecting diversity dimensions - both visible and invisible - which constitute who we are. It is this intersectionality which makes it challenging to fully embrace diversity in our workplaces and thereby be truly inclusive. Addressing just one, or even several dimensions of diversity, does not yield the positive results we expect because we continue to experience bias and discrimination in other dimensions.

A truly inclusive organisation embraces diversity holistically, so that each of us can bring our whole diverse selves to work while minimizing the biases experienced. This is the key to transforming our workplaces to fit our talent, rather than expecting our talent to fit our workplaces.

In this book, the word *talent* is used to refer to a company's entire workforce.

Diversity, and its closely related terms equity, equality, and inclusion, are certainly having their moment in the limelight and rightfully so. These terms may be widely used in today's context but understanding the nuances between them is crucial to developing a thorough understanding of the subject.

When we diversify diversity, we stand to gain the commitment from those unable to fully relate to the vision of Diversity and Inclusion (D&I), even if they themsleves have experienced some form of discrimination. Many see inclusion only as empathizing with someone else's experiences of bias and discrimination. When

**Diversity-Equity-Equality-Inclusion**

*Diversity* is everywhere. Embracing diversity implies understanding that each person is unique and recognizing that people have differences across a range of human qualities or dimensions. *Surface-level diversity dimensions* are those that are visible and include, but are not limited to, sex, race, age, body size, or visible disabilities. *Deep-level diversity dimensions* are those that are invisible and include, but are not limited to, thinking styles, perspectives, experiences, values, and beliefs.

*Equity* implies understanding and acknowledging differences to ensure that support is provided to level the playing field. Equity acknowledges the existence of systemic biases and makes amends for those.

*Equality* has to do with fairness, but does not take into account differences. In a just, ideal world free from systemic biases, everyone would have fair and equal experiences, and therefore equal access to tools and opportunities.

*Inclusion* is embracing an environment where everyone is respected and appreciated as valuable members, where their voice is heard, and where they feel a sense of belonging.

it comes to human behaviour, however, nothing makes us want to change the things around us more than when we personally connect with them. By expanding the dimensions of diversity we look at, we can garner active support from much larger groups of people - as allies of inclusion - who can better connect to D&I through their own personal stories of discrimination and exclusion.

I recall a training session during which a White, male leader of a large global company shared: "Most people think of me as an old, White man. I want people to stop thinking of me *only* as a White man. For me, the fact that I am from Portugal matters more to me than being a White man; the fact that I have had a major surgery matters to me more than being a White man. And yet, all people see is an old, White man".

If each one of us can see that we all have dimensions of diversity which make us different from others, we are likely to be more motivated to make concrete efforts, both individually and collectively, to ensure inclusive cultures. This requires a fundamental mindset shift in the way we think about D&I. At its core, we must begin to recognise the breadth of dimensions across which each person is different. In order to create value for all, we need organisations to be ready, in both their D&I strategy and workplace culture, to embrace all the dimensions of diversity which their talent brings to the workplace.

In her book *Invisible women: Exposing Data Bias in a World Designed for Men*, Caroline Criado Perez forces us to consider a world created and built by men.[1] In Chapter 9, titled 'A Sea of Dudes', she highlights that when a woman is involved in a car crash, she is 47% more likely to be seriously injured than a man. Why? One of the main reasons is that the crash test dummy used for car safety tests is much taller and heavier than the average woman. The implication? The cars we drive were never tested to be safe for women.

When reading this aloud to my husband who is ethnically Indian, he pointed out that the crash test dummy's constitution did not represent him - and millions of other men - either.

This made me wriggle in discomfort. We need to create and nurture a world that is built and functions for all, not just the privileged few who make up the core of decision makers. Our organisations, and in fact our societies, have been created by and for the majority. The expectation is that "others", those who are not part of the majority groups, must make substantial efforts to "fit in" with the prototype or model of an ideal employee. This needs to change.

## Why are we not there yet?

Historically, the human race has made significant progress only when we have come together as exactly that – a human race – to address big issues such as war, disease or economic crises. D&I is no different. We are at a unique point in human history. We have the chance to shape the world our children and their children grow up into – a world where the diversity of human beings is fully embraced, where inclusion is assumed. A world where the different basis for biases and discrimination are minimised. We need a broader view of diversity, and a deeper understanding of what is required to be fully inclusive. For that to happen, we need everyone on board. In our workplaces that means that alongside minority groups we need White men and women; we need majority nationalities; we need straight people; we need able-bodied persons; we need those who are neurotypical; and we need the old and the young. To really move the needle on D&I, we need the

**The fallacy of "fit"**

vast majority of talent in our workplaces, regardless of position and role, to commit to being an ally of inclusion.

In our workplaces, we are facing two major challenges with D&I: (1) we are not looking at diversity broadly enough, leaving significant dimensions of diversity and bias ignored and (2) we do not have everyone on board as an ally of inclusion.

Before we go further, it is a good idea to have a common understanding about who an ally of inclusion is. An *ally of inclusion* is someone who demonstrates inclusive behaviours even if the issues at hand do not directly affect their personal identity. An *active* ally of inclusion is one who has a deep understanding of the issues surrounding D&I, has the right attitude towards making workplaces more inclusive for all, and demonstrates frequent and consistent behaviours that are inclusive. We will develop this idea further in the upcoming chapter on the Active Ally of Inclusion (AAI) model.

While it is important that those who form the majority step up as active allies for inclusion, they are not the only ones who are not fully onboard as allies. In particular, we need minorities in positions of power and influence to be on board as allies. Many are not. In my experience, one reason is that many have had to alter their natural behaviour to "fit in" with the majority. I speak from experience, I have done this as well. Minorities are crucial for inclusion progress because we have often felt and experienced discrimination and can act as a bridge to greater understanding. We need minorities to be actively on board.

So how do we get everyone - the minorities and the majorities - on board? Until now, not everyone has felt a personal connection or identified with their organisation's D&I efforts. D&I is often perceived as an issue for the minority and the few active allies who think it is 'the right thing to do'. Often, I have observed that when we place emphasis on inclusion for women in D&I strategy, we end up losing the interest of men. This is not necessarily because they do not want to support women, but simply because they do not fully connect with the strategy, know how to support it, or both. Similarly, when we address ethnic diversity, we alienate the majority ethnic groups. Again this could be because they feel "it doesn't concern me" or "I don't know what I should be doing". How do we change this way of looking at diversity? At the same time, how do we encourage everyone to be active allies?

The answer to these questions and challenges lies in *diversifying diversity.* We need to approach diversity holistically and in a way that everyone feels personally invested. Many people are genuinely looking for ways in which to be an intentional ally of inclusion, but they may lack the understanding on how to be an *active* ally. I have often heard my corporate trainees, those who belong to the majority groups, express a feeling of lacking the vocabulary and knowledge to engage in conversations with their minority colleagues about biases and discrimination.

In the first half of 2020, following the Black Lives Matter movement and the resulting protests in the wake of the murder of George Floyd, I found myself further reflecting upon why we are not making adequate progress towards equity and equality for women and ethnicity minorities. My conversations with clients and colleagues revealed that most people outside of The United States of America - be it White men and women in Europe, members of the Chinese community in Singapore or Indians in Mumbai - were condemning the discrimination suffered by African Americans, but nothing really substantial beyond that. Very few, beyond those leading major organisations, were looking for ways to do something concrete and meaningful about discrimination. Some had check-ins with their African American colleagues or held a meeting to discuss the issue. Few offered anything more than that. Why? Why were these majority groups not doing more?

At that time, I came across an article written by a Singaporean Chinese woman living in Australia. The author shared her experiences of discrimination when, simply by virtue of looking Oriental, she was viewed as the cause of the COVID-19 pandemic. She certainly was not alone. During the pandemic, those who looked Oriental faced COVID-19 related racial slurs, and even violence, in London, Paris and New York. What struck me was her statement that she had never faced racism until that point. This was a shock. I grew up in Singapore and experienced plenty of racism. How is it that she and I had such varied experiences of the same country? The reality is that the majority, in any context, do not experience situations the same way as the minority. They are therefore often unable to identify with aspects of bias and discrimination; until, that is, they face discrimination themselves. While conceptually many know D&I is the right thing to do; it still isn't seen as something that concerns them directly. This way of thinking is problematic. This mindset is a barrier to inclusion; it leads to indifference and inaction.

This book helps address these challenges by defining diversity broadly enough to represent us all, whilst providing people with the knowledge and tools to be an active ally. The purpose is to help us all - individually and collectively - become more active allies in order to nurture inclusive workplaces that harness the benefits of the diverse talent in our organisations. Whether you are an individual employee, manager of a team, or leader of an organisation, this book will help you on your path towards and in active allyship.

# The 12 Dimensions of Diversity

*"Diversity drives innovation –*
*when we limit who can contribute,*
*we in turn limit what problems we can solve."*

Telle Whitney,
former CEO and President of the Anita Borg
Institute for Women and Technology

# Making the Case for Diversification

While the concept of diversity has existed for decades, we need a new way to define the concept to reflect both the visible and invisible diversity of talent in our workplaces. We need to address a wider range of biases and discrimination in order for everyone to be personally invested and thereby see themselves as allies of inclusion. This involves *diversifying diversity.*

So, what are the dimensions of diversity which will enable organisations to do this?

Recently there has been increased discussion in business related publications like Harvard Business Review regarding the need to address biases in our workplaces; biases based on sexual orientation, physical disabilities, age and most recently, neurodiversity. With gender and ethnicity being the predominant dimensions in organisations' efforts to make their workplaces more diverse and inclusive, these other dimensions have not yet received the attention or traction needed. Gender and ethnicity are extremely important, and we need to continue the work being done in these areas. At the same time, the diversity of human beings is so much more than our gender and ethnicity; it includes age, physical abilities, physical appearance, our educational background, skills, ways of working, learning and thinking, our sexual orientation, beliefs and values, socio-economic background and the choices we make about marriage and parenthood.

These visible and invisible diversity dimensions can be divided into three categories: *physical and physiological*, *cognitive* as well as *social and lifestyle*. Gender, sexual orientation, and age, along with physical abilities and appearances, constitute the physical and physiological dimensions of diversity. The cognitive dimension looks at diversity in education, experiences and skills, personality, and ways of working, as well as ways of thinking and learning. Finally, the social and lifestyle category includes the diversity of ethnicity and culture, beliefs and practices, and marital and parenthood choices in addition to socio-economic background.

These dimensions of diversity affect many aspects of organisational life for employees. They play a role in who gets hired - and who does not - how employees progress through the organisation, the opportunities they are given, how they are assessed and how they are rewarded. A cultural dimension may affect how someone dresses for work, or the food they eat. It may affect which companies, organisations, or locations are appealing, their working hours and their work habits, along with what motivates them. Diversity dimensions can affect how someone prefers to be led or how they lead others, the ways they communicate and how they prefer to receive or provide feedback. Diversity dimensions may influence a person's ability to identify with the strategy of the company, or with its products and services. It can even affect the way the phys-

**Does your meeting room look this diverse? If not, who is missing?**

**Diversifying Diversity (DD) Model**

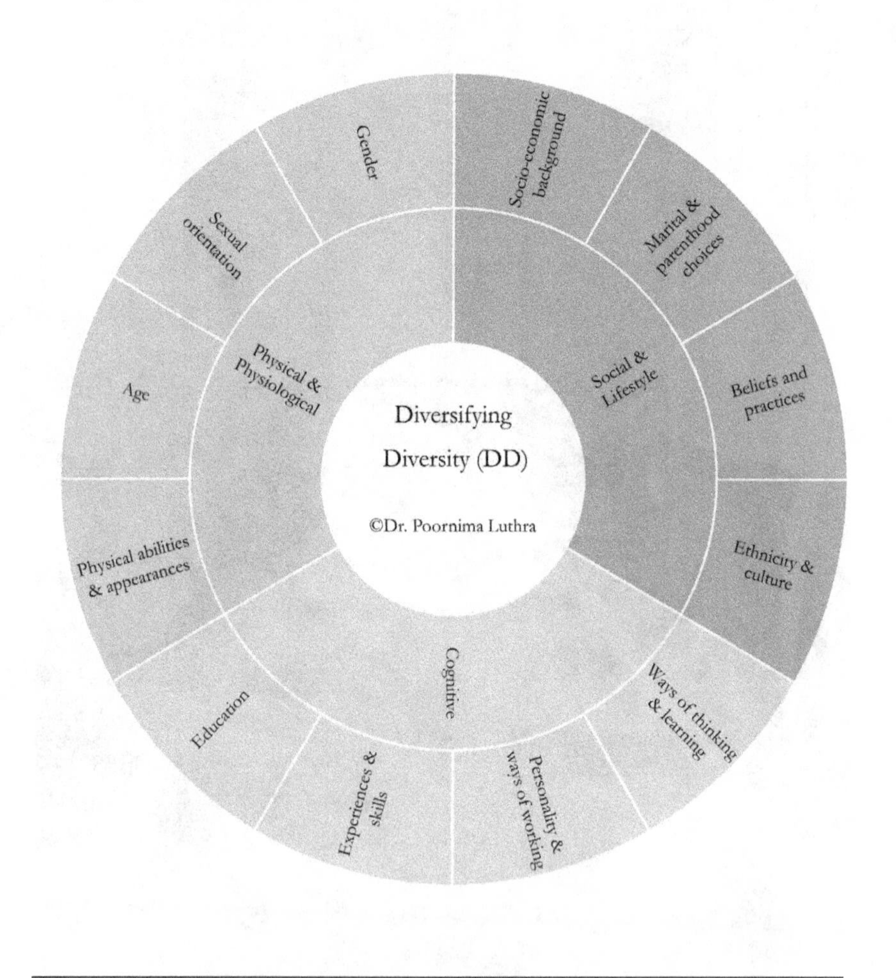

ical space of the workplace is laid out, making provisions for those with physical disabilities, those with neurodiverse needs, or those with religious requirements such as the need for prayer rooms.

## Intersectionality of Diversity

Dimensions of diversity do not exist in isolation; they intersect with each other to form the complex weave of diversity which is unique to each person. In embracing diversity and nurturing inclusive workplaces, we must recognise this intersectionality. We must acknowledge the interplay between dimensions, for these multiple dimensions of diversity influence each other to define our thoughts, attitudes and behaviour.

In 2010, Black feminist Moya Bailey coined the term *misogynoir* in a blog post where she discussed misogyny toward Black women in hip hop music. Bailey combined the terms misogyny and noir to describe the anti-Black sexism faced by Black women, encompassing more than one dimension of diversity. In this case, race and gender. Within our organisations, there are many groups of talent who are similarly living multiple dimensions of diversity. The interaction between those dimensions makes one's experiences much more complex, yet no less important, to address.

On the next page is a short list of some of the intersectional diversity dimensions that may be present in your organisation, amongst your fellow team members and colleagues. Do you recognise any of them in your colleagues? Your leadership? Perhaps even yourself? While intersectionality makes diversity even more complex to unpack, understand and manage, to truly have inclusive workplaces for all, it is even more necessary for us to do so.

**Intersectionality of diversity**

Before we begin to look at diversity diversely, it may be a good idea to step back and ask ourselves why do we want diversity in our workplaces at all? What are the advantages? Is diversity really all it is made out to be? Before we proceed, we need to be convinced of the need for diversity. For those of you already sure of the necessity of diversity, the next section should serve as a reminder. For those who need or want to be convinced, or even those who may be curious to learn just how far the benefits extend, the next section is for you.

# The Benefits of Diversity

Embracing diverse talent means there is the real possibility for intergroup tensions and competition. Conflict and misunderstandings, culture clashes, and even distrust may arise. This can lead to lower morale and productivity, absenteeism and even turnover. It does not seem like I am making a robust case for diversity, does it? These negative outcomes are further heightened for individuals who are not able to bring their whole diverse selves to work. Such negative outcomes of putting inclusion in the spotlight are real possibilities, but if managed well, the *positive* impact of diversity in workplaces almost certainly outweighs the negative.

Glassdoor, the world's largest job and recruiting site, conducted a 2019 survey in the United States (US), United Kingdom (UK), France and Germany, in which 64% of the workers surveyed said their company was investing more in Diversity and Inclusion (D&I) than in prior years.[2] For many organisations, this has meant creating new roles within the company to spearhead change. Globally, from 2015 to 2020,[3] there has been a 107% increase in the number of companies hiring talent into Head of Diversity roles, a 75% increase in companies with Director of Diversity roles, and a 68% increase in companies with Chief Diversity Officer roles. Coca-Cola, Mastercard, Bank of America, British Petroleum, Netflix, General Motors, Walmart, Harvard University, Accenture, and Adidas are just a few of the large global companies who have specific senior leadership roles for D&I. And while the US seems to be the bedrock of recent D&I movements, it is interesting to note that the UK employs almost twice as many D&I workers (per 10,000 employees), with Australia, the US, Ireland, and Canada rounding out the top five.

There is no doubt companies are increasingly investing more resources into D&I. But why?

One of the most important underlying drivers for embracing diversity is that it is perceived as the *right thing to do*. One could argue that is reason enough. However, for those who need something more than being 'the right thing to do' to justify investing resources, the business case for embracing diverse talent and nurturing inclusive workplaces is strong, and, in recent years gained widespread acceptance.

## Improved Financial Performance

A 2020 McKinsey & Company's global study of more than 1,000 companies in 15 countries found that organisations in the top quartile of gender diversity were 25% more likely to perform better on profitability (measured through average EBIT margins) if they had gender diverse executive teams. The percentage rose to 28% if the organisation had gender-diverse boards. Organisations in the top quartile for ethnic/cultural diversity among executives were 36% more likely to achieve above-average profitability. At the other end of the spectrum, companies in the bottom quartile for both gender and ethnic/cultural diversity were 27% *less* likely to experience profitability above the industry average.[4]

There is more. A 2017 BCG study shows that companies with more diverse management teams have 19% higher revenues due to innovation.[5] Credit Suisse Research Institute found that companies in which women held 20% or more management roles generated 2.04% higher cash flow returns on investment than companies with 15% or less women in management roles.[6] Bloomberg reports that companies with gender-balanced teams have a higher

**The benefits of D&I**

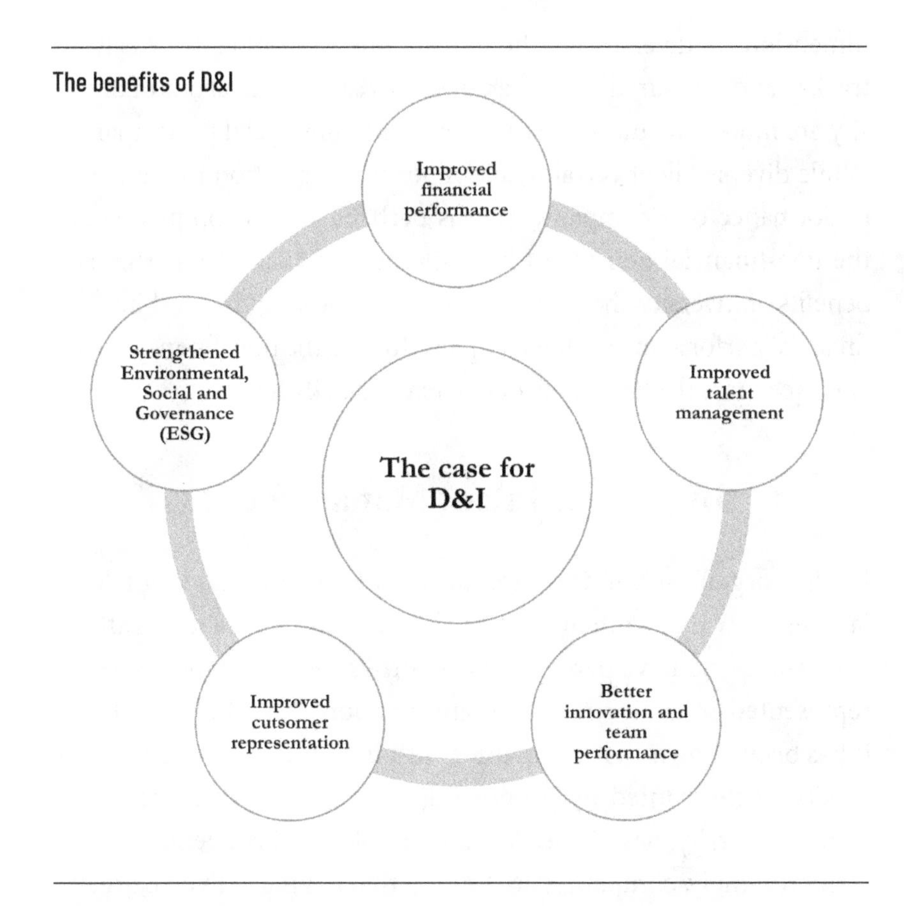


return on equity; and large UK firms whose executive boards were one-third female were 10 times more profitable on average than all-male boards.[7] Many other studies show similar improved financial performance in gross and net margins, internal rate of return, investment performance, market value, operating profit margin, Return on Assets (ROA), Return on Equity (ROE), Return on Sales (ROS) and sales performance[8] from having diverse talent.

One thing to note is that the research to date has focused on assessing the financial impact of gender and ethnic diversity. These two dimensions of diversity are the visible dimensions that can easily be tracked and measured. However, many invisible dimensions of diversity are more difficult to measure and link to financial performance. While diverse talent certainly has a positive impact on the financial performance of a company, what is perhaps just as compelling are the non-financial benefits of having a diverse talent pool. The true benefits of diversity should be viewed more broadly, beyond just the financial performance of the company. In fact, the non-financial benefits are where the true value of diversity actually lies.

## Improved Talent Management

Diverse organisations are better at recruiting and retaining talent. Studies show that women are more likely to apply for a job in an organisation, and have perceptions of fairness, when women are well represented in senior management positions.[9] At the same time, it has been shown that companies with higher levels of gender diversity, accompanied by supporting HR policies which promote gender diversity, have lower levels of employee turnover.[10]

Increasingly, companies are finding that having a diverse organisation and inclusive workplaces is a key factor in attracting younger talent. A 2016 survey by Weber Shandwick, one of the world's leading global public relations firms, shows that 47% of Millennials are actively looking for diversity and inclusion when sizing up potential employers.[11] Managers and leaders I have worked with have reported an increase in younger talent asking prospective employers questions related to diversity and inclusion. Questions such as: "What does your company actively do to increase diversity?" or "What has your company done in the past year to create a more inclusive culture internally?". Even "How do you ensure your product line is able to meet the needs of your diverse customer group?". The 2020 Deloitte Millennial Survey shows that Millennials and Gen Z expect leaders to ensure "diversity and inclusion across the organisation"[12] and that diversity/ inclusion is seen as being essential to keep these generations "happy" at work.[13]

While diverse organisations certainly attract more diverse talent through their doors, also worth noting is that employees' experience of inclusion - also known as a company's "diversity climate" - plays a key role in improved job satisfaction and commitment to the company,[14] as well as greater trust,[15] employee engagement and retention.[16] *Diversity climate* is defined as "inclusive work cultures characterized by appreciation of individual differences and the adoption of practices to advance underrepresented groups".[17] Research shows evidence that organisations with incluisve work cultures have reduced incidents of interpersonal aggression and discrimination, with women experiencing less discrimination and episodes of sexual harassment in such inclusive cultures.[18] What is really interesting is that just a 10% increase in perceptions of inclusion reduces absenteeism, adding nearly one day a year in work attendance per employee.[19] A little change certainly goes a long way in this case.

## Better Innovation and Team Performance

One of the most significant non-financial benefits of a diverse talent pool is the richness of creative thoughts and breadth of ideas, insights and approaches. Having talent with different backgrounds, experiences and perspectives results in innovative solutions. A 2017 BCG report showed that diversity in gender, nationality, career path, and industry background among managers are all highly linked to innovation.[20] The same report also showed that companies with diverse, innovative management teams earned more as a result of that innovation. Over a three year period, companies with more diverse management earned, on average, 38% more of their revenues from innovative products and services than those companies with lower diversity.

Why is this the case, you ask? Well, homogeneous groups tend to succumb to groupthink.[21] *Groupthink* is a psychological phenomenon where people within a group engage in dysfunctional or irrational decision making in an effort to maintain harmony or conformity. The American Psychological Association defines groupthink as "a strong concurrence-seeking tendency that interferes with effective group decision making. Symptoms include apparent unanimity, illusions of invulnerability and moral correctness, biased perceptions of the outgroup, interpersonal pressure, self-censorship, and defective decision-making strategies".[22] Homogenous teams are more likely to design and solve problems in a way that is most helpful to users and customers who sound and behave like them. Diverse teams, on the other hand, leverage the variety of perspectives and experiences and consider information more thoroughly and accurately,[23] resulting in faster problem solving,[24] as well as decisions and intellectual output of higher quality.[25]

It should be emphasized that it is not just about diversity in a company's talent pool, but ensuring there is an inclusive culture which supports this variety of perspectives. It is the merger of these perspectives which results in synergistic benefits. In fact, employees' overall experiences of inclusion may help explain 49% of problem-solving in teams and 18% of employee innovation.[26] Companies with such an inclusive culture and accompanying D&I policies are shown to have a 59.1% increase in creativity, innovation, and openness.[27]

**Why don't we have new ideas?**

## Improved Customer Representation

The drivers for diverse talent extend beyond the organisation itself. Many companies today do not just have customers from their local or regional markets. Their customers are global and diverse. To truly understand the needs of various markets requires companies to bring aboard talent and leadership which represents the diversity of their customers. This diverse talent would have the ability to (1) create products and services which meet the diversity of customers' needs and preferences in the various markets the company operates, or is seeking to operate in; and (2) create inclusive marketing and advertising campaigns which represent the diversity of customers. The result is improved customer satisfaction[28] and enhanced brand image.

At a speech at New York University's Tandon School of Engineering and the Stern School of Business in February 2017, Microsoft's Satya Nadella shared that, "an aspect we are focused a ton on is we say we want to empower the world, everyone and every organization. That means we have got to look like everyone and every organization in the world". This involves embedding an inclusive mindset into design thinking while maintaining diverse representation within the organisation, one which reflects the organisation's customer base.

There are numerous companies in a variety of industries that have made efforts - some in response to the continued Black Lives Matter movement in 2020 - to have products and services that better reflect the diversity of their customers. Mattel has certainly evolved in the diversity of its Barbie dolls over the past six decades. The brand now includes dolls that reflect 9 body types, 35 skin tones, 94 hairstyles, and over 200 professions. The line includes a doll with vitiligo, (a loss of skin pigment cells), a doll with no hair, and dolls in wheelchairs. Lego chose bright yellow as a neutral skin colour for its figurines, and includes figures that are gender-neutral, have different mobility needs, and that are neutral of physical shape and size. Lego has also made conscious efforts to have female characters in STEM (Science, Technology, Engineering and Math) roles.

Many clothing manufacturers have created more inclusive product lines, sensitive to the variety of sizes within their customer base. Others have moved away from using models that perpetuate outdated and dangerous stereotypes of an ideal shape or size. J.Crew and American Eagle now cast models of different sizes. In 2019, plus-size brand 11 Honoré opened New York Fashion Week. H&M, ASOS and Balenciaga are increasing efforts to include gender-fluidity in their campaigns.

In May 2020, Crayola introduced "Colours of the World", a box of 24 or 32 crayons created to represent the rich diversity of skin tones and eye colours. In June of the same year, Band-Aid followed suit and unveiled a new line of plasters in varying shades of Black and brown. Some of you may be wondering what took Crayola and Band-Aid so long? I hear you, but I am glad those companies finally recognized the need for representation. Now children like mine can proudly - and accurately - colour themselves in their drawings or choose a bandage that matches their skin colour to help heal their wounds.

At the same time, some industries still have a long way to go. In the global fintech industry, only 12% of employees are women. In the UK, less than 30% of the fintech workforce are female[29] and women make up only 17% of senior roles.[30] Of the founders of fintech50 companies, only 5% are women.[31] Coin Dance, a company that tracks bitcoin users, found that females account for only 5.7% of investors.[32] A study by the OECD found that women entrepreneurs face biases from the outset.[33] Having just one woman on a startup founding team reduces the probability of securing funding by 5-10%. Those women-led teams who do succeed in securing funding receive, on average, one-third less than their all-male counterparts.

A comprehensive study by Boston Consulting Group (BCG)[34] shows that despite women controlling 32% of the world's wealth, "women remain largely underserved by the wealth management community. Too many banks and firms rely on broad assumptions about what women are looking for, resulting in products, services, and messaging that can feel superficial at best and condescending at worst". The results of the study reveal that women's investment priorities differ from men's, but in ways that go beyond conventional assumptions – for women, wealth is a means to an end and not an end in itself; women make decisions based on facts not gut; millennial women are taking charge of their own wealth; and cultural differences play a crucial role in shaping investment behaviour. The study also revealed that firms in this industry view women as a homogeneous group, ignoring the vastly different needs and preferences of different female clients, instead relying on prevailing stereotypes. The result? Tone-deaf products and services. Within this sector, women are a revenue base that remains largely untapped. Founded in Denmark, a company called Female Invest[35] aims to close the financial gender gap by educating and empowering women on how to manage their finances, but industry-wide, such efforts are far and few between.

In many cities around the world, discrimination in the hospitality industry is rampant, particularly in clubs and bars. The main basis of discrimination lies in the following: ethnicity, gender, age, dressing or fashion, physical appearance, and status and wealth. In London and Manchester, clubs deny entry to ethnic groups and male only groups, while charging a different entry fee for men and women.[36] In 2017, in Portland Oregon, an African American man faced discrimination for wearing "excessive matching clothing" because it could signal being a part of a gang.[37] In fact, discrimination based on "strictly enforced dress codes" are surprisingly common.[38] In other clubs that cater to older, more sophisticated clientele, younger customers are turned away. The reverse takes place in nightlife establishments meant for youth. At Scandal in London, management describes the establishment as "the ultimate nightlife experience for a privileged few", discriminating on the basis of wealth and status. In Denmark, night clubs and bars justify discrimination on the basis of ensuring the safety and security of their other customers, turning away clients from certain ethnic groups that have in the past been shown to engage in disruptive behaviours.[39]

What about the inclusivity of marketing and advertising campaigns? We have all heard of campaigns that have gone terribly wrong, often lacking gender or cultural sensitivity. Luxury fashion houses like Prada have embarked on cultural sensitivity training to avoid cultural misappropriation after a window of a Prada shop in downtown New York was filled with Pradamalia figurines that resembled monkeys in Blackface. Similarly, Gucci faced backlash after launching a Blackface sweater and Dolce & Gabbana faced strong criticism for trivialising Chinese culture after they released a video of a Chinese model trying to eat pasta and pizza with chopsticks as part of its Shanghai campaign. It is not just high-end brands that commit such faux pas. In 2019, Zara was criticised for drawing freckles on its Chinese models (Asian people typically do not have them), and in 2018, H&M had to apologise after an advertising campaign showed a Black child in a "coolest monkey in the jungle" hoodie.

Also in 2018, Heineken had to withdraw their 30-second advertisement "Sometimes Lighter is Better". The advertisement featured a bartender sliding a bottle of Heineken Light towards a White woman. The bottle passed several men and women of colour before it reached her, at which point the slogan "Sometimes Lighter is Better" appears. Back in October 2017, Dove removed a three-second Facebook video that was racially insensitive showing a Black woman morphing into a White woman who then transitioned to another woman of colour. In 2020, in response to the Black Lives Matter movement and backlash against brands promoting negative stereotypes of dark skin tones, FMCG (fast-moving consumer goods) companies like Johnson & Johnson pulled their whitening range of products off the shelves in Asia and the Middle East.

Such grave mistakes have led to many companies paying greater attention to inclusive marketing: ensuring the tone and language is respectful and not offensive to their diverse customer base, avoiding appropriation and stereotypes while ensuring diverse representation in their campaigns. The reality is that customers tend to purchase brands in which they see themselves represented in campaigns as it makes them feel empowered, inspired, and heard. In 2019, Adobe conducted a research report[40] with more than 2,000 consumers. Their results showed that 66% of African Americans, and 53% of Latino and Hispanic Americans feel their ethnicity is portrayed stereotypically in advertisements. The same report showed that 61% of Americans find diversity in advertising important, and 38% of consumers are more likely to trust brands that show diversity in their advertisements.

The pressure to be inclusive is growing. Recent research shows that consumers are more likely to purchase, or consider purchasing, a product after viewing an advertisement perceived to be diverse or inclusive.[41] 70% of Millennials say they would choose one brand over another if it displays diversity and inclusion in its marketing.[42] Some companies have taken inclusive marketing a step further, acting as a voice for their customers to further positive societal change towards inclusion and inclusive mindsets. P&G's "Black is Beautiful" and "Proud Sponsor of Moms" initiatives depict African American mothers in multiple decades as they have difficult conversations with their children about racism. A Pixel 2 commercial called "The Picture-Perfect Life" shows real photos of Google Pixel users from different backgrounds, while also tackling the tough topic of mental illness. In the spot, Google aims to show that although someone might seem happy in photos or videos, they may still be struggling with mental distress.

Gillette changed its old slogan "the best a man can get" to "the best men can be" showing support for the #MeToo movement, which aims to combat sexual assault and harassment. ThirdLove is a lingerie company committed to making bras and loungewear for all different body types. To enforce this brand message, their marketing campaigns feature real women of all ages, shapes, and races, rather than touched up, high-fashion models. In 2016, Axe launched a commercial that embraced all men who used its body spray. While many commercials targeted at men in the past related masculinity to physical strength, Axe's ad argued that masculinity is more about being confident with your own identity than being a stereotypical, buff athlete.

Achieving this level of inclusive marketing requires the same level of diversity and representation within the teams creating the campaigns. Often a lack of diversity in marketing teams results in serious oversight, which in turn shows a lack of inclusivity in the campaigns produced. *Marketing Week*'s data[43] shows that "a staggering 88% of the 3,883 respondents surveyed identify as White, with just 4% identifying as mixed race, 5% as Asian and 2% as Black." At senior levels, on boards with marketers, 51.8% were male, versus 48.2% being female. From a socio-economic standpoint, despite only 10% of respondents defining themselves as coming from an upper middle-class background, these marketers made up a whopping 52.6% of senior positions. Diverse marketing teams are better able to create campaigns that are representative of their customers' diversity, spot insensitivity and lack of representation before campaigns hit the published stage. In turn, a strong brand image of a company that truly is inclusive to diversity is built.

## Strengthened Environmental, Social, and Governance (ESG) Performance

When corporate boards include members with diverse backgrounds and experiences, they can better recognize the needs and interests of different stakeholder groups. Women board directors are more likely than men to identify social issues like human rights, climate change, and income inequality as critical to corporate strategy.[44] Gender-diverse boards also tend to adopt more progressive organisational management practices, such as work-life support programs, to increase employee satisfaction.[45]

It has been shown that mixed gender boards have fewer instances of fraud. Adding women to a board can improve investment efficiency and prevent risky overinvestment decisions[46] as well as reduce the overconfidence of male CEOs.[47] At the same time, having women on boards has been shown to result in fewer financial reporting mistakes,[48] controversial business practices such as fraud and earnings manipulation,[49] and fewer operations-related lawsuits.[50]

# The Human Barrier to Inclusion

D&I reports and data by McKinsey & Company, Deloitte, and Harvard Business Review show that D&I efforts do in fact result in significant positive financial and non-financial benefits to the organisation. More recently we see companies intentionally investing resources into D&I talent, teams and initiatives to drive business results, innovation and inclusive workplace cultures.

More than just an "HR initiative", these efforts are now seen as a key strategic priority for organisations. D&I teams are holding leadership accountable and getting D&I on the agenda right at the top; they are educating the talent in their workplaces through professional development and company-wide initiatives to increase awareness, while providing support; and they are working with partners to make workplaces more inclusive and diverse.

Given that 35% of an employee's emotional investment to their work and 20% of their desire to stay at their organisation are linked to feelings of inclusion,[51] it is fair to say that inclusion is key.

Yet, nurturing inclusion remains the biggest challenge for workplaces. A 2020 report by leading consulting firm McKinsey & Company states that: "While overall sentiment on diversity was 52% positive and 3% negative, sentiment on inclusion was markedly worse at only 29% positive and 61% negative - which encapsulates the challenge that even the more diverse companies still face in tackling inclusion. Hiring diverse talent isn't enough - it's the experience they have in the workplace that shapes whether they remain and thrive".[52]

The challenge lies in the fact that this experience is significantly influenced by *bias*. Deloitte's 2019 state of inclusion survey of 3000 American professionals found that despite organisations making significant progress in inclusion, 63% witnessed bias at least once a month, 61% experienced bias at least once a month and 83% categorise the biases they experienced in the workplace to be subtle and indirect.[53] What is important for us to bear in mind is that this presence of bias can affect productivity, well-being and employee engagement: 84% of those surveyed said the biases had a negative impact on their happiness, confidence and well-being. A further 70% reported a negative impact on their engagement.

So, what is bias?

*Biases* are our stereotypes and prejudices towards others, both individuals and groups. These biases are developed over time through our early family and educational experiences and then through adult life experiences. We are *socially conditioned* - the sociological process of training individuals in a society to respond in a manner generally approved by the society and by peer groups within society - to hold these biases.

In some of my corporate training sessions, I am confronted by participants – usually, though not always, White men - who question the idea that everyone is biased. They do so in defensiveness, and on the basis that they are not racist, sexist, ageist or ableist. They assume that if one is biased, they must be racist, sexist, ageist or ableist. This is incorrect. If you are racist, sexist, ageist and ableist, you are biased. That is correct. However, having biases does not make you racist, sexist, ageist or ableist.

We all have biases; some of them we hold consciously, others unconsciously. Even those of us who may think we are not biased – are. Yes, each and every one of us. If you have a brain, you are biased. That is something we must come to terms with and accept. In that humble acceptance, we can allow ourselves to become vulnerable to unpacking our biases.

**Understanding the terms associated with bias**

A *stereotype* is an exaggerated belief, image or distorted truth about a person or group. It is a generalization that allows for little or no individual differences or social variation. Stereotypes are based on images in mass media, or reputations passed on by parents, peers and other members of society. Stereotypes can be positive or negative.

A *prejudice* is an opinion, prejudgment or attitude about a group or its individual members. A prejudice can be positive, but in our usage refers to a negative attitude. Prejudices are often accompanied by ignorance, fear or hatred. Prejudices are formed by a complex psychological process that begins with attachment to a close circle of acquaintances or an "in-group". Prejudice is often aimed at "out-groups".

*Discrimination* is behaviour that treats people unequally because of their group memberships. Discriminatory behaviour, ranging from insults to hate crimes, often begins with negative stereotypes and prejudices.

*Racist:* A person showing stereotyping, prejudice, and discrimination against people on the basis of their membership in a particular racial or ethnic group, typically one that is a minority or marginalized.

*Sexist:* A person showing stereotyping, prejudice, and discrimination on the basis of sex.

*Ageist:* A person showing stereotyping, prejudice, and discrimination against a person's age.

*Ableist:* A person showing stereotyping, prejudice, and discrimination against people with disabilities based on the belief that typical abilities are superior.

## Conscious and Unconscious Bias

Our human brain receives an extraordinary amount of information – 11 million bits of information every, single second.[54] We consciously process about 40 bits of information per second. Not 4 million; not 400,000; not 40,000; just 40. This means the remaining 99.9% of information is covered by our unconscious mind. We use algorithms and heuristics that we have developed over time to help us make sense of the overwhelming amount of information coming our way. We use these mental shortcuts to help us interpret and predict the happenings in the world around us. Our brains connect dots and fill in gaps, extrapolate and make assumptions based on incomplete information or similarity to previously recognized patterns. To be efficient and conserve our mental energy, our brain fits new information into existing frameworks, rather than reconstructing it from scratch every time we receive new information.

These mental shortcuts help us survive. Yes, survive. Imagine you are a cave person hunting for food. You come across a large animal. If you consciously processed the 11 million bits of information every second – the animal is from the cat family, is very large, has a mane, claws, etc. etc. – you would likely end up being dinner. This same instinctive decision making helps us cross the road or avoid dangerous situations by choosing the more populated train carriage at night or avoiding a deserted lane.

The problem is that we use similar mental shortcuts or biases when we meet and interact with people. The information we receive is so cognitively overwhelming, we sort people into groups. To save time and effort we arrange these groups based on stereotypes, the cultural environment around us and our personal experiences. So, instead of meeting the whole diverse self of people, we meet them in the boxes that we sort them into. The reality is that our unconscious thoughts occur between 200 to 400 milliseconds[55] before our conscious processes engage, and the unconscious categorisations have implications on the accuracy and fairness of our decision making.

*Conscious* or *unconscious biases* are also referred to as explicit or implicit biases. Conscious, or explicit biases, are biases in which we are aware of the prejudices and stereotypes we hold. Unconscious, or implicit biases, are just that, unconscious. They are deeply ingrained mental associations that comprise accidental, unintended, subtle, unexamined, and completely unconscious choices and judgements, made by everyone, all the time without our awareness and control - making awareness of them challenging. It is important to note that conscious and unconscious biases can be held collectively as well. *Collective biases* are prejudices and stereotypes held by groups of people about other individuals or groups. The more homogeneous a group is, the greater the collective bias that can potentially exist.

Both conscious and unconscious biases affect the way we think. More importantly, they influence our words and actions. This has consequences, often negative, in our interactions with others and, particularly, in interactions with those who are different from us. Our biases cause misunderstandings, mistrust and uncomfortable situations. They create non-inclusive environments. Within the workplace environment, conscious and unconscious biases affect (1) the process of decision making and the outcome of that process, (2) how we lead and manage other people in the workplace – people reporting to us, our colleagues and those we report to, and (3) our relationships with others – how we communicate, provide feedback and handle conflict.

*Cognitive biases* are systematic errors in thinking. These occur when people process and interpret information in the world around them resulting in decisions and judgments that deviate from the norm and/or rationality. The notion of cognitive biases was introduced by Amos Tversky and Daniel Kahneman in 1972.[56] These systematic errors affect our thought process and in turn affect the way we work and live. There are over 50 cognitive biases. Here we will focus on 13 of the most common cognitive biases at work.

**Common cognitive biases in workplaces**

*Fundamental Attribution Error:* We judge others on their personality or fundamental character, but we judge ourselves on the situation.

*Self-Serving Bias:* Our failures are situational, but our successes are our responsibility.

*Intergroup Favoritism:* We favor people who are in our in-group as opposed to an out-group. (In-group is a social group to which a person psychologically identifies as being a member. By contrast, an out-group is a social group with which an individual does not identify.)

*Groupthink:* Due to a desire for conformity and harmony in the group, we make irrational decisions, often to minimize conflict.

*Halo (Horn) Effect:* If you see a person as having a positive (negative) trait, that positive impression will spill over into their other traits.

*False Consensus:* We believe more people agree with us than is actually the case.

*Anchoring:* We rely heavily on the first piece of information introduced when making decisions.

*Confirmation Bias:* We tend to find and remember information that confirms our perceptions.

*Belief Bias:* We judge an argument's strength not by how strongly it supports the conclusion but how plausible the conclusion is in our own minds.

*Framing Effect:* We often draw different conclusions from the same information depending on how it's presented.

*Stereotyping:* We adopt generalized beliefs that members of a group will have certain characteristics, despite not having information about the individual.

*Authority Bias:* We trust and are more often influenced by the opinions of authority figures.

*Blind Spot Bias:* We do not think we have bias, and we see it in others more than ourselves.

Unconscious biases can be triggered by four factors:

- Task
- Numbers
- Clarity
- Perceiver

**Task: We associate certain jobs with a certain type of person**

Teachers and nurses are female. Scientists and engineers are male. Skydiving and adrenaline sports are for the able and young. These implicit associations are created and compounded by what we see and hear around us. In the 1980s and even 1990s, washing detergent commercials usually involved a frustrated woman, often a mother, with the dirty and stained laundry in front of her. In walked a man, often a White man in a white coat - assumed to be a scientist - who had the answer: a washing detergent which would magically remove that stain. Social conditioning like the example above deepens the associations we have.

**Numbers: Use biases when analysing people in outlying demographics**

When we are interacting with people from minority groups we are unfamiliar with, we use stereotypes and generalizations.

In my training sessions I am often asked about the role of stereotypes and generalizations. Is there a role for stereotypes in our interactions with others? Does it do more harm than good? My answer is simple. Stereotypes and generalizations certainly do help us when we are confronted with ambiguity and uncertainty posed by someone or a group of people having unfamiliar characteristics.

There are three things we need to keep in mind when relying on stereotypes and generalizations: (1) we have to be conscious we are holding and relying on a stereotype or generalization, (2) the stereotype and generalization must be descriptive, without judgement associated with it, and (3) we must be conscious and willing to go back and modify the stereotype or generalization to accommodate individual, regional and generational differences. Stereotypes and generalizations per se are not bad – we all have them and they do help make interactions with others smoother. In our initial interactions with others, they provide a foundation and reduce the occurrence of misunderstandings, miscommunication, and conflict. However, they can be problematic when we are not aware we are holding them, they are judgmental and we do not make the effort to modify them as we interact with someone more frequently.

**Clarity: Our brain fills gaps with what we expect**

---

**Do you see a white equilateral triangle?**

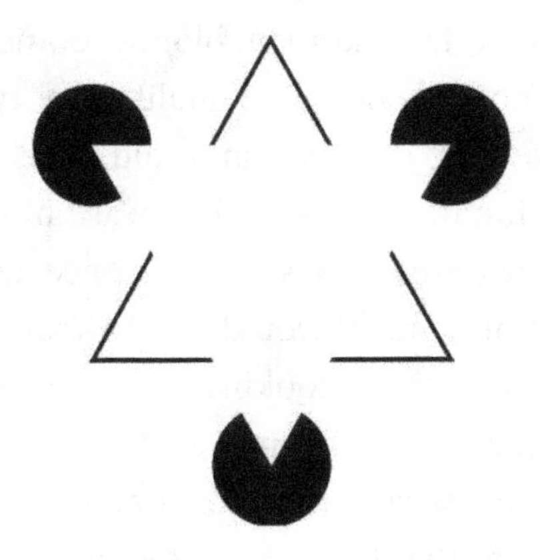

---

This is the Kanizsa triangle, the famous illusion created by Italian psychologist Gaetano Kanizsa in 1955. As shown in the image above, a white equilateral triangle can be clearly perceived even though there are no explicit lines or enclosed spaces to indicate such a triangle. Psychologists use this illustration to show how we perceive objects as whole even when they are incomplete; we ignore gaps and complete contour lines to form familiar figures and shapes. In a similar way, when we meet people we seek to fill gaps with what we expect. This reduces ambiguity and uncertainty while trying to enhance clarity.

A few summers ago, I was on the beach in the south of France with my family. After having spent a large part of the morning in the water with my children, I was really looking forward to some "me-time". I settled myself down with a glass of wine and a book. Just as I opened the cover, a lifeguard approached. He proceeded to ask me, "So, where are you from?". I really wanted to enjoy these precious minutes of "me-time", so I answered "from Denmark" to which he replied, "No, you aren't from Denmark, where are you *actually* from?". To him, I certainly did not fit the profile of a Danish woman – I am not White skinned, blonde, do not have blue eyes and am certainly not tall enough to qualify as a "typical" Dane. So, I put my book down, grudgingly, and said, "Well, I am originally from Singapore", hoping that would appease him. It did not. He looked puzzled. I assume it was because once again I did not fit the image of what he thought would be a woman from that region – perhaps someone Oriental looking--which I am not. Before he could repeat his question yet again, I said "I am ethnically Indian". Now clearly *this* was what he expected and was hoping to hear, given the excitement that followed as he told me about the wonderful Indian restaurant down the street that we should definitely try. Like the lifeguard, we all seek to gain clarity by filling in gaps with what we expect.

**Perceiver: A heightened emotional state can cause the conscious mind to be distracted**

What happens to our biases when we are upset, angry, frustrated, elated, or excited? Think about an incident when you last experienced any of these emotions. In these episodes of emotional outbursts, our ability to be rational and conscious of our thoughts, words and actions reduces. This heightened emotional state can certainly result in our unconscious mind taking over and defining what we think, say, and do. These are the times we risk saying or doing something driven by our unconscious mind rather than our conscious mind.

## Microaggressions: Subtle Unconscious Biases

While biases can certainly manifest themselves as overt and obvious aggressions, there are many times when our unconscious biases express themselves as *microaggressions*. Microaggression is a term coined by Dr. Chester Pierce in the 1970s in his work with African Americans. Microaggressions are subtle and indirect. From assuming a new female colleague is an intern or asking someone "Where are you actually from?" or "Is that your natural hair?", to commenting "Wow, I didn't expect you to speak so well", microaggressions like these are expressions of our biases.

Microaggressions are often expressed unintentionally by people who may be well-intentioned. They can be mistaken for a casual comment or even be brushed aside as humour. They may go unnoticed; even by the receiver. Microaggressions are communicated through subtle language, making it difficult to know if you are committing one. However, microaggressions - when experienced repeatedly and frequently - make people feel undervalued, unappreciated, and generally offended.

> *Microaggressions* are brief, subtle and commonplace biases that unintentionally or intentionally communicate hostile, derogatory or negative attitudes towards others, and are often mistaken for a casual comment or even get brushed aside as humour. When experienced repeatedly and frequently, they make people feel undervalued, unappreciated, and generally offended.

When microaggressions are pointed out, the response the receiver gets is "Oh come on, I was just joking" or "You're just being over-sensitive". Very often, those on the receiving end of microaggressions even rationalise the microaggression as being a "one time thing". Perhaps they think "I'm sure they didn't mean it that way" or even "I'm sure I'm overthinking this". Have you witnessed a colleague experience a microaggression during a meeting or at lunch? Or have you had a colleague come to you distressed about a microaggression they experienced? What did you say to them? Did you try to help them forget about it, or diminish their experience, telling them they might be too sensitive? Unfortunately, these brush-asides - by those of us who could be active allies - serve only to discount feelings of discrimination and support the continued perpetuation of such microaggressions.

**What do microaggressions at work look like?**

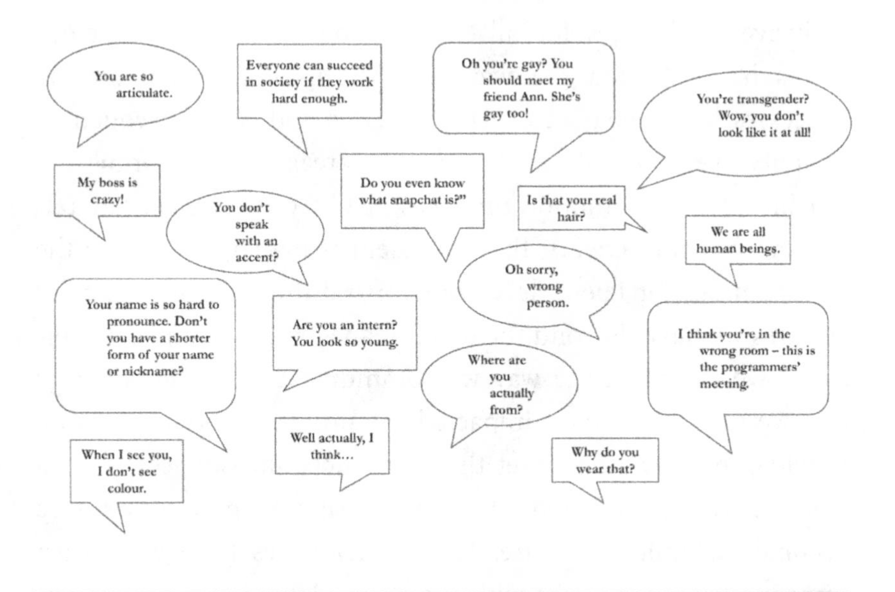


Microaggressions have always existed in workplaces and societies. Recognising their role in perpetuating non-inclusive behaviours has only received greater attention recently. We have organizational policies in employee handbooks for overt acts of racism and sexism. These provide guidelines on what constitutes inappropriate behaviours and language. What is missing are policies to address microaggressions that create toxic, non-inclusive, unsafe, and uncomfortable workplace environments.

## Systemic Biases

*Systemic biases* embedded in workplace structures and processes are a significant barrier to achieving the vision of diverse and inclusive workplaces for all. Unconscious and even conscious biases have affected the way our organisational systems and processes have been set up. These biases and the consequential inequity are especially evident in key areas of our workplaces: our hiring and promotion practices; the way we compensate talent and provide benefits; the way talent is managed and led; the opportunities for talent development; and the kind of workplace cultures we have. Beyond the talent management realm, these biases have impacted the way we communicate and the language that we use. Biases have impacted the products and services we provide, the way we market these products and services, and to whom they are marketed. Over time, many of these biases have become systemic in nature. How many times have you heard someone bat away a bias with the excuse "this is the way things have always been done", without genuine critical questioning of the biases that lie beneath? Some systemic biases have even gone completely unnoticed and accepted as a norm. This has to change.

## Quotas: Positive Discrimination vs Positive Action

While we probably all agree that something needs to drastically change – the 'how' is more challenging. A question that often comes to mind as we think about increasing diversity in our workplaces is "Should companies use quotas or not?" This question often generates some rich debate. Quotas in the recruitment process involve hiring and promoting a specific number of people within a minority group, and are part of what is known as positive discrimination or affirmative action. *Positive discrimination* is the process of increasing the number of employees from underrepresented groups - such as ethnic minorities, women or disabled people - in workplaces from which they have been excluded, by preferentially selecting recruits with those characteristics.

How and where quotas are used? Let's start with gender quotas. In December 2005, Norway passed a quota-law requiring that women make up a minimum of 40% of corporate boards. Companies had two years to comply with the law, and as a result the ratio of women directors increased from 5% in 2001 to 40% in 2008. Following Norway's introduction of quotas, more than a dozen countries set similar quotas, usually requiring between 30% and 40% female representation. In Belgium, France and Italy, firms that failed to comply could be fined, dissolved, or banned from paying existing directors. While Britain opted for guidelines, Germany, Spain, and the Netherlands preferred soft-law quotas, with no sanctions.

In 2015, Germany set gender quotas for supervisory roles, which resulted in a significant increase in the proportion of female board members. As a result, by 2020, women accounted for 36% of non-executive board roles in large companies.[57] In November 2020, Germany's coalition government agreed to a mandatory quota for women on the boards of listed companies to end women-free boardrooms. This was in an effort to increase female board representation given that none of Germany's biggest companies were led by women, and only 12.8% of the members of management boards of Germany's 30 largest listed companies were women at the time.

How do other countries fare? Better it seems, at least in terms of the percentage of women in senior leadership roles in leading companies: 24.5% in Britain, 24.9% in Sweden, and 28.6% in the US.[58] California state passed a bill requiring publicly listed companies with their headquarters in California to have at least one female board member by the end of 2019.

What about ethnic quotas? In the US, the sacking of two African American football head coaches led to the establishment of the "Rooney Rule" in 2003, requiring National Football League teams to interview at least one minority candidate for all head coach and general manager roles. In education, we see quotas being used in Brazil and France to provide opportunities for indigenous, minority or disadvantaged students.

One of the world's oldest positive discrimination policy lies in India, where it is known as the "reservation" policy. Put into place in 1950, it was designed to address the prejudices of India's caste system, setting quotas in education, the workplace, and positions of governance for those considered to be part of the lower castes. The quotas, which vary across India, have been partly successful. In 1965, Dalits (tribes that live in remote areas of the country) who formed the lowest rung of the Hindu caste system, occupied 1.6% of the most senior positions in the civil service. By 2011, that had risen to almost 12%, just 4% lower than their 16% population share in India. Race quotas have also been woven into Malaysian society since 1971, when ethnic Chinese and Indians dominated the upper classes: a legacy of British colonisation. Sweeping changes were introduced under the Bumiputera (indigenous Malay communities) policy designed to ensure that the majority Malays would no longer be discriminated against. These quotas still persist across the public sector, in NGOs and elements of the business sector, but have become contentious.

While positive discrimination is practiced in many countries including the US, it is illegal in the UK under the Equality Act of 2010.[59] In the UK, positive action became legal in April 2011 to ensure measures are taken to support the recruitment and promotion of underrepresented minorities, without the risk of hiring candidates who are not qualified for the job, resulting in qualified candidates missing out on jobs.

You must be wondering: What is the difference between positive action and positive discrimination? The terms are often used interchangeably, though they are different. *Positive action* involves measures that are taken to support the recruitment and promotion of underrepresented minorities. It comes into play when a company is deciding who to hire or promote between two equally qualified candidates. In this instance, an employer can choose to hire an individual from the underrepresented group. Positive action can also include an employer taking measures to address any imbalance within the company to encourage and enable members of underrepresented groups to overcome disadvantages and avoid discrimination.

This is different from positive discrimination. The somewhat subtle difference lies in the fact that positive discrimination involves hiring an individual purely based on their protected characteristic, rather than experience or qualifications. Protected characteristics can include race, gender, age, disability, religion, and sexual orientation.

The challenges with positive discrimination lie in the the legal, moral and economic questions that arise from the preferential treatment of certain groups of people in society. Underlying the debate between the use of these two actions are various concerns about the notion of reverse discrimination, or the unfair disadvantage to individuals who bear no responsibility for past or present discrimination practiced by others.

While quotas may increase the numbers of minority groups, there is the risk of it being seen as tokenism or nothing more than a symbolic effort. *Tokenism* involves hiring a person who belongs to a minority group only to prevent criticism and give the appearance of people being treated fairly. If you are in a company where there are very few people like you, it could be regarded that you were hired as a "token". In fact, quotas do a major disservice to minority groups by perpetuating the bias that they "only got the job because they are a minority" and not because of their skills, competencies and behaviours. In turn, quotas cause resentment amongst those who are not part of the minority group, making nurturing an inclusive environment more difficult. Women, minority ethnic groups and those with disabilities have long experienced the casual comments and microaggressions insinuating they were only hired or promoted because of positive discrimination.

I can share a personal story. When the announcement came out on social media that I was chosen to speak at a TEDx event, I was approached by an acquaintance when doing the daily school pick-up. She politely congratulated me and asked what I was planning to speak about. When I replied "diversity" as the broad topic of my TEDx talk, not wanting to give away too much and being conscious of picking up my younger child, she gestured towards me with her hand and said "Of course they would pick you to speak about that" - immediately negating all my years of experience and hard work. With one gesture, she implied that I had been chosen only because as a woman of colour, I ticked two diversity boxes.

One of the comments I get from corporate clients and students in my Masters level university courses is that companies do not see minority groups adequately represented - be it women or people of colour or those with disabilities - because there are simply not enough of them within that industry. A closely related comment that also comes up is that the few candidates who do apply from minority groups lack the same level of experience as those from the majority, which makes it harder to justify hiring for example, a less-qualified woman compared to a more-qualified man.

The question we should be asking when confronted with such comments is *why is there a dearth of candidates from minority groups in the first place*? What biases, including systemic ones, exist in our society, culture and educational systems are causing this, and how do we help address those issues in partnership with relevant organisations? One area to look for ideas is the Science and Technology sector. STEM companies who have recognised the source of their diverse talent shortages are working closely with educational partners to nurture a more robust talent pipeline of women and minority ethnic groups by supporting, encouraging and promoting STEM courses in schools and universities. Leaders in these companies from underrepresented groups can act as powerful role models to encourage young talent to pursue careers in this field.

When it comes to hiring practices, diversity enters the picture far too late in the process. Diversity of thought, experience, background and skills should be a part of the early job analysis and description stage, and be key criteria for the roles candidates are being hired for or promoted into. If we only discuss diversity after shortlisting candidates, or hiring a minority or underrepresented candidate, we risk the perception of tokenism. That is, no matter what strengths an individual brings to the role, they will be perceived as a token hire.

## The Issue of Privilege

*Privilege* is a loaded word these days. In the D&I training sessions I conduct for my corporate clients, things can sometimes get uncomfortable. Questions come up such as "Why should I feel guilty for being White?", "Why should I feel guilty for the privileges that come from being male?" or "I didn't ask to be born this way, why should I feel guilty about it?. Yet, one cannot have a deep discussion about our unconscious biases without addressing the role of privilege.

What is privilege? McIntosh (2003) defines privilege as the "invisible, weightless knapsack" of special advantages carried by persons native to the majority, but denied to those who form the minority.[60] Privilege is assuming something is not a problem because it is not a problem for **you**.

Privilege does not arise only from affluence or having a better socio-economic background. Adopting a broad view of the term, privilege can stem from any single or combination of (but not limited to) sources shown in the figure on the next page.

Acknowledging one's privilege means recognising that your circumstances and situation play a crucial role in defining your experiences. It is about empathy, not defensiveness. It is recognising the paths we take are different, depending whether we come from a majority or minority group. Majority groups likely have not experienced biases and discrimination, or racism, sexism, ageism or ableism, or not to the same extent. That is the privilege one has. It is not just White men who experience privilege. Many of us have some degree of privilege, some more than others. Awareness of privilege means acknowledging the existence of systemic biases and discrimination. The ability to empathise with someone who

**Sources of privilege**

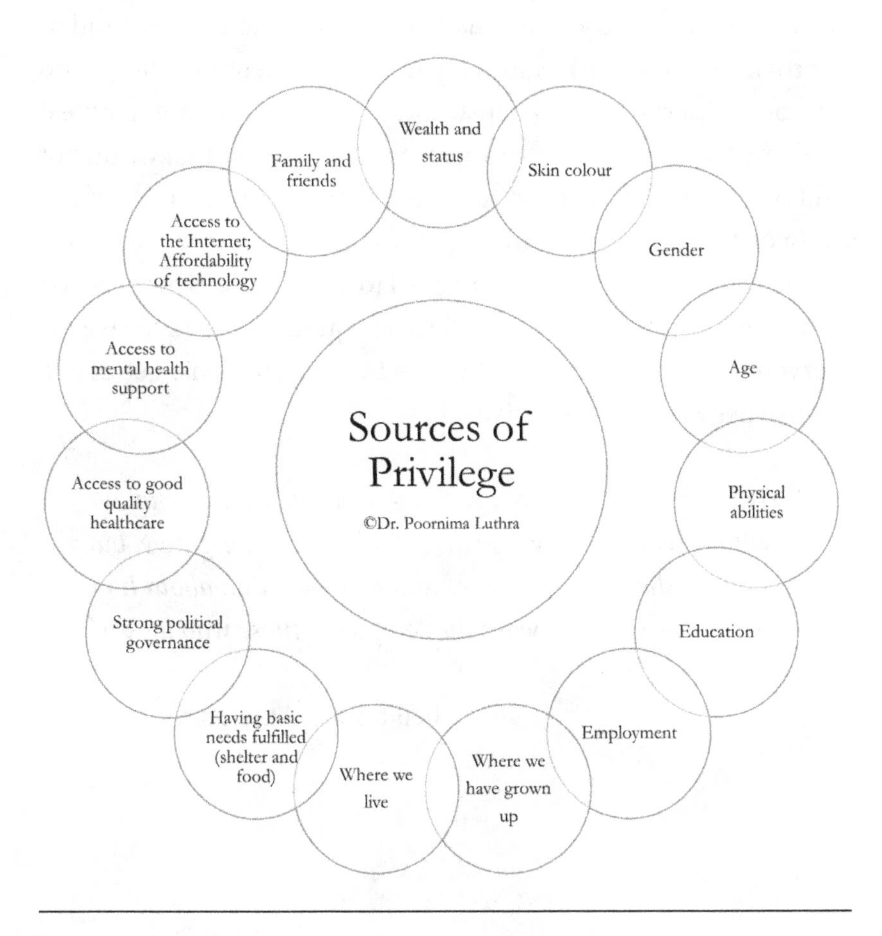


has experienced discrimination acknowledges that the world is, indeed, not equal, and our experiences, even of the same context, are different. Those who are unable to demonstrate empathy or acknowledge privilege are the biggest roadblocks to inclusion. That is the harsh reality. In the words of Brené Brown: "Avoiding difficult conversations is the definition of privilege".

History books can shed a light on the seeds of certain dimensions of privilege - colonialism, supremacy, and slavery. The purpose of history should be to remind us why we are where we are today, to provide context and legitimacy to the experience of those who have been discriminated against, and to remind us to not to repeat those mistakes again. At the same time, it is prudent that we do not fight bias with bias. We must recognise that the vast majority of talent in our workplaces are willing to do things differently and have positive intentions. We therefore need to adopt a positive approach to creating workplaces that are diverse, equitable and inclusive for everyone. Let us do better, not create further divisions. Let us use our privilege to be more active allies.

> *"Privilege is not in and of itself bad; what matters is what we do with privilege... Privilege does not have to be negative, but we have to share our resources and take direction about how to use our privilege in ways that empower those who lack it."*
>
> bell hooks, American author

## Managing Bias

So, how do we manage bias? How do we solve something that is often unconscious? How do we address something that is a result of social conditioning? Here is a set of strategies:

- Equip ourselves with the skills and training to recognise biases - in and around us. We will need to jump off the hamster wheel of social conditioning and become more aware.
- Think honestly and critically about where the biases in our companies lie and make concrete efforts to address them.
- Create workplace cultures where people feel psychologically safe and are motivated to be an active ally of inclusion by calling out biases and microaggressions without repercussion.

Professor Amy Edmondson, from Harvard Business School, coined the term *psychological safety*, defined as "a belief that one will not be punished or humiliated for speaking up with ideas, questions, concerns or mistakes". In an inclusive culture with psychological safety, biases are openly addressed and minimized. Talent will feel that they are able to bring their whole diverse selves to work.

The idea of bringing our whole selves to work was made popular by Mike Robbins in his 2018 book titled *Bring Your Whole Self to Work: How Vulnerability Unlocks Creativity, Connection, and Performance*. The idea behind this concept is that each of us has a diverse set of personality traits, backgrounds, skills and circumstances. When we are able to be ourselves in our work environments and not have to leave anything behind, we can give of ourselves fully to the organisations we work for. A 2020 You-

Gov study, conducted amongst 2,000 employees and 500 business leaders, undertaken by Mental Health First Aid (MHFA) England, reveals that almost one in five workers – about 6.5 million people – feel they cannot be their whole self at work, with people of colour reporting this most frequently.[61]

Many working mothers feel pressured to leave their motherhood "behind" when they enter the revolving doors of their offices in order to be seen by others as professional and an equal contributor. Minority ethnicities will tell you that they need to leave their cultural background behind and make conscious efforts to "fit-in" with the majority's norms of behaviour. A White, single dad will tell you that he feels the pressure of needing to leave fatherhood out of the office to be seen as a team player. A gay employee will likely tell you how frustrating it is to have to leave his sexual orientation in the closet.

Unfortunately, at present, our workplaces do not celebrate our talent's whole diverse selves. In fact, our workplaces seem to celebrate talent that conforms to a certain prototype or model of an ideal employee. Very often, the prototype is a White, heterosexual, able-bodied male. As Caroline Criado Perez writes in *Invisible Women,* the world as we know it is one that was created by and for the White man.[62]

This prototype has had a tremendous impact on many aspects of organisational life, from our ideas of successful leadership styles to views on the best way to manage others or make decisions. It influences who we hire to join the team or lead the company, the hours we work, when meetings are scheduled, and crucially, workplace culture. We have been socially conditioned to accept these without question; until now that is.

Think of the successful people in your organisation. Do they seem to have more in common with each other than differences?

Do they have the same skin colour, age, gender, or sexual orientation? Have they had similar educational and socio-economic backgrounds? Do they have similar leadership qualities? Are they all able-bodied and conform to what is accepted as "normal intelligence"? Do they outsource childcare and household responsibilities to others? Ask yourself – what is the prototype of the successful person in your organisation? Now ask yourself what that means for those who are outside the prototype boundaries?

Women in senior leadership positions often display many of the same traits and behaviours as their male counterparts. Minority ethnic leaders make significant efforts to conform to their majority colleagues. Women minority leaders - given the intersection of gender and ethnicity - face even more pressure to conform to the majority prototype.

When the talent in our organisations feel compelled to conform to the organisation's prototype to "fit in" to be accepted, this puts a tremendous emotional and mental strain on them, which can lead to resentment. This contributes to feelings of not belonging.

So, how do we ensure that our organisations are inclusive for all, while keeping biases at bay? How do we ensure that everyone feels like they can bring their whole diverse selves to work? How do we encourage everyone on board to be an ally of inclusion? This is where the Active Ally of Inclusion™ (AAI) model comes in.

# Maersk Tankers

## Diversity and Inclusion as a Strategic Lever for Transformation

Maersk Tankers operates vessels for owners in the product tanker industry with the purpose of pioneering shipping solutions for its partners and the planet. The company operates more than 220 vessels globally on behalf of owners, employs 3,000 employees and has offices in Copenhagen, Mumbai, Singapore and Houston. Maersk Tankers was founded in 1928 and was part of A.P. Moller - Maersk until 2017 when it was acquired by A.P. Moller Holding and became an independent company. Since the acquisition, the company has been transformed from that of an asset owner to an asset-light service company.

To help owners optimise performance of their assets, which reduces the industry's emissions and increases its earnings, innovation is needed, which, in turn, requires diversity of thought. Therefore, the company is investing in digital know-how and solutions and is increasingly attracting talent outside the maritime sector, bringing in new skills and mindsets. It is also working to ensure an inclusive work culture that can unleash the potential of an increasingly diverse workforce.

The cultural transformation started with an analysis of the current levels of inclusion. A consultant was hired to conduct an audit on the three dimensions of inclusion: belonging, covering and equal opportunities. Feedback was sought from current and past employees.

### Belonging-Covering-Equal Opportunities at Maersk Tankers

*Belonging:* The extent to which people feel part of their team.

*Covering:* The extent to which people can voice their opinions and express themselves freely.

*Equal opportunities:* Refers to people's experiences being equal and fair.

The survey indicated that employees had a high sense of belonging, but scores were medium to low on both covering and equal opportunities. The trend was more acute among female employees, which, given the lack of female role models in leadership roles, perhaps comes as no great surprise.

On some indicators such as age, education and nationality, the workforce was diverse. However, only 26% of onshore employees were women and just 11% were in leadership roles. Gender was selected as the area of diversity on which to focus during the first phase of the people and culture strategy. The decision was based on evidence-based research that gender diversity in corporate settings and leadership roles can lead to significant innovation, better decision-making, and higher employee retention and satisfaction, as well as greater productivity.

The new diversity and inclusion strategy was based on four pillars and one principle – that all employees can thrive, no matter their background.

The first pillar is managing talent. The talent pipeline, primarily male-dominated in the maritime sector, posed challenges for recruiting female talent. Changes were made to focus on hiring for actual capabilities and skills rather than previous experience such as working for specific companies or having sailed at sea, thus broadening the hiring talent pools.

Maersk Tankers is committed to hiring fairly and has set a 50-50 gender-hiring target. This will encourage hiring managers and recruiters to invest significant effort in sourcing and developing talent, redesigning job descriptions, and creating an attractive employer brand with key audiences and networks locally, such as the newly established Women in Shipping network.

The second pillar is developing an inclusive leadership style and culture. A leadership development programme was designed and rolled out to support this initiative. All leaders were trained in identifying and reducing unconscious biases in hiring and promotion decisions and asked to create an environment where employees can be their best selves.

The third pillar is CEO and leadership advocacy, which is crucial to win the support of leaders and employees and create a positive employer brand in the talent market. The CEO and other senior leaders have been at the centre of networking events, workshops and panel debates that aim to promote gender diversity in the industry.

The fourth pillar is developing a more inclusive workplace. Maersk Tankers amended its parental leave policies to encourage all fathers in all locations to take four weeks of paternity leave. Managers were trained to support employees going on or returning from maternity/paternity leave. Events to promote diversity, such as Pride Week, were celebrated in Maersk Tankers offices as a visible symbol of a changing culture that is becoming more inclusive.

The company has also shaped a more progressive flexibility working policy for its employees. The policy's aim is to remove bias associated with flexible working, including working from home. Flexibility in time and location is important for much of today's workforce, including young parents.

The company has made progress: in one year it has increased its ratio of women to 30% and the number of women leaders from 11% to 18%. Its ambition is to reach 35% on both counts by the end of 2023, focusing on hiring diverse talent.

Maersk Tankers will continue to make the case for greater diversity and inclusivity in the shipping industry.

## Key Takeaways:

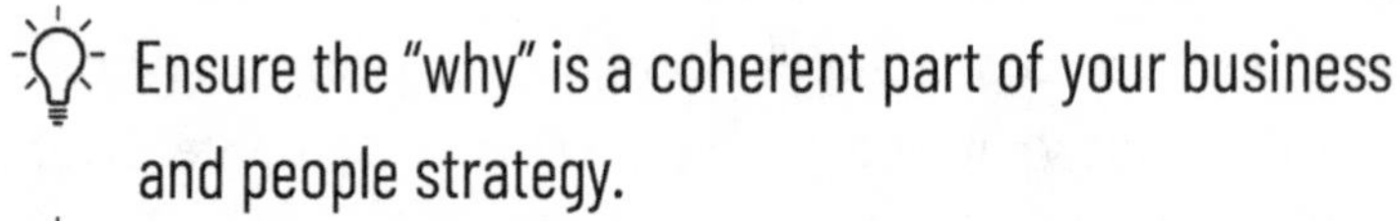

- Ensure the "why" is a coherent part of your business and people strategy.
- Conduct a third-party diversity and inclusion audit to understand how inclusive the current organisation is, and define the desired state. Set bold targets towards the desired state from the start and establish robust reporting to track and project progress.
- Ensure that senior leadership are visible and committed advocates of diverse talent and an inclusive culture.
- Expand the talent pool from which new hires are recruited from and hire for capability, not background.
- Make sincere efforts to address unconscious biases across the organisation, particularly amongst those making hiring decisions.
- Review and revise policies and practices to make them inclusive for not only diverse, but all employees.
- Celebrate the diversity you already have, bring people closer through events and communities where you can highlight the differences that make us unique.

Explore more about Maersk Tankers at https://maersktankers.com/

# Active Ally of Inclusion (AAI) Model

*"The ultimate measure of a man is not where he stands in moments of comfort and convenience, but where he stands at times of challenge and controversy."*

Martin Luther King, Jr.,
American civil rights activist and leader

If we want to work in truly diverse and inclusive workplaces, we need each and every one of us to become *active allies of inclusion.* Simply saying "I am not racist, sexist, ageist or ableist" is not enough. Many of us are far too passive, and in that passivity, we risk becoming an accomplice and co-conspirator, permitting discrimination and biases to continue to exist and even thrive. If we want to see real change and progress in D&I, we need every human being to stand up and be an *active ally***.** This cannot be an issue for the minority to deal with. It isn't an issue for women, it isn't an issue for minority ethnic groups or the LGBTQ+ or the disabled or neurodiverse communities to deal with – this is a human issue for all human beings to deal with. Individuals from majority and minority groups alike need to actively stand up.

What does it mean to be an *active ally of inclusion*?

An *active ally* is one who is acutely aware of their own identity and its intersection with the identities of others. An *active ally of inclusion* is one who has a deep understanding of the issues surrounding D&I, has the right attitude towards making workplaces more inclusive for all and demonstrates frequent and consistent behaviours that are inclusive.

Active allyship requires an authentic curiosity and hunger to understand and expand our knowledge of D&I. It means making sincere efforts to learn more about D&I issues amongst colleagues, in our workplace and in wider society. It is this knowledge and understanding of the issues that shapes our attitudes and behaviours. It involves questioning the mental shortcuts we take and our unconscious biases; calling out microaggressions when we witness or experience them; engaging in honest and open dialogue based on a robust understanding of the issues at hand; acknowledging the role of privilege; and taking action to correct the systemic biases that exist in our workplaces. To effectively address unconscious and systemic biases requires the active allyship of every person in the organisation. Does it seem daunting? It is. Yet in order to achieve inclusion, it is exactly what we must do.

It is not enough for leaders to implement a D&I strategy, to make public statements of support or to set and monitor quotas. Leaders need to believe D&I is the right thing to do, and understand the positive benefits for the organisation. Leaders need not only 'talk the talk', but 'walk the talk'. They must be true active allies themselves: holding themselves accountable; actively demonstrating inclusive behaviours with zero tolerance for micro-aggressive and biased behaviours; making concrete efforts towards eliminating systemic biases in hiring and promotion process; correcting flaws in organisational systems to make them equitable for all; and nurturing a truly inclusive organisational culture for all employees.

The buck does not stop there. Leaders are certainly instrumental in setting the tone, demonstrating inclusive behaviours and being role models. But the responsibility lies with everyone – each and every person in the organisation. Inclusion requires all hands-on-deck. Active allyship cannot be imposed, it must come from within. You may be wondering, *what do I need to do to become an active ally*?

---

**Active Ally of Inclusion (AAI) model**

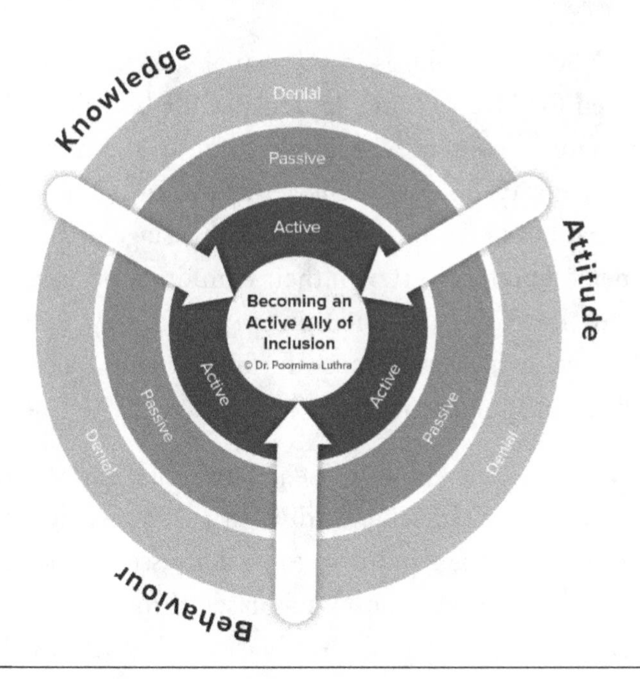


---

The *Active Ally of Inclusion (AAI)* model is a comprehensive way to gauge where we are at present, and what it will take for us to move towards or further on in active allyship. There are three stages of allyship: denial, passive, and active. The model is based on the Knowledge-Attitude-Behaviour (KAB)[63] approach and applies to all the dimensions of diversity we will be looking at in the chapters ahead. In order for us to become active allies, we need to develop an understanding around the issue (Knowledge), have the needed beliefs and ways of thinking behind our actions (Attitude), and engage in observable actions that demonstrate our knowledge and attitude (Behaviour).

**Stages of Allyship**

***Denial:*** Someone who is in the denial stage does not see the need for diversity and appreciates the benefits of homogeneity; is content with conforming to the norms set by the majority; does not believe that discrimination is an issue that needs to be addressed. At this stage of allyship, this person prefers to stay in their comfort zone, interacting with those who look and think in similar ways to them. Such a person is usually uncomfortable around those who are different from themselves.

***Passive:*** Someone who is in the passive stage understands the need for and benefits of diversity, acknowledges the lack of inclusion is a problem to be addressed, is open to unpack their own unconscious biases through training, and is able to identify their own biases and privileges. At this stage of allyship, this person interacts with people who look and think differently from themselves; seeks opportunities to be around people who are different; can identify biases and microaggressions around them; and is able to recognise systemic biases in processes and systems.

***Active:*** Someone who is in the active stage keeps themselves well-informed about the latest happening in the areas of diversity, equity and inclusion, advocates for effective unconscious bias training, believes that being inclusive is the right thing to do, and is fully certain of the benefits of diversity. At this stage of allyship, this person is very aware of their own unconscious biases; engages frequently in open and honest dialogues about diversity and inclusion; makes conscious efforts to correct systemic biases in processes and systems; actively includes, sponsors and mentors those in minority groups; calls out biases and microaggressions and pressures for change.

# Being an Active Ally of Inclusion

To use the Active Ally of Inclusion model (AAI), the most important step is to identify your current stage of allyship: Denial, Passive or Active. Where we are along this journey towards active allyship can vary across the three components of Knowledge-Attitude-Behaviour. We may have the knowledge and attitude to be an active ally, but our behaviour may be more passive in nature. Or we may have the knowledge about being an active ally but need to develop our beliefs and attitude to help us make our behaviours more active.

Spend some time reading the descriptions for each stage over the next few pages and mark where you are at present for each component - Knowledge, Attitude and Behaviour. We must be honest with ourselves. Only when we know and recognise where we are at the moment can we decide where we want to go. Next, read the descriptions across the three components of Knowledge-Attitude-Behaviour to decide where you would like to be. This should provide a starting point for your journey towards active allyship.

## Knowledge

One of the key enablers of change in behaviour is having a clear and deep understanding about the issue(s) at hand. To develop this depth of understanding, we need to make sincere efforts towards building our knowledge base about issues in the area of diversity, equity and inclusion.

Educating ourselves to truly understand the complexity of diversity could involve reading books like this one, reading credible articles and reports that are widely available to us, being a part of relevant social media groups, or being a part of D&I communities of practice in your organisation.

*Communities of practice* in the workplace bring people together to discuss D&I issues in a psychologically safe environment. These communities can act as a forum for the exchange of ideas or can be action-oriented in their mandate. Engaging in conversations with colleagues, or even with our network outside, can help expand our knowledge base and build our understanding around the issues in the area of D&I.

**AAI model: Knowledge**

**Knowledge**

**Denial:**

- ❑ I do not understand the need for D&I and see no necessity to make an effort to understand more about D&I.
- ❑ I do not know D&I vocabulary.
- ❑ I appreciate the benefits of homogeneity and make efforts to find evidence to support this.
- ❑ I recognize the benefits of conforming to the accepted norms defined by the majority.

**Passive:**

- ❑ I have a basic understanding of D&I.
- ❑ I have basic command of D&I vocabulary but hesitate to use it.
- ❑ I understand and appreciate the need for D&I.
- ❑ I understand the limitations of homogeneity.

**Active:**

- ❑ I have a deep understanding of D&I.
- ❑ I have a good command of D&I vocabulary and feel comfortable to use it.
- ❑ I keep myself well-informed of the latest developments in the area of D&I, locally and globally, through books, articles and reports.
- ❑ I organise and/or participate in communities of practise to share what I know and learn.

## Attitude

An active ally is one who is acutely aware of their unconscious biases, and understands the statement 'If you have a brain, you are biased'. An active ally appreciates that even those who claim to be without bias, are, indeed, biased. We are all biased. We all have preconceived ideas, stereotypes, and prejudices about people, individuals, and groups. While we are aware of some of these biases, there are many others we are not conscious of. The problem arises when these unconscious biases manifest themselves in our attitudes and into our words and behaviours.

There may be times when we are unsure if we are being biased or if we are failing to recognise our own biases. Having a trusted, diverse group of colleagues with whom we are comfortable asking for feedback is extremely beneficial. This group of colleagues become our compass as we navigate our own biases. I call this group our *'bias compass circle'* and it is within this group that we can determine if our actions and ways of thinking or communicating are biased. This circle can provide us with constructive and motivational feedback. If we are being non-inclusive, our circle can help us understand more about a dimension of diversity we may not yet fully comprehend. This bias compass circle provides a psychologically safe zone to help us become more inclusive. At the same time, giving those in your bias compass circle the mandate to give you feedback implies that they will be more observant themselves, and more likely to act as active allies in contexts beyond the circle.

*Bias compass circle:* A trusted, diverse group of colleagues with whom you are comfortable asking for feedback about your biases.

Who would you invite to be part of your bias compass circle? Is it as diverse as you would like it to be? If not, consider nurturing relationships at work with those who could be a part of your bias compass circle.

**Who would you invite to be in your bias compass circle?**

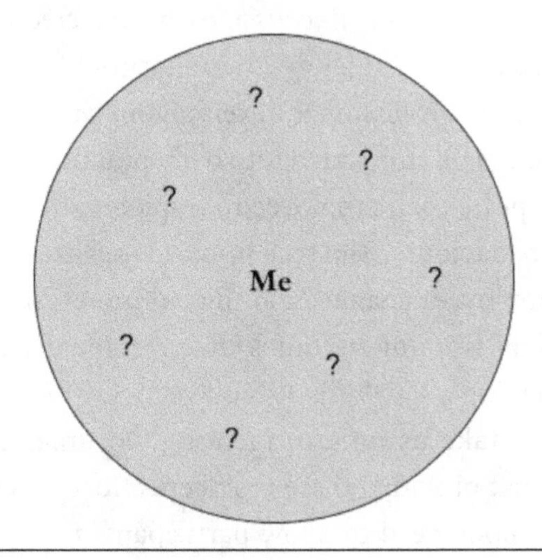


Addressing our unconscious biases requires us to make sincere efforts towards discovering what those unconscious biases are, and being mindful of how these biases affect what we say and what we do.

As a starting point, it can be beneficial to do an Implicit Association Test. While such a test can help us identify and understand what unconscious biases are at a theoretical level, to truly be able to reduce our unconscious biases requires us to take time to reflect and introspect.

Recently, there has been some criticism around the effectiveness of unconscious bias training. Some research has shown that one-time bias training is not enough to change behaviour, that anti-bias training may, in fact, perpetuate more stereotypes, and that it creates unrealistic expectations of antidiscrimination programs.

Unconscious bias training is often seen as a way to protect the reputation of decision makers and leaders by demonstrating that something is being done: a tick-box exercise.

Companies, leaders, and individual talent need to be reassured that reducing bias takes time. Real change in what we say and do happens through being mindful. We need to start paying *conscious* attention to the *unconscious* biases creeping into our words and behaviours. Therefore, training should be ongoing, one part of continuous professional development programs. Personal reflections need to be embedded into daily practices through a disciplined attempt by each employee to implement their reflections into changed behaviours. The true impact is realised when the behaviours of employees change, and the culture becomes inclusive. This is when bias training becomes effective. Many companies get it wrong, expecting a quick fix. It took years for us to develop our biases; and will take us time to identify and unlearn them. The good news is that provided there is sincere effort, it is possible.

Training sessions need to allow participants to engage in open and honest conversations about uncomfortable issues that go beyond a theoretical knowledge about the different types of biases. Training needs to tap into the emotive aspect of D&I and enable participants to experience life as another person through activities or even virtual reality experiences. Ideally, these sessions should be face-to-face, to allow for the rich sharing of ideas and thoughts that are sometimes very personal. Crucially, the trainer needs to be skilled at creating a psychologically safe environment where trainees feel comfortable with vulnerability.

Finally, for diverse talent to be convinced about the need to put in sincere effort towards addressing their biases, bias training sessions should use a combination of relevant research, credible data, simulation exercises, visuals including videos and imagery, honest and open discussions, and time for introspection. Ultimately, trainees should walk out of bias training sessions feeling *positively motivated* to make conscious efforts to confront their own biases and the biases of others, to make workplaces truly inclusive.

---

**AAI model: Attitude**

**Attitude**

**Denial:**

- ❑ I believe that D&I do not concern me.
- ❑ I do not believe that discrimination is an issue that needs attention.
- ❑ I believe I am unbiased.
- ❑ I do not believe in the need for bias training.

**Passive:**

- ❑ I believe that D&I are needed.
- ❑ I feel comfortable with bias training.
- ❑ I view discrimination as an issue that needs to be addressed.
- ❑ I keep an open mind to being aware of my own biases and privileges.

**Active:**

- ❑ I believe in the value of diversity and that being inclusive is the right thing to do.
- ❑ I believe in the benefits of effective unconscious bias training.
- ❑ I have a positive mindset towards being aware of my own biases and privileges.
- ❑ I believe in the power of having a bias compass circle.

---

## Behaviour

While we have made some progress in becoming more aware and politically correct in the language we use and our behaviours when it comes to more obvious biases, we are sometimes oblivious to the micro-aggressive words and actions in ourselves and in those around us. These microaggressions are a silent enemy when it comes to creating inclusive societies and workplaces. If we do not address these, we do not stand a chance at progressing towards more diverse and inclusive environments.

To reduce the presence of microaggressions, we need talent to call them out. Calling out biases means pointing out biases, whether they are your own or those of others. While 'calling out biases' seems harsh, it does not have to be. No one likes to be confronted, and the human reaction to confrontation is to become defensive. Given this, microaggressions - and biases more generally - need to be called out in a non-confrontational way – our tone matters. Asking questions in the right tone - what I call *empathetic questioning* - can be a powerful tool for getting ourselves and those around us to have an "aha" moment, one in which we discover a bias we, or they, weren't aware of. These questions could include:

- "How did you get to that decision?"
- "Why do you think that?"
- "What led you to that conclusion?"
- "That's an interesting way of looking at it, why did you say that?"
- "Can you help me understand why you reacted that way?"

Initially, being an active ally can feel like we are walking on eggshells, fearful of our biases being called out and hesitating to call out the biases of others. At times, we may get it right and have positive bias experiences where we are able to recognise biases and call them out respectfully - in ourselves and in others. At other times, we may fumble and find ourselves in negative bias experiences. This is natural. In fact, it is healthy and demonstrates movement in the right direction. We need to get uncomfortable first - and go through a period of flux - before we reach a new equilibrium. In the *inclusion comfort zone*, we have more consistent positive bias experiences where we are able to identify biases in ourselves and others, and call them out respectfully. In this zone, our fear and hesitation has reduced significantly, and our confidence and comfort with calling out biases has increased.

---

**Getting to the inclusion comfort zone**

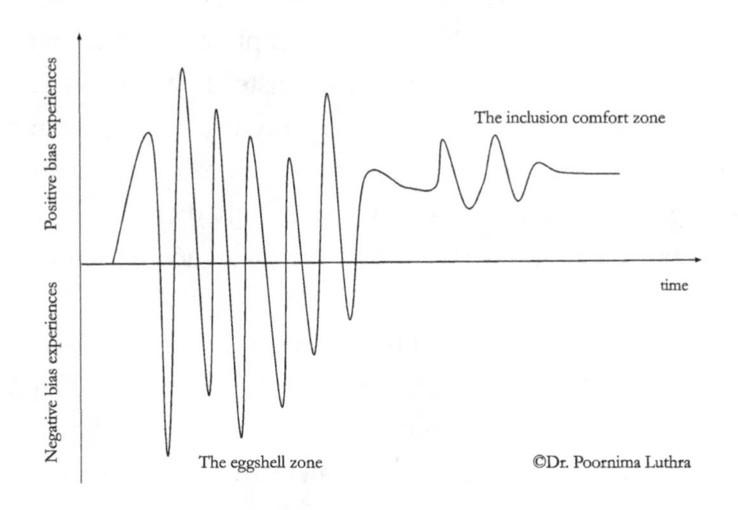


---

To support each other in reaching the inclusion comfort zone will require a psychologically safe environment in our workplaces. There must be a deep understanding that everyone is biased, and that we are all on a journey towards becoming more inclusive. It should never become a blame game. *Empathetic questioning* becomes a very useful tool to avoid pointing fingers. An inclusive organisation is one where everyone is encouraged to call out biases, ignorance and microaggressions and all individuals - leaders and talent alike - are willingly vulnerable in their efforts to discover their biases.

We need to stop avoiding difficult conversations, uncomfortable as they can be. This may be especially true the first few times we engage in them. We need to push ourselves and those around us to have those conversations. One barrier to having these deep conversations is the lack of know-how when it comes to the language and vocabulary we can and should use when engaging in dialogues about sensitive issues. We need to stop being fearful to talk about difficult bias related issues simply because we do not have the language framework to do so. Instead, we should accept that sometimes we may use the wrong language or engage in microaggressions, but we must allow ourselves to be vulnerable to those microaggressions being called out. Only then can we make changes and move towards constructive dialogues and conversations.

My hope is that as you read this book, you will develop a solid understanding of each dimension of diversity, and with this knowledge and vocabulary, feel confident to engage in open, honest, and courageous conversations. Through these frequent dialogues, we have the opportunity to shape the language and narrative we use around these issues in our workplaces and communities.

In addition to calling out biases and engaging in honest, open and courageous conversations, an active ally ensures that minority groups are included in all organisational processes. Every meeting, committee, and task force that is set up must have adequate representation. Authentic leaders show empathy, and even emotions, when openly speaking about uncomfortable issues[64] and make conscious efforts to have an inclusive communication style. This includes using audience-centred language, which demonstrates a deep understanding of D&I. It also goes a long way in showing not only that they care, but they are determined to create an inclusive culture.

For those in positions with responsibility over resources and decisions, being an active ally involves sponsoring those from minority groups who may not otherwise have access to resources. These resources can include leadership training or other opportunities for career growth and development. Sponsorship could also take the form of setting up and actively supporting Employee Resource Groups (ERGs) for minority employees. Finally, being an active ally means mentoring those who are from minority groups to provide advice, guidance, and wisdom of experience to help them achieve their career aspirations.

For us to normalise being an active ally, we need to celebrate active allyship. We need to recognise our colleagues who are demonstrating the kind of behaviours that are representative of being an active ally. This will in turn provide the needed motivation to move those who are passive allies to becoming active allies. We need to celebrate not just the grand gestures of active allyship, but should in fact be focused on smaller gestures and actions; inspiring those who are hesitant to become active.

**AAI model: Behaviour**

## Behaviour

**Denial:**

- ❑ I do not notice biases and microaggressions, and am unable to identify them.
- ❑ I feel uncomfortable when discussing discrimination and bias.
- ❑ I interact with others who look and think like I do.
- ❑ I feel unsure of what to say and do when there are people who are different from me.
- ❑ I prefer being in situations that are familiar to me.
- ❑ I actively avoid being amongst diverse groups of people.
- ❑ I get uncomfortable when there are minority groups around me.
- ❑ I am uncomfortable with D&I initiatives and do not think they are necessary.

**Passive:**

- ❑ I can identify biases and microaggressions but feel uncomfortable calling them out.
- ❑ I am comfortable interacting with others who look and think differently than me.
- ❑ I seek opportunities to be amongst diverse groups of people.
- ❑ I am comfortable being a part of uncomfortable discussions on discrimination, though I do not actively participate in them.
- ❑ I recognise systemic bias in systems, processes and practices.
- ❑ My way of supporting minority groups and D&I initiatives involves not opposing it.
- ❑ I notice when those from minority groups feel excluded, though I am not sure what to do about it.
- ❑ I celebrate others who are being an active ally.

**AAI model: Behaviour**

**Behaviour**

**Active:**

- ❑ I actively speak about the benefits of D&I.
- ❑ I call out biases and microaggressions using empathetic questioning.
- ❑ I engage frequently in open and honest dialogues about D&I with those around me.
- ❑ I make sincere efforts to make decisions that support diversity and foster inclusion.
- ❑ I make conscious efforts to correct systemic biases in systems, policies and practices.
- ❑ I actively include, sponsor and mentor those from minority groups.
- ❑ I set up and/or participate in Employee Resource Groups for minority groups.
- ❑ I put pressure on managers and leaders to take concrete actions.

In the upcoming chapters, we will explore the 12 dimensions of diversity that will help organisations embrace diversity and nurture inclusive workplaces to drive innovation, better talent management and improved financial results. At the end of the book, specific tools and strategies to be an active ally at the individual, team and organisational level are suggested so that each of us will be better equipped to be confident in our quest to be a sincere active ally of inclusion. We begin with *Physical & Physiological* dimensions before we move into *Cognitive* dimensions, and then, *Social & Lifestyle* dimensions.

Join me on this journey towards active allyship. It won't be easy, and at times it will be frustrating and require us to be vulnerable, but the reward – diverse and inclusive workplaces for all – should act as a motivation for all of us to become active allies of inclusion.

# Carlsberg Group

## Creating a Community of Allies

The Carlsberg Group is a Danish multinational brewery, established in 1847 by brewer J.C. Jacobsen. Enriched by a great history where tradition and innovation have always co-existed, today the Group is powered by more than 140 strong brands from all over the world, each unique in their values, local products, and cultural heritage.

"At Carlsberg, we are brewing for a better today and tomorrow. In addition to looking for new ways to make our beers even better, we are also constantly in pursuit of new ways to support innovations that create a better future for our planet and humanity. Examples of these can be found in our ambitious sustainability programme 'Together Towards Zero' and in the work carried out by The Carlsberg Foundation in support for science, art, culture and society" shares Myriam Shingleton, Vice President for Product Development and member of the D&I council in Carlsberg Group.

In September 2019, Carlsberg began more active efforts in Diversity and Inclusion (D&I) across their commercial functions (what is known internally as Group Commercial), knowing the direct benefit it would have on the business, as well as interactions between colleagues in headquarters as well as the markets in which the company is present. The first step involved conducting a D&I audit across Group Commercial to understand the D&I issues facing the organisation. Based on the data collected, the next step consisted of providing D&I training to all Group Commercial employees through a program known as the "Carlsberg D&I Lab"; the program was named to honour the company's rich history of research. Over a period of 18 months, 222 employees were trained. The training program focused on developing knowledge of different cultural practices and worldviews, becoming aware of personal attitudes towards cultural differences, increasing awareness of unconscious biases, and developing cross-cultural skills. Over 4 weeks, each employee spent a total of 12 hours in training, with a week of self-reflection between each of the sessions.

These training sessions created a desire amongst colleagues in Group Commercial for more ongoing D&I efforts. This resulted in the creation of a D&I Allies of Inclusion, consisting of volunteers across Group Commercial who were passionate about the topic, wanted to contribute more, and continue to be active allies of inclusion. The group meets every 6 to 8 weeks at breakfast sessions, and what started with 14 active members has grown to 20 volunteers.

Myriam explains: "It is amazing to see how through the year, the maturity and engagement of this group of people increased. We started by brainstorming on concrete actions to continue to create awareness outside the training and continue to build an inclusive workplace. This included weekly 'mix-up lunches' where employees were asked to sit with colleagues that they did not know to increase inter-function interaction.

"More recently we had intense discussions on a range of issues from how to be inclusive through times of lockdown due to COVID-19 to what are the forms of harassment, how to detect them and act on them. I am amazed at how every D&I Allies of Inclusion group member decided to become a more active ally of inclusion in their own team by offering to be available for the others when needed, driving regular D&I updates in their team meetings, or organizing a reflection among their communities on unconscious bias and how to be comfortable to call biases out.

"I am really thrilled to be able to facilitate such an engaged group of allies of inclusion, supported by my colleague from Human Resources, Camilla Mikkelsen: it is so rewarding to see an active group, willing to move the needle on our D&I journey in the Carlsberg Group and having the courage to step up. This small group is surely creating a true D&I movement across the commercial functions in the organisation".

## Key Takeaways:

- Behavioural change takes time: Allow for time in between training sessions for self-reflection.
- Understand the D&I needs of your organisation: A D&I audit helps to uncover the most pressing D&I needs and issues that need to be addressed in your organisation.
- Awareness is key: The more awareness that is created about this topic, the more you raise expectations and engagement from the teams.
- Communities of Allies are key to enabling change: At Carlsberg, the D&I Allies of Inclusion was not just a learning and knowledge group but also a forum for true active allyship to be nurtured.
- Diversity amongst the members of the Communities of Allies is very important: At Carlsberg, the members of the breakfast group comprised a diverse group of employees covering a good mix of gender, levels in the organisation, background, field of operations, nationalities, and cultures. This brought a lot of richness and knowledge sharing.

**Explore more about the Carlsberg Group at https://www.carlsberggroup.com/**

# Physical & Physiological Dimensions of Diversity

# Gender

*"Gender equality is a human fight, not a female fight."*

FREIDA PINTO, Indian actress

Much of the focus of diversity to date has been on gender so it feels right to begin here. At a global level, we have made progress in gender equality since the early 1900s. More girls go to school, fewer girls are forced into early marriage, and women have secured voting rights.[65]

Sadly, egalitarian trends seem to have stalled since the 1990s[66] and many challenges remain. Discriminatory laws and social norms remain pervasive with 2.5 billion women living in countries with at least one discriminatory law or practice.[67] It is hard to believe that in 59 countries there are no laws prohibiting sexual harassment in the workplace,[68] or that in 18 countries husbands are legally allowed to prevent their wives from working.[69] 40% of economies have laws constraining women's decision to join and remain in the labor force.[70]

Outside the workplace, one in five girls and women between the ages of 15 and 49 report experiencing physical or sexual violence by an intimate partner in the past year.[71] While extreme poverty has declined between 1990 and 2015, 25% more women aged 25-34 years are likely to live in extreme poverty than men, and half a billion women above the age of 15 remain illiterate.[72] This is a staggering two-thirds of the world's adult illiterate population.[73]

Each year, the World Economic Forum releases their Global Gender Gap Report (GGGR)[74] which benchmarks 153 countries on their progress towards gender parity across four areas: economic participation and opportunity; educational attainment; health and survival; and political empowerment. The 2020 report reveals that gender parity will not be attained for 99.5 years. Yes, it will take us close to a century to achieve gender parity.

While a century feels like an eternity, the news is not all grim, and we seem to be on the right track. Since 2018, the timeframe to achieve gender parity has decreased from 108 years. 101 of 149 countries have seen their scores increase yearly, and it is projected that we will reach gender parity in education in just 12 years. Iceland, followed by its Nordic neighbours Norway, Finland and Sweden, lead the pack, ranking among the most gender-equal countries in the world.

Sobering, however, is the likelihood we will not witness full gender parity in our lifetimes, and neither will our children. The report says: "Without the equal inclusion of half of the world's talent, we will not be able to deliver on the promise of the Fourth Industrial Revolution for all of society, grow our economies for greater shared prosperity or achieve the UN Sustainable Development Goals. At the present rate of change, it will take nearly a century to achieve parity, a timeline we simply cannot accept in today's globalized world, especially among younger generations who hold increasingly progressive views of gender equality".

What about in the political arena? How are we doing there? If a photo of the G20 Summit in Osaka in 2019 is anything to go by, the situation is bleak. Just 3 out of the 38 world leaders pictured are women. Yes - three. In 2020, out of 193 countries, only 21 women sat as heads of state or government.[75]

While these facts are concerning, what is most concerning is data in the area of economic participation and opportunity, where instead of progress, there actually has been regression from previous gains. Gender parity in this realm is at a low of 57.8%. It will take an astonishing 257 years before gender parity can be achieved in economic participation and opportunity.

If you are wondering how this can still be the case, you are not alone. The GGGR report sheds some light, citing three primary reasons for this dismal outlook: women are overrepresented in roles that are being automated; not enough women are entering professions where wage growth is the most pronounced (e.g., technology), and women face the perennial problem of insufficient childcare infrastructure and access to capital.

At the start of the year 2020, the representation of women in corporate America was headed in the right direction. In senior management roles, between January 2015 and January 2020, representation of women in senior-vice-president positions grew from 23% to 28%, and representation in the C-suite grew from 17% to 21%.[76] In 2020, the number of women running America's largest corporations hit an all-time high with 37 Fortune 500 companies led by female CEOs. On the other side of the pond however, only 5% of FTSE (Financial Times Stock Exchange) 100 CEOs in 2020 were women. The FTSE 250 was even further behind, with the number dropping to 2%[77] and in the FTSE 350, only 10% of roles were held by female executives.[78] Though the number of women on executive committees has improved by 2.7% in 2020 compared to 2019, a deeper look at the data shows that these women tend to be in non-P&L (profit and loss) roles like human resources, marketing and legal.

Worth noting is that the representation of women of colour at senior levels still remains very low. With Indra Nooyi stepping down as CEO of PepsiCo in October 2018, the total number of Fortune 500 CEOs who are women of colour became 0.2%. The number of female African American and Latina CEOs? Zero.

You might think the Nordic countries, who top the list of gender-equal countries, have a magic solution for achieving a greater number of female managers in organisations. After all, with healthy female labour-force participation[79] and generous public parental leave, as well as childcare intended to encourage women's economic participation, they must have some secrets for the rest of the world. Unfortunately, they do not.

In Denmark, in 2018, only 28% of managers were female, while in Finland and Norway it was 32%, and 36% in Sweden. The only Nordic country with a higher share of female managers was Iceland, at 40%.[80] In contrast, the percentage of female managers in the United States for the same period was 43%. In the Nordics, the figures fare better in the political arena thanks to a history of female involvement in politics. The proportion of women in parliament ranges from 37% in Denmark to 44% in Sweden.[81] In 2020, four out of the five prime ministers in the region were women, with Sanna Marin being the youngest female state leader in the world. In 2019, Marin, also Finland's youngest-ever prime minister, formed a coalition government of five female political party leaders.

At a global level, gender equality at senior leadership levels and on boards remains low and has increased only incrementally. In 2019, 9% of senior management roles were held by women, the highest number ever on record. That same year, 87% of global businesses had at least one woman in a senior management role.[82] The GGGR states that "on average, only 55% of adult women are in the labour market, versus 78% of men, while over 40% of the wage gap (the ratio of the wage of a woman to that of a man in a similar position) and over 50% of the income gap (the ratio of the total wage and non-wage income of women to that of men) are still to be bridged".

When 50% of the population are female, why are these numbers so skewed?

While some of the data points we have seen until now are certainly disappointing, there is some room for hope. In July 2020, New Zealand passed an Equal Pay Amendment Bill. Paying men and women equally for the same work has been in effect in the country since 1972, but this bill goes beyond that. It focuses on pay equity by "ensuring women in historically underpaid female-dominated industries receive the same remuneration as men in different, but equal-value work." The bill creates a pathway for collaborative resolution of gender related pay gaps.

Despite the data, the case for embracing gender diversity is clear. Research shows there is significant improvement in financial performance for organisations that have greater gender diversity at the top level. Companies in the top-quartile for gender diversity are 15% more likely to have financial returns above their respective national industry medians.[83] The benefits go beyond financial performance - improved reputation, improved ability to understand the customer base, increased perspectives and ideas for problem solving, and a diverse range of management styles. Greater gender diversity at all levels is crucial in today's organisation for attracting and retaining talent: 61% of women look at the gender diversity of the employer's leadership team when deciding where to work.[84]

So, what is standing in the way of companies having equal gender representation at all levels, equal pay and equal opportunities for promotion to managerial roles? The challenges for women moving up the corporate ladder start early, often with the first managerial step. In 2020, for every 100 men promoted to a managerial position, only 85 women were promoted. The gap is larger for women of certain ethnic groups, with only 58% of African American women and 71% of Latina women promoted.[85]

A 2017 Harvard Business Review study may give us some clues why we see this pattern.[86] Researchers collected data from a large, multinational firm where women were underrepresented in higher management. Data included email communication and meeting schedules of hundreds of employees, and sensorial data from 100 individuals who were given sociometric badges to track in-person behaviour. What they found is very interesting.

They found no perceptible difference in the behaviours of men and women - both had as many contacts, similar access to seniority, comparable amounts of time with senior leadership, similar work patterns, and even received similar performance evaluation scores. The data dispelled the common belief that women do not advance at the same rate as men because they do not engage in informal networks known as the "boy's club". So, what explained the differences in outcomes? The study concluded gender inequality is not because of differences in behaviour, but because of *biases*. So, what do gender biases and microaggressions look like in today's workplaces?

## The Socialisation of Gender Biases

*Gender biases* have existed for as long as humanity has – more so in some societies than others. History shows us that in most ancient civilisations, the male members of society were depicted as stronger and more powerful than female members. The primary role of women, by default, was procreation and caring for the family. One ancient example where relatively greater gender equality was present were in the Norse societies of the Viking age. Norse societies, though patriarchal, are generally regarded as having greater gender equality with women having significant influence, power, and rights.[87] This relative egalitarianism continued as the region progressed into capitalism in the 18th and 19th centuries. In these communities, women were independent and enjoyed rights like inheriting land and property, controlling their dowry, and owning a third of the property they shared with their spouses.[88] However, even in the most egalitarian of ancient societies, they did not hold political positions, which were reserved for men.

To really make sense of the situation today requires us to step into the past. With the global shift to trade-based capitalism in the 16th and 17th centuries, unions of the time - which were known as trade guilds - defined labour as men's work. Brewing and weaving - which were, at one time, regarded as women's work - became more highly valued when they became the work of men. Industrial capitalism of the 19th century dictated that women did the unpaid work in the home - caring for the predominantly male workforce and children. On the rare occasion that women worked outside the home, they were paid less than men. Work that involved advanced technology of that time was seen as "too complicated for women". These social and economic norms were imposed by Europeans on the nations they colonized, overriding indigenous ways of viewing gender. The combination of colonialism and capitalism emphasized class differentiation alongside gender, and regarded White men as the superior class of societies.[89]

Did you know that gender stereotypes and biases begin in childhood and are at their peak around the age of ten?[90] The 'Draw-a-scientist Test' has become a classic piece of social science research. Over 50 years, researchers have learned much about when gender stereotypes begin, just by examining children's drawings. At the age of six, when asked to draw a scientist, girls draw 50% of scientists as women. By age 10 to 11, the proportion flips, and by age 16, approximately 75% of scientists drawn by girls are male. Boys draw only 5% of scientists as women to begin with.

Similarly, studies in the UK[91] and Denmark[92] show that children's stereotypes regarding gender roles at work begin between the ages of five to seven, where they begin to associate certain jobs like firefighter, surgeon, fighter pilot, chief engineer, or ship captain with men. When young children were asked what it means to be a boy, they commonly used phrases and words such as "to be tough", "athletic", "confident", "to not cry", "aggressive", and "play and watch sports". When asked what it means to be a girl, young children used phrases and words such as "play with dollies", "make-up", "dressing up", "baby-making machines that stay at home".[93]

Cultural differences play a significant part in defining the role of women and men in societies. In patriarchal societies, men hold the power as the primary breadwinner and head of the family, as well as in politics and workplaces. This means that power in governance, moral authority, social privilege, and control of property lies in the hands of men.

In the Confucian societies of East Asia and China, patriarchy is very much a part of the philosophy or way of life – women are seen as subordinate to their fathers, husbands and brothers. Korean Confucianism has been described as "the enemy of feminism" with some feminists arguing that Confucianism is the source of patriarchal societies.[94] Historically, women's roles in these societies were primarily kinship roles: daughter, sister, wife, daughter-in-law, mother, and mother-in-law. Women were expected to fulfil the needs of their fathers when young, husbands when older, and sons when widowed. While there is certainly greater equality between men and women amongst younger generations in urban areas of China and East Asia, the patriarchal mindset is one that is deeply embedded in the traditions of societies in the region. In Africa, rural Nigerian women continue to suffer subordination.[95] In South Africa, the patriarchal system, based on the powerful role of the father as the head of the household, affects family life and is a significant risk factor for intimate partner violence and family disintegration.[96]

In India, the preference for male children over female children reinforces the patriarchy. This preference is responsible for the high rates of female infanticide or the deliberate killing of female children. Although sex-selection or disclosure of the sex of the foetus has been criminalized in India, India continues to have one of the highest rates of female foeticide incidence in the world. The UN State of World Population report for 2020 shows that India accounts for 45.8 million of the world's 142.6 million missing females - girls who went missing at birth - over the past 50 years. Between 2013 and 2017, about 460,000 girls in India were "missing" at birth each year. Weak law enforcement and illegal abortions remain the key challenges for addressing this, alongside the lack of education and the prevalence of the dowry system, which makes having a female child a financial burden for the family. While the dowry system has been prohibited since 1961, the implementation of this law has been ineffective. In essence, dowry is the payment of gifts or cash to the bridegroom's family from the bride's family during marriage. Dowry is also a major contributor of violence against women, the most extreme example being dowry murder, in which the bride commits suicide or is killed by the husband and/or his family due to the dissatisfaction with the dowry given.

Why is this relevant for understanding workplace bias? A 2019 study of Nigerian organisations found that patriarchy shapes women's behaviour in ways that undermine their performance.[97] The study found that patriarchal attitudes, often practiced at home, are frequently transferred to organisational settings. It is this transference that affects women's workplace behaviour and maintains men's self-perceived superior status quo. Women continue to be dominated, discriminated against, and permanently placed in inferior positions. In other words, the biases which start at home when we are young follow us as adults, this time into our organisations.

## Gender Biases at Work

Gender biases take many forms. When it comes to biases and microaggressions against women in workplaces, the list is endless.

Ask any woman if she has experienced biases or microaggressions in her professional life. You will be hard pressed to find a woman who does not have multiple experiences to share. A 2020 report, based on a survey of nearly 256,700 women around the world, shows that while discrimination and crimes against women exist across the world, the intensity and volume vary from country to country, from culture to culture.[98] The report used these key attributes to assign a gender equality ranking to each country: gender equality, percentage of legislative seats held by women, sense of security, income equality, care about human rights, women empowerment, average years of education among women, women age

25 and older who are engaged in paid work, and women's inclusion in society.

So, what do biases and microaggressions against women look like? Let us begin with sexist slurs against women or "locker room" talk as it is commonly referred to. A 2019 study found that over a one week period, 2.9 million tweets contained instances of gendered insults - "bitch," "cunt," "slut," or "whore" - averaging 419,000 sexist slurs per day, with the vast majority of these tweets being negative in tone and sentiment.[99] The authors of the study argue that online aggressions towards women through social media platforms reinforce traditional feminine norms and stereotypes.

The #MeToo movement has undoubtedly raised greater awareness around the need to call out gender biases, sexual abuse, and sexual harassment in our workplaces. While the term "Me Too" was initially used in 2006 by sexual harassment activist and survivor Tarana Burke, it gained momentum after high-profile sexual abuse allegations against American film producer Harvey Weinstein were exposed. Women across the world began sharing their own stories of sexual abuse and harassment, highlighting just how ubiquitous the problem is. Allegations ranged across a variety of industries in the US - fashion, finance, technology, sports, music, and the military. The movement gained significant momentum across the world – in the UK, India, China, Pakistan, Spain, South America, Afghanistan, Australia and many more – with women in all these countries coming forward with their own #MeToo stories of sexual abuse, some going against heavy societal pressures not to talk about these incidents. While the movement has forced men to be more conscious about their language choices and behaviours, the prevalence of "locker room" talk, often disguised as humour at office social events, is still very much present. The less talked about side of the #MeToo movement are the less frequent, yet still harmful, incidents of false allegations against men, prompting the creation of the term #HimToo, a movement against false rape and sexual misconduct allegations.

Biases against women are not only sexual in nature. They go beyond sexual harassment. While many organisations have a zero tolerance stand and policies for sexual harassment, biases against women continue to exist in other forms. Have you heard about 'bropropriating' and 'mansplaining'? Bropropriating is a colloquial term for a commonly described occurrence: when a man takes credit for a women's idea. Mansplaining is when a man tries to explain something to a woman in a condescending or patronizing tone, based on the assumption that the woman does not have the capability and knowledge about the issue at hand, or is emotional and lacking rational thinking abilities. The latter term, mansplaining, was made famous in 2008 by author Rebecca Solnit's famous essay, 'Men Explain Things to Me'.

Added to this mix is 'manterrupting' – when a man unnecessarily cuts off a woman who is speaking. This happens astonishingly often. In 2009, on the most public of stages, the MTV Video Music Awards, Kanye West lunged onto the stage and grabbed the microphone from Taylor Swift. During a 2015 panel discussion, Google's chair Eric Schmidt was called out for manterrupting by his colleague Megan Smith, the US CTO and Google executive at that time. Several studies show women are interrupted far more frequently than men during meetings and panel discussions - 33% more frequently, in fact.[100] Observe the next few meetings you are in and see if you can identify these behaviors. They may be occurring more often than you think.

**Bropropriating**

The argument that women and men are biologically different, and that women are less physically capable than men, is often used when it comes to barring women from certain tasks and jobs traditionally reserved for men. In the sporting arena as well as industries requiring physical strength, the assumption is that women will not be able to cope with the physical demands required by the job itself. When engaging with clients in industries where there is a requirement for lifting of heavy goods, operating of machinery, or usage of industrial tools, I am told by women that they are often disregarded during the hiring selection process itself. These women express that they see themselves as being capable of handling the requirements of the job, but are not given the opportunity to showcase that ability. These female clients feel that selection committees, usually composed of able-bodied men, assume that hiring a woman will put additional strain on the men to compensate for the assumed lack of their female colleague's strength.

Occasionally, gender biases about the role of women in the household permeate the office environment and generate causal comments or microaggressions. Let me share a story. A woman got into a lift at work, heading down to the lobby. A few floors down, another woman got in; they exchanged pleasantries as the lift door shut. The lift stopped a floor below that, and a man got in. He had his work shirts draped over his arm, ready for the office dry cleaners. He pressed the 'door close' button on the lift, and turned to the two women - who were the only two other people in the lift - and said "Which one of you two ladies will help me do my laundry today"? Before the women could respond, the doors opened and the man confidently strode off, leaving two women stumped for words. You may be thinking, come on, this doesn't happen anymore, does it? It does – in 2020: this is a real story, narrated to me by one of the women in the lift.

A recent personal experience highlights just how deeply ingrained social conditioning is. I was sitting next to a White, male colleague during a virtual meeting with our client, a woman. During the meeting, the woman interrupted me several times whilst I was speaking and diverted the conversation back to my male colleague. Each time, my colleague handed the ball back to me, saying I would be better suited to answer those questions. After the meeting, my colleague expressed his frustration at the number of times I had been interrupted. What bothered me was that I hadn't noticed it! One would think that given my immersion in this field, I would have noticed, but I didn't. As I reflected upon this, I realised that such experiences are normalised in my world. If someone like me, who is acutely aware of biases and non-inclusive behaviours missed this, imagine how many such biased microaggressions in workplaces must go unnoticed.

It is a good time to pause for a moment here and answer this - Who *first* comes to mind when you think of someone brilliant?

Was it a man? A 2018 study[101] involved five experiments in which over 3,000 people from 78 countries, including American children between 9 and 10, were surveyed on what gender they most associated with "brilliance". Using an implicit association test, the researchers asked participants to sort stimuli into categories like "male" and "brilliant" or "female" and "brilliant". While few participants *explicitly* associated men with brilliance, 70-75% of the participants had an *implicit* bias that associated the concept of brilliance with men rather than women.

What is most troubling is that these implicit associations begin very early in life. In a 2018 study, children were asked to go through a stack of photos of other children they did not know and select "really, really smart" potential members for their team to play a game. The study found the children consistently chose boys.[102] In another study in 2019, it was found that children aged five or six, when asked to choose a photo of someone they thought was "really, really smart", tended to choose photos of men over women.[103]

Have you observed how often the words "chairman", "foreman", "businessman", "salesman", "seaman" or "landlord" are used, even when referring to a female person in that role? It is only recently that new terminology like 'firefighter' or 'police officer' have been introduced to replace fire or policeman. These gender-specific occupational titles have certainly played a part in being able to attract, hire and retain diverse talent in these industries. In the US, only 3.3% of firefighters are women, and it is only in September 2020 that a fire department in Florida had a female captain, driver, firefighter, rescue lieutenant and a medic working together in an all-female crew.

In STEM fields, despite more girls being in school than ever before, the same opportunities available for girls to pursue their chosen path in education are limited. UNESCO's report 'Cracking the Code: Girls' and Women's Education in STEM' shows that globally, only 35% of STEM students in higher education are women, and of that, further differences are observed within STEM disciplines.[104] In 2017, 2,174 students across the UK were surveyed, comprising an equal number of males and females. Prior to going to university, 64% of female students studied a STEM subject in school (for male students that number was 83%), yet only 30% studied a STEM subject at University, and a meagre 3% of female students chose a career in technology as their first choice.[105] At home and through school, girls have been conditioned to believe that certain jobs and industries are better suited for them - think education and childcare, nursing and being a homemaker - while others like science and engineering are not. This is changing, and efforts are being made by governments, educational institutions, and parents, but one could argue based on the data, it is not changing fast enough.

In the workplace, there has been some progress. We see more women rising to the top: Ginni Rometty, CEO of IBM; Susan Wojcicki, CEO of YouTube; Sheryl Sandberg, COO of Facebook; Amy Hood, CFO of Microsoft; Roshni Nadar Malhotra, CEO of HCL Technologies and Gwynne Shotwell, President of SpaceX. These women are great role models, but they are the minority: only 5% of leadership positions in the technology industry are held by women in the UK[106], and just 14% of US start-ups have a female CEO. 70% of start-ups in China have at least one woman in an executive position, which is higher than the US and UK which stand at 53% and 57% respectively.[107]

The reason? Biases, social norms and expectations. In workplaces within the STEM industries, the biases run deep. Women in technology (Tech) companies face biases and microaggressions both at the recruitment stage and after they enter the workplace. I have heard of women being told they must be in the wrong meeting, the one "for the programmers". What is worrying is that women who do enter the Tech industry quit their jobs almost 2.5 times more frequently than their male co-workers.[108] Women are expected to behave more like men to "fit in" but also expected to be feminine. This is amplified for women of colour with gender's intersection with ethnicity.[109] More than a third (34.1%) of scientists surveyed reported feeling pressure to play a traditionally feminine role, with Asian Americans (40.9%) more likely than other groups of women to report this. About half of the scientists surveyed (53.0%) reported backlash for displaying stereotypically "masculine" behaviours like speaking their minds directly or being decisive.

Girls and young women also lack sufficient female role models across the fields of STEM.[110] Between 1901 and 2019, the Nobel prize for physics has been awarded 213 times but only three times to women; between 1901 and 2019, the prize for medicine has been awarded 219 times with only 12 being women; and only five women have ever won the prize in chemistry, two of those, Emmanuelle Charpentier and Jennifer A. Doudna, in 2020. While there might be fewer women researchers within these fields – an issue that needs to be addressed in and of itself - we need to ask if this accounts for the low number of female Nobel laureates. Jocelyn Bell Burnell, Esther Lederberg, Chien-Shiung Wu, Lise Meitner, Rosalind Franklin, Nettie Stevens are all female scientists whose research was instrumental to the development of science for which they never received recognition.

Gender biases are deeply ingrained; we are socially conditioned to associate certain tasks with certain people. Despite being in this field for so many years, and training others in unconscious biases, even I am prone to succumbing to our deeply conditioned biases. Let me share an embarrassing incident that happened a few months ago. I was having dinner with my family on a normal Thursday evening. My 11-year-old son was telling me, my husband, and his younger brother about a talk that he had listened to at school by a guest speaker from Google. I asked him, "Was he a parent at school"? As the words rolled out of my mouth, I immediately realised my bias. What was so heartening was my son's immediate reaction in calling out my bias: "Mom, the speaker was a woman and that was so biased of you!". It is encouraging to know that the younger generations are growing up aware of the biases in and around them, while having the confidence to call them out. I consoled my deep embarrassment with a renewed hope: that with the younger generations, the world may be heading in the right direction.

Have you ever heard a male colleague complain, "my (female) boss is crazy and hysterical"? The insinuation is that her actions are emotional and illogical rather than rational and critical. Did you know the word "hysteria" comes from the Greek *hystera*, meaning uterus, signifying that this so-called disease was unique to women?! How many times have you heard a man comment that a woman who is expressing emotion must be "having her time of the month", delegitimizing those emotions? In my corporate training sessions, I am shocked at the number of times I have had male trainees declare "Women are not in leadership positions simply because they don't want to be there. If they wanted it, they could, but they don't". This biased thinking reflects a lack of understanding, a disregard for the challenges faced by women, and the ignorance that inequity exists.

Speaking of leadership, what do you think are the characteristics we associate with being an effective and successful leader? It turns out they are largely "male characteristics", and these associations are held equally by men and women. In a 2018 study in *Frontiers in Psychology*, 249 men and women were asked to do a self-reflection on what kind of attributes would be needed for them to be effective in either a leadership role or an assistant role.[111] Here, both men and women equally think they should have primarily agentic characteristics - capable, competent, confident, common sense, intelligent, ambitious, assertive, competitive, decisive, and self-reliant - in order to be a successful leader. In contrast, they view communal attributes - good-natured, sincere, tolerant, happy, trustworthy, cooperative, patient, polite, sensitive, and cheerful - as important to help them succeed in low-power assistant positions. "Our results underscore that women internalize a stereotypically masculine view of leadership," says author Andrea C. Vial. "Although women seem to value communality more than men when thinking about other leaders, they may feel that acting in a stereotypically feminine way themselves could place them at a disadvantage compared to male leaders." Women are expected to be not just competent, but also warm. At the same time, when women express emotions, they are seen as emotional; when a man shows emotion, he is seen as intense and passionate.

The biases against women and "female traits" certainly do not stop there - from biases that question the capability of women of child-bearing age or the commitment of mothers with young children, to what is considered appropriate dress for women in senior roles. I recall a female CEO being "recommended" to wear a pantsuit for her first day as CEO rather than a dress so as to be taken "more seriously". She showed up in a pink dress. Kudos to her. I know competent and ambitious women who have been told "Don't you think it's time for you to have children now?" by their male managers. If that has got you feeling uneasy, wait - there is more.

Men and women even face biases based on their voice; yes - their voice. Research shows that male and female leaders with lower-pitched - read masculine - voices are generally preferred by both men and women.[112] Lower-pitched voices tend to be perceived as more attractive, physically stronger, and more dominant. Even for women, while higher-pitched voices tend to be considered more attractive, those with lower-pitched voices are perceived as more dominant.[113] I had a trainee who is Black African British who says he often faces stereotyping because he speaks with a loud voice, which gets louder the more passionate he is about the topic. He shared that he speaks that way because he comes from a large family where he had to speak loudly to get attention from his parents. However, he is often thought of as being aggressive and angry, which is far from reality. Who would have thought that our voice would have such an impact on the perceptions about us at work?

While women do face significantly greater biases and microaggressions in the workplace, men experience them too, especially if they are from minority ethnic groups. In certain fields like human resources (HR), early years teaching as well as in nursing, men face biases based on the perceived qualities needed for those roles. For example, in HR, being "warm" and "personable" with higher emotional intelligence are characteristics that are seen as being integral to success. Men wanting to enter into this field or move up in the hierarchy are often seen as less capable because these traits are, stereotypically, more prevalent in women than men. Unfortunately, many of these biases against men are reinforced in childhood with phrases like "don't cry like a girl" or "boys don't cry, act like a man"; indicating that boys should show less emotion and be "tough". In fact, these stereotypes are so widely reinforced that author Keith Negley has written a book to counteract them. *Tough Guys (Have Feelings Too)* is a beautiful book which I read to my sons.

Biases exist in hiring in the field of education. Kindergarten and primary school educators tend to be women. Of the 506,400 full-time teachers in the UK, 30.5% of teachers are male and 69.5% are female.[114] What is interesting is that at the primary school level, this rises to 82.4% female. In the US, in 2018, about 76% of public-school teachers were female and 24% were male, with a lower percentage of male teachers at the elementary school level (11%) than at the secondary school level (36%).[115] Similar data can be found across other OECD[116] countries.

Why is this? Several studies state that men are underrepresented in early childhood education because of a low salary, perceived lack of status, fear of child abuse allegations, and scarcity of male camaraderie in the field.[117] In addition, early childhood education has been traditionally considered to be a female-oriented profession.[118] As a society we are conditioned to believe that women are better suited to be more nurturing or "motherly" towards younger children, resulting in fewer men applying for those roles, and hiring committees making choices that prefer female candidates over men. Again, a bias against men. Part of this bias centres around the belief that early childhood teaching is somehow less "important" or prestigious than other jobs. The skew of male educators in early childhood education is not just a result of hiring decisions and job-candidate fit, but rather decades of social conditioning which has resulted in an association with women in those roles. The result is an imbalance in the number of men who actively choose early childhood education as a career path, creating a talent pool which is heavily weighted toward women.

As a result of these biases, teachers face microaggressions like "Is this an actual job or are you a glorified babysitter?". In some countries, it does not help that the salaries of teachers are lower than other professions, cementing the belief that these jobs are less worthy than others, prompting fewer men - who are often seen as the primary breadwinner of households - to go into these careers. Early childhood teaching roles were, and perhaps still are, thought to be more amenable to the needs of women juggling their own motherhood roles and household responsibilities. Shorter work days and time off during school holidays, which usually align with their own children's holidays, may also be a factor.

Stay-at-home dads are often met with confusion and disbelief that they would voluntarily stay at home and take care of the children. They face stigmas which stem from a lack of familiarity with the role, religious beliefs, opposing attitudes about gender roles, and ignorance.[119] Even dads who show an active interest in their family - who leave work to pick their children up from school, watch their child play basketball or are involved in household chores - are not spared the stigma. Some are seen by others as "weak" or worse still, "whipped" (a sexist slur indicating that the partner is forcing the man to engage in these activities, and the man is obliging out of fear). I know plenty of dads, including my husband, for whom being actively involved in their family - by their own free will - brings them great joy.

So, what do we do? Fighting gender bias with more bias is certainly not the strategy that will result in more inclusive workplaces for all. At the same time, saying that one is 'gender blind' is not right either. Gender blind implies that one does not acknowledge or recognise the systemic biases that result in either gender facing biases and discrimination. What we need is active allies of gender - those who actively recognise where biases exist in our workplaces and make conscious efforts to correct them. That begins with diversifying the term 'gender' itself.

## Diversifying Gender

Much of what has been written and studied about gender as a dimension of diversity in societies and workplaces has focused primarily on addressing the lack of equality for women - rightfully so - and 'male' and 'female' have dominated our categorisations of gender. *Gender* is a social construct referring to whether an individual sees themselves as male, female or identifies with another gender entirely. Gender is different, though often used interchangeably, with sex – the latter being biologically defined.

As we look ahead, we need to adopt a broader view of gender that would require us to consider the variety of gender identifications in societies including male, female, transgender, gender-neutral, non-binary, agender, pangender, genderqueer, third gender, gender-fluid and many more. Did you know that there are 58 gender options on Facebook[120] that users can choose from? Generation Z, those born between 2001 to 2015, are the most likely to say forms or online profiles should include options other than "male" or "female". Roughly six-in-ten Gen Zers (59%) hold this view, compared with half of Millennials and four-in-ten or fewer Gen Xers, Boomers and members of the Silent generation.[121]

Gen Zers[122] are more likely than Millennials to say they know someone who prefers that others use gender-neutral pronouns to refer to them: 35%, compared with 25% of Millennials. There is a noticeable generational shift. Among each older generation, the share drops: 16% of Gen Xers, 12% of Boomers and just 7% of Silents say this. These findings seem to speak more to exposure than to viewpoint, as roughly equal shares of Gen Zers and Millennials say society should be more accepting of people who don't identify as either a man or a woman. Gender-neutral pronouns include "they", "them", "that person", and "their". More recently, I have noticed this shift on LinkedIn with more people highlighting their preferred pronouns "He/Him" or "She/Her", paving the way for those who are non-binary to feel more comfortable sharing their preferred pronouns "They/Them".

In 2019, I was fortunate to hear a heart-breaking and inspiring talk by Cecilia Jacobsen, a transgender woman from the Faroe Islands. From experiencing gender-biased slurs to having stones thrown at her to being called "it", Cecilia shared her horrific experiences as someone who identifies as transgender. She shared how often she faces comments like "Oh, you're transgender? You don't look it at all!", reflecting the view that being transgender is somehow undesirable.

**Gender identifications**

*Cisgender:* People whose gender identity matches their sex assigned at birth.

*Transgender*: People have a gender identity or gender expression that differs from the sex that they were assigned at birth.

*Gender neutral/ non-binary:* People whose gender is not male or female use many different terms to describe themselves, with non-binary being one of the most common.

*Gender-fluid:* People whose gender changes over time. A gender-fluid person might identify as a woman one day and a man the next. They might also identify as agender, bigender, or another nonbinary identity.

*Agender*: People ('a-' meaning "without") who identify as having no gender or being without a gender identity. Also called genderless, gender-free, non-gendered, or ungendered.

*Pangender/ Omnigender:* A gender identity in which a person either identifies as a countless number of separate identities that they are fluid between over time, or that they identify as one all encompassing identity.

*Genderqueer:* A gender identity that's built around the term "queer." To be queer is to exist in a way that may not align with heterosexual or homosexual norms.

*Third gender*: A concept in which individuals are categorized, either by themselves or by society, as neither man nor woman. It is also a social category present in societies that recognize three or more genders.

In the workplace, toilets are one of most glaring examples of discrimination against anyone who does not identify with "male" or "female". An increasing number of organisations are modifying toilets to be gender-neutral to eliminate the need for individuals to make an uncomfortable choice, often in front of others. The topic has even made it into the latest season of the popular Netflix series *Suits,* highlighting the relevance and the surprising challenges faced, with different generational views presented. Some companies have addressed this by creating individual, soundproof cubicles, with individual sinks and a mirror, so while it is gender-neutral, privacy is maintained. In schools and universities, younger generations are dialling up the pressure for gender-neutral bathrooms. I remember the first time, a few years ago, when I entered a gender-neutral bathroom at Copenhagen Business School where I teach, and the discomfort of having to wait in line and chat with a male student of mine. Over time, I have certainly gotten used to it and don't even think of it as an issue anymore.

Workplace dress codes are another area where we need to change the language and terminology we use to be inclusive to all the gender identities within our organisations. During a virtual training program with two White, middle-aged, male trainers, a client of mine - also a white male - noticed that the trainers said, "for our session on Thursday, please wear a suit and tie", completely disregarding the women on that call. The client, who was undergoing unconscious bias training with me at that time, identified the microaggression and raised it with HR, suggesting that more gender-neutral terminology could have been used instead, for example 'business formal'.

## Impact of Gender Bias

Gender biases influence who we hire, how they progress through our organisational hierarchies, how their performance is assessed and how they are rewarded. This leads to a lack of equal gender representation within our organisations, which in turn, has an impact on the kinds and range of products and services provided to customers, as well as how these products and services are marketed to the gender diverse population.

With positive discrimination/affirmative action and equal employment laws in most economies around the world, explicit biases in job descriptions are rare. However, the implicit or unconscious biases through the words used in job descriptions are prevalent, and affect the candidates' perception of the job itself as well as the perception of inclusion of the organisation as a whole. Language, and the use of certain words, has been found to have a significant impact on who applies for the job in the first place.

A 2011 research study showed that job advertisements for male-dominated sectors like construction, security, and Tech used greater masculine wording than advertisements within female-dominated sectors.[123] The study found that when job advertisements were constructed to include more masculine than feminine wording, more men applied for these roles, and importantly, women found these jobs less appealing. In the study, masculine words in job descriptions included active, adventurous, assertive, aggressive, ambitious, analytical, athletic, autonomous, challenging, competent, decisive, determined, independent, objective, principled and self-confident. Feminine words, on the other hand, included affectionate, nurturing, committed, compassionate, considerate, cooperative, empathetic, interpersonal, supportive, understanding, trustworthy, kind and dependable. Many companies today use gender bias decoder software to help remove gender bias in their job descriptions with the hope of attracting a diverse pool of talent in the hiring process.

We cannot discuss the impact of gender biases in the workplace without addressing the presence of glass-ceilings. This metaphor is used to represent an invisible barrier that prevents women from rising beyond a certain level in a hierarchy. These glass-ceilings are still very much present in many workplaces today. Bias – affinity and intergroup – are key causes. We tend to hire people who are like us. With men being over-represented in many professions and at leadership positions in our workplaces, it is not surprising that we see a dearth of women in these professions and leadership positions. *Intergroup bias* means that we tend to hire for "fit" with the prototype. I frequently hear personal accounts of women who did not get promoted to a more senior role because they did not "fit in" with the current team. Most of the time, the current team is made up of a rather homogenous group of men.

In a recruitment training exercise conducted by the HR team of a large global alcohol manufacturer, line managers involved in recruitment decisions were asked to provide examples of questions they would use to assess the following in a candidate: (1) if they were the right person for the company; (2) if they were a team player; and (3) if they had resilience. One manager's responses were: (1) ask them if they drink beer; (2) ask them if they played a team sport; and (3) ask them when they cried in the office last. Who do you think this manager was likely to hire? A man who enjoyed drinking beer and playing or just watching football? In other words, a man exactly like himself and many others in leadership positions in the company.

It may be hard to believe that men are given higher performance ratings than women, even when their qualifications and behaviours are identical,[124] but it is true. In fact, high performing men and women are described differently in performance appraisals.[125] Performance appraisals are shown to contain nearly twice the amount of language describing niceness or warmth for women than for men. While men are allowed to focus on their own objectives, women are expected to also care for others, "shouldering an unfair load".[126] Such biases, over time, harm a women's career progression and contribute to gender gaps in earnings and the underrepresentation of women in top-level positions.

As we explore decision making in hiring and promotion, there is a commonly held 'belief' that the lack of confidence is what is holding women back.[127] This is simply untrue. A 2018 study by *Harvard Business Review* shows that this confidence gap between men and women is a myth - women are not lower in confidence overall, but they do tend to appear less confident because of our biases in how we expect confidence to manifest.[128] This perceived lack of confidence is what makes hiring managers tend to hire men, because men are perceived to have greater confidence than women. In his TED talk,[129] book and *HBR* article[130] titled 'Why Do So Many Incompetent Men Become Leaders?', Tomas Chamorro-Premuzic explains that the reason why women are underrepresented in workplaces across the world, barring Iceland perhaps, is because of our inability to discern between confidence and competence. We mistake confidence for competence and get "fooled into believing that men are better leaders than women",[131] and we choose leaders who are narcissistic, confident, and charismatic rather than talent with the traits that are actually needed for effective leadership - competence, humility and integrity.[132]

To see what we can do differently in our hiring and promotion processes, we can draw inspiration from the music industry. Since the 1970s, as part of revisions made to hiring practices, a number of orchestras have adopted "blind" auditions in which screens are used to conceal the identity and gender of the musician from the jury panel.[133] The results of these changes were significant. In 1970, female musicians made up less than 5% of all players in the top five symphony orchestras in the United States. In 2000, that number was 25%. The research study found that the screen increased the probability of a woman advancing from preliminary rounds by 50%.[134] The screen also enhanced, by several fold, the likelihood a female contestant would be the winner in the final round. The study concluded that the switch to "blind" auditions can explain between 30% and 55% of the increase in the proportion of females among new hires, and between 25% and 46% of the increase in the percentage of females in the orchestras since 1970.

Blind auditions are certainly a good strategy. What about quotas? There has been a lot of discussion around the use of quotas as part of positive discrimination efforts in organisations to increase the number of women in more senior positions of leadership. With projections suggesting that it would take 30 years before we get 30% of female representation on boards of directors, some argue that quotas are necessary to kickstart the process of achieving equal representation. Melinda Gates says on Harvard Business Review's podcast *Ideacast* that quotas can be helpful if they are temporary. For quotas to be effective, critical mass is needed – marginalization becomes difficult when 40% are women, or better still, 50%. In addition, expanding the search criteria and scope helps to increase the pool of candidates to choose from. While there may be some discomfort in the beginning, with adequate support, these quotas could help increase gender representation.

On the other hand, these quotas are likely to be seen as unfair and unjust where one group, in this case women, are being favoured over another group, in this case men. The other bigger issue with quotas is the stigma that women who are selected into the role face. They may be perceived to be less qualified, even when being adequately qualified, and there because of quotas to fulfill a "tick-box" exercise. I have met numerous women in senior leadership roles who faced casual comments that their presence is part of the hiring manager's "diversity quota for the year". Quotas, though well-intended, can reduce genuine support for D&I efforts as employees feel that the company is telling them what to do, rather than doing it because it is the right thing to do.

In 2003, the Norwegian government passed a law that required companies to have at least 40% of their board members be women. After an initial grace period of two years for existing companies, a failure to achieve the 40% quota led to the delisting of the company. On a positive note, this ruling meant that organisations in Norway widened the criteria from traditional parameters of selection for board positions to looking more broadly at other relevant criteria, in order to expand the pool of women who could take on these roles. This law had a knock-on effect as companies not required by law also began to recruit and hire more women. While there were certainly positive effects in the boardroom, these did not trickle down to lower levels and underrepresentation persisted there.[135] In addition, these quotas did not necessarily address the underlying causes of discrimination and bias. The initial, small group of women who were appointed to various different boards were nicknamed the "golden skirts"; implying that they were there only to fulfill the government requirement rather than to harness their competencies and add value to the board.

In more recent times, there has been increased attention on the gender pay gaps that exist in workplaces. In 2017, the gender pay gap between the BBC's top presenters was publicly brought to light, and top female presenters demanded equal pay. While the BBC's pay gap of 9.3% was lower than the UK average of 18% at that time, the public outcry prompted one of the world's leading news organisations to make concrete efforts to close the pay gap between men and women.[136] The news is not much better across the Atlantic Ocean, with Goldman Sachs, Twitter, Microsoft, Google, Disney, and Nike all facing recent lawsuits alleging the companies paid women less than men or passed them over for promotions.

It is hard to believe that the raw gender pay gap, which looks at the median salary for all men and women regardless of job type or worker seniority, shows that women in America in 2020 earned 81 cents for every dollar earned by men.[137] This is a 7% improvement from 2015, when the median salary for men was roughly 26% higher than the median salary for women. In the EU, data from the European Commission showed that in 2019, women earned 16% less, or 84-euro cents for every €1 men earned.[138] While progress is being made, at differing rates across the EU, the gap has only decreased by 1% over the past seven years. The gender pay gap in 2019 stood at 20.8% in the UK, 14.7% in Denmark, and 21% in Germany.[139] What is perhaps most surprising is that gender pay gaps begin right after university. In the UK, men earned 10% more on average than women 15 months after they left university. Even among graduates with similar qualifications, there remained a wide gap in pay.[140]

What about elsewhere in the world, how do these figures look? While China has witnessed a widening gender pay gap in the past two decades[141] and data is limited, a recruitment website[142] claimed that in 2019, China saw a decrease in the wage gap for the first time, with women earning 77.5% of men's average wage compared to 72.3% in 2016. The main reason stated for this was that more women were moving into management because of stronger work capabilities and greater desire in women to succeed professionally. In 2020, India slipped to the 112th position (from 108th in 2018) in the World Economic Forum's Gender Gap Index, with a 19% wage gap between men and women in 2019.

Surely things must be better when all compensable factors, such as experience, industry and job level are accounted for, right? Well, they are not. Even when men and women with the same employment characteristics do similar jobs, women in America earn $0.98 for every dollar earned by an equivalent man. In other words, a woman who is doing the same job as a man, with the exact same qualifications, is still paid 2% less for no attributable reason. This has not changed by any significant amount since 2015. Do things get better at the top? Unfortunately not. In fact, the pay gap widens as women progress in their career, with women at the executive level making $0.95 to every dollar a man makes when all compensable factors are accounted for, and a shocking $0.69 to every dollar when these factors are not accounted for.[143]

It is easy to assume that this gap must be due to the fact that many women may take a career break to have children. Some may look for jobs in industries like health care and education that offer flexibility to manage their family, and those are likely to be of lower pay.[144] This does not fully account for the gap. Neither do differences in education, experience, and occupation. Women earn less pay per hour across all sectors and occupations for the same jobs, and do a significantly larger share of unpaid work.[145]

Women with children also make less than men with children or women without children. This is often called the motherhood penalty[146] - the penalty for women having a family. No such penalty exists for men. In fact, the opposite is true.

So, how can companies address the impact of gender bias internally to ensure gender representation? Through active allyship at all levels.

To find out how to be an active ally as an individual, team, and organisation, turn to the chapter titled 'Active Allyship in Action'.

# IKEA RETAIL (INGKA GROUP)

## Building a Gender Balanced Business

IKEA is guided by one single, yet powerful vision: creating a better everyday life for many people, including customers, co-workers and all who work with the company. Introduced in 1976 by its founder, Ingvar Kamprad, IKEA's vision and purpose will continue to guide the company into the next decade and beyond. As a company, IKEA is on a journey to become more accessible, affordable and sustainable. With a reach of approximately 706 million customers in 378 IKEA markets worldwide, IKEA has an incredible opportunity to make a positive impact.

IKEA's vision goes beyond home furnishing. The company wants their business to have a positive impact on the world, from communities where materials are sourced, to the way products help customers to live a more sustainable life at home. By sharing what the company does, and speaking up for what they believe in, IKEA sees itself as part of the movement for positive change in society.

According to IKEA: "We are committed to Equality, Diversity & Inclusion (ED&I) and we recognize that equality lies at the heart of human rights. At IKEA Retail, we welcome all dimensions of diversity, because we understand that an inclusive workforce is good for our co-workers, our customers and ultimately, our business. Here you are free to be yourself and to have equal say regardless of your background, age, or gender. Equality is felt at every corner of the office, the stores, and can even be seen when people speak to each other daily.

"Today however, there is a new reality. Many movements are having a large effect in society, such as technological disruption, increased demand for social activism, unprecedented demographic changes, social polarization, and most recently due to the pandemic, increased economic regression for minorities, and unfavored conditions for females in the workforce, among others. It is therefore crucial that large organizations such as IKEA make a substantial footprint and become a guiding light for others to follow.

"We know that a diverse and inclusive workplace is good for people and for the business. In order to foster an environment that doesn't simply tick compliance boxes, IKEA has made a conscious effort in three key areas: our co-workers, our business, and society as a whole.

"At IKEA, our co-workers are at the heart of our business, and we have closed the gender gap by achieving a 50/50 gender balance in leadership roles in all levels and functions, and we are placing focus on new growth roles such as positions in STEM. Every day we are getting closer to our goal, and examples can be seen across the organization, such as our Digital Design Operations team, where females hold at least 50% of leading positions. In 2019 we rolled out a common global approach to achieve equal pay across 30+ countries where we ensured paid maternity leave, and where we continuously contribute in addressing inequality of caring, nursing and housework responsibilities. We are anchoring ED&I throughout the co-worker journey, integrating equality dimensions into all people processes. This includes all recruitment activities, where hiring is based on our values."

Barbara Martin Coppola, Chief Digital Officer (CDO), is an inspiring example of equality in the workplace, as she has seen and experienced imbalance firsthand. "The importance of a diverse and gender equal workforce is very close to my heart. It's a commonly known fact that companies that are gender and ethnically diverse outperform their peers- I've seen and experienced this personally. I have spent my career in the technology sector which is gender imbalanced. Coming to IKEA made an impact on me and I am experiencing first-hand the benefits of a balanced work environment."

"We are fostering equality throughout our business practices. Research shows us that diverse teams showcase more innovation and companies with gender diversity have better financial performance. In Digital at IKEA we are fostering a stronger workforce with different points of views, skill sets, approaches and experiences, in order to produce innovative solutions. We created an ED&I ambassador knowledge program that empowers co-workers in every market to increase their cultural knowledge and understand unconscious bias, to better serve a diverse customer base.

"As a humanistic, values-driven company, IKEA is committed to having a positive impact on societal development. By 2030 our ambition is to improve the wellbeing of millions of people by becoming truly an inclusive and a people-centered company and employer. We want to provide safe and meaningful employment across our value chain, playing our part in creating a fair and equal society for co-workers, workers in our supply chain and people facing barriers to enter the labor market in our communities. As part of that commitment we are working towards changing the global recruitment industry by eliminating recruitment fees charged to migrant workers by 2026 and enabling social entrepreneurs to drive social change locally. Currently, we have partnerships with 21 social enterprises."

## Key Takeaways:

- It is essential to stress the importance of making ED&I a strategic priority for all businesses. This helps better understand customers to offer more creative and relevant home furnishing solutions.
- Diversity is an asset in teams (like technology), where fostering new ideas drives innovation, and attracts more talent by creating a better place to work.
- ED&I practices should be embedded in every facet of the organization, to create a positive contribution towards society, as it sets a benchmark of how companies should be operating. Equal opportunities are a human right, and they make business sense.

Explore more about IKEA Retail (Ingka Group) at https://www.ingka.com

# Sexual Orientation

*"Everybody has the right to love and be loved, and nobody on this earth has the right to tell anyone that their love for another human being is morally wrong."*

Barbara Streisand, American singer

Many of us have come to recognise the rainbow flag - often referred to as the gay pride or LGBT pride flag - as a symbol of lesbian, gay, bisexual, transgender, and queer (LGBTQ) members of our societies. Maybe some of you have taken part in a pride parade in your city or neighbourhood to celebrate the rights of the LGBTQ+ community and show your support. If you are a fan of the Emmy award winning mockumentary *Modern Family*, you may have fallen in love with gay dads Mitchell Pritchett and Cameron Tucker as they battle stereotypes within their own families and communities, while also making parenthood work. The public display of rainbow colours and our favourite TV characters have tried to normalise sexual orientations that are non-heterosexual. In reality though, who we have a physical, romantic and/or emotional attraction with can be a real source of discrimination and bias, and is a dimension of diversity that continues to generate polarised views in some parts of the world.

While sexual orientation is closely related to the gender dimension of diversity, gender and sexual orientation are two separate things. Sexual orientation includes being straight, gay, lesbian, bisexual or any of the other sexual orientations. An acronym that has become synonymous with representing people who identify with the various sexual orientations other than heterosexuality is LGBTQ+ referring to Lesbian, Gay, Bisexual, Transgender/ Transsexual, Queer while the plus refers to additional sexual identities including pansexual, intersexual, and asexual.

Sexual orientation is a dimension of diversity that has historically been seen as controversial, stemming from deeply embedded social and religious beliefs of what sexuality should look like, and what is considered to be an appropriate sexual relationship. In 18th and 19th century Europe, same-sex behaviours were socially unacceptable and even criminalized. The LGBT movement only really began in the beginning of the 20th century and picked up steam after the end of World War II in Western Europe, Scandinavia, and the US. The Homophile Movement from 1945 to 1969 led to some pivotal steps towards equal rights. In 1967, the Sexual Offences Bill passed in England and Wales, which decriminalised homosexual acts between two men over 21 years of age in private.

The Gay Liberation Movement from 1969 to 1974 resulted in The American Psychiatric Association removing "homosexuality" from the diagnostics manual of mental illness in 1973. LGBT activists were inspired by Black Power and Women's Liberation movements of the time and became more radical following the Stonewall Uprising of 1969, during which a group of gay men, transgender women, lesbians, and drag queens at the gay club Stonewall Inn in New York resisted a police raid. The raid sparked a riot that lasted for six days with protests and violent clashes with law enforcement. This Stonewall Uprising was a catalyst for the gay rights movement in the US and around the world. In fact, it was after the Stonewall Uprising that the word "gay" was used as an antonym for straight and what was thought to be appropriate sexual behaviour.

## What Has Been Done

In 1972, Sweden became the first country in the world to allow people who were transsexual by legislation to surgically change their sex, and provided free hormone replacement therapy. Sweden also changed the age of consent for same-sex partners to 15, making it equal to heterosexual couples. The LGBT Rights Movement from 1972 to the present is where the most headway has been made in securing equal rights for its members.

The Netherlands was the first country to allow same-sex marriage in 2001. This was followed by Belgium in 2003, and Spain and Canada in 2005. By 2020, same-sex marriages were also recognized in South Africa, Norway, Sweden, Portugal, Iceland, Argentina, Mexico, Denmark, Brazil, France, Uruguay, New Zealand, United Kingdom, Luxembourg, Ireland, the United States, Colombia, Finland, Germany, Malta, Australia, Austria, Taiwan, Ecuador and Costa Rica. South Africa became the first African nation to legalize same-sex marriage in 2006 and is currently the only African nation where same-sex marriage is legal. In contrast, in Somalia and northern Nigeria, homosexuality is punishable by death. In a landmark and historic decision, the Indian supreme court ruled in 2018 that gay sex was no longer a criminal offense.

**Sexual Orientations**

*Heterosexual:* Romantic, sexual attraction or sexual behaviour between persons of the opposite sex or gender.

*Pansexual:* Pansexuality is sexual, romantic or emotional attraction towards people regardless of their sex or gender identity.

*Demisexual:* Sexual attraction towards people that they have close emotional connections with.

*Transexual:* A transgender person, especially one whose bodily characteristics have been altered through surgery or hormone treatment to bring them into alignment with their gender identity.

*Monosexual (Heterosexual/Homosexual):* Romantic or sexual attraction to members of one sex or gender only.

*Queer:* An umbrella term for sexual and gender minorities who are not heterosexual or cisgender.

*Bisexual:* Romantic attraction, sexual attraction, or sexual behaviour toward both males and females, or to more than one sex or gender.

*Asexual:* Not engaging in sexual activity, feelings, or associations.

*Grey-Asexual*: An area between asexuality and sexuality, in which a person may only experience sexual attraction on occasion.

*Autosexual:* Someone who has a great deal of trouble responding to someone else sexually but can respond fairly or very well to their own touch. They usually are attracted to others and fantasize about others, but what they respond to is their own touch.

*Intersexual:* A variety of conditions in which a person is born with a reproductive or sexual anatomy that does not seem to fit the typical definitions of female or male.

A report in June 2020 by the OECD provided a comprehensive overview of the extent to which laws in OECD countries ensured equal treatment and inclusion of LGBTI (lesbians, gay men, bisexuals, transgender and intersex) individuals.[147] As of 2020, 29 countries officially recognise same-sex marriage – and five of them are the Nordic nations.[148] Nordic countries are known for being the most LGBT-friendly nations with a more liberal mindset, high degree of social acceptance and tolerance. Norway was one of the first countries in the world to enact an anti-discrimination law explicitly including sexual orientation in 1981. In 2009, Sweden voted with an overwhelming majority to support same-sex marriage, and in 2010, Iceland voted unanimously to legalize same-sex marriage. As the law came into effect, Jóhanna Sigurðardóttir, Iceland's Prime Minister at the time, married her long-time partner Jonina Leosdottir. Denmark was the first country in the world to allow same-sex partners to register as domestic partners in 1989, and legalized same-sex marriage in 2012. The Nordic countries are certainly leading the way in implementing legislation that would help inclusivity for the LGBT community.

In the corporate sector, some companies have taken strong stands to actively support their LGBTQ+ employees and customers. IBM is one organisation which has a long history of LGBT+ workplace equality. From as early as 1984, IBM has promoted and defended LGBT+ rights around the world and actively influenced legislation and policy in the US states of Louisiana, North Carolina, and Texas. The company has also engaged in Northern Ireland, Taiwan, Israel and Japan to support marriage equality referenda. Visa has expressed support for the United Nations Standards for LGBTI, a best-practice guide for policies and practices for LGBTI employees and inclusive workplaces. Starbucks' CEO Howard Schultz famously put his money where his mouth is when he told an anti-gay shareholder he was free to sell his stocks and invest somewhere else.[149] Google created the Employee Resource Group (ERG) 'The Gayglers' which is comprised of LGBT Googlers and their allies. This group leads the way in celebrating Pride around the world, but also provides advice on programs and policies.

Uber has also taken a leading role by globally prohibiting its drivers from discriminating against LGBT passengers, even if state laws might allow it in the countries where they operate. Internally, through UberPride, the company is building a diverse and inclusive workplace specifically focused on making LGBTQ individuals feel welcomed. During Pride month in 2017, Adidas released a rainbow-flag makeover of its iconic Stan Smith trainer, devoting a portion of the sales to an Oregon-based charity supporting homeless LGBT teens. Ikea devoted the year 2018 to transgender inclusion and in 2019, the IKEA Group celebrated International Day Against Homophobia, Biphobia and Transphobia. Microsoft was one of the first companies in the world to offer employee benefits to same-sex domestic partners, starting in 1993. GLEAM (Global LGBTQI+ Employees and Allies at Microsoft) is the ERG at Microsoft, where members interact through programmes such as talks, lunches, cross-corporate LGBT+ networking, sporting events, cultural activities, discussions with community leaders about gender and sexuality, volunteering, and fundraising for local LGBT+ organisations.

While we have become much more accustomed to seeing rainbow-coloured ads, particularly during Pride month, this has not always been the case. In the 1980s, with stigma surrounding HIV/AIDS, many companies that had introduced LGBTQ+-inclusive advertising in response to the Stonewall uprising in 1969, stopped. In the 1990s, things began to change when companies realised the untapped potential of the "gay affluent consumer". Marketers estimated the total annual income of the gay community at that time to be over $500 billion.[150] In 1994, Ikea launched the first television ad to feature a gay couple. In the commercial, the two men tease each other about their taste in furniture. The ad was viewed as radical at the time. Not everyone liked it, however, and the IKEA store in New York received a bomb threat. In 1994, AT&T launched a direct-marketing mail campaign which made them the first US phone company to openly target lesbian and gay customers. Subaru, in the late 1990s, realised the value of what was termed the "pink dollar" of their lesbian consumer base and launched a lesbian-focused marketing campaign. More recently, we have seen more representation of transgender and gender-neutral consumers, with Gillette's commercial featuring a young trans man and his dad, and Uber running a campaign featuring trans, genderqueer, and bisexual pride flags.

In the early 2000s, companies faced backlash for gay/lesbian-focused marketing; thankfully, the landscape is very different today. Companies have recognised the growing support for the LGBTQ+ community and their considerable buying power, which has triggered increasing interest from marketers in the LGBTQ+ market.[151] Where in the past alcohol and travel were typically leaders in LGBTQ-inclusive campaigns, we now see retail, cars, banking and financial services, food and beverages, and youth-oriented brands[152] following suit.

Even then, companies often are seen using superficial tactics to reach out to the LGBTQ+ community. Some use what is known as 'gay window' advertising where advertisers use special cues, signals and markers that allow their ads to be specifically noticed by gay consumers but pass more or less unnoticed by the general consumer. Alternatively, companies may use 'gay vague' advertising, which is when the relationship or sexual orientation of the people appearing in an ad is not 100% clear. There is certainly room to do better.

## The Business Case

Studies that have focused on quantifying the gains and positive financial effects of adopting LGBT-friendly policies focus on two aspects: financial savings on personnel costs, and positive effects on stock prices. In 2015, *Out Now* conducted a survey in Australia, Brazil, Canada, France, Germany, India, Italy, Mexico, UK and US. The study revealed that among LGBT people who have '*come out of the closet*' at work, meaning they are open with others about their sexual orientation, there are 16.6% fewer people who are thinking about leaving their job in the near future than among those that are not 'out'.[153] This is called the "retention dividend".

Other studies have demonstrated a positive relationship between the adoption of LGBT inclusive policies and the value of company shares in the stock market. A study on 258 publicly traded firms in 2002-2006 in the US found that the stock prices of companies with more progressive LGBT non-discrimination policies – as measured by their score on the Corporate Equality Index - outperformed otherwise equivalent firms in the same industry.[154] Another study found that LGBT-friendly workplace policies are at worst value-neutral, and firms' stock value is not penalised for supporting LGBT workforce diversity.[155] A 2016 Credit Suisse study found an association between the presence of LGBT people in senior roles, and company stock market performance.[156] The bank took 270 companies with openly LGBT staff as leaders or senior managers and compared their performance to a stock index tracking North America, Europe and Australia. They found that LGBT-led companies had outperformed the other index companies by 3% annually since 2010. Nearly 60% of the LGBT companies Credit Suisse tracked come from one of three sectors: information technology, financial, and consumer staples.

Beyond the financial benefits, from a business performance standpoint, companies that have an inclusive workplace for LGBTQ+ colleagues are able to attract and retain talent, be more innovative, and improve customer orientation and brand reputation. Happier, confident employees are more productive and less likely to resign. A diverse workforce broadens business perspectives and fosters creativity, and has greater collaboration with increased trust and open communication. A workforce which reflects the makeup of society appeals to a broad range of potential employees and customers. Improved brand reputation makes companies more attractive to employees, customers, and suppliers.[157]

A 2016 report by the European commission highlights that LGBT-supportive policies are "good for people, good for business" and draws on studies that show that having LGBT-supportive policies reduces incidences of discrimination, thereby improving psychological health and increasing job satisfaction, while also improving relationships between LGBT employees and their colleagues.[158] For LGBTQ+ employees, open, diverse, and inclusive workplaces mean that they can be authentic to their whole selves, rather than concealing important parts of their identity. When employees are emotionally and mentally drained from leaving a part of themselves outside the office doors because of non-inclusive workplace cultures, it prevents them from performing at their best. On the other hand, inclusion leads to greater motivation, and having an inclusive workplace for LGBTQ+ individuals means that employees feel like they can bring this dimension of diversity to work. This boosts engagement and productivity,[159] motivation and the willingness to go above and beyond what is required of them in their jobs.[160]

Among consumers and job-seekers who value LGBT-inclusive diversity practices, businesses with LGBT-supportive policies may be seen as better companies from which to buy products or for whom to work, thereby increasing their customer base and pool of prospective employees.[161] A Boston Consulting Group (BCG) LGBTQ employee survey in 2020 showed that LGBTQ employees who were open about their sexual orientation experienced two times greater psychological safety, felt 1.5 times more empowered, and 1.5 times more able to take creative risks.[162]

When it comes to brand reputation, the Human Rights Campaign Foundation's Corporate Equality Index (CEI)[163] in the US is the national benchmarking tool on corporate policies, practices and benefits pertinent to lesbian, gay, bisexual, transgender, and queer employees, and was launched in 2002. The CEI criterion has three pillars: non-discrimination policies across business entities; equitable benefits for LGBTQ workers and their families; and supporting an inclusive corporate culture. 91% of the Fortune 500 - including both companies that participate in the CEI survey and those that do not - have gender identity protections enumerated in their non-discrimination policies (up from 3% in 2002) and 98% of the entire CEI universe of businesses offer explicit gender identity non-discrimination protections (up from 5% in 2002).

Companies that are openly supporting LGBT rights are certainly reaping the benefits from loyal LGBT customers. In the US alone, the spending power of the LGBT community is calculated to be in the region of $800 billion a year.[164] A report by *Out Now* estimates the US economy could add an extra $9 billion a year if companies improved their ability to retain LGBT talent through the implementation of inclusive policies.[165]

"Almost 70% of homosexuals, both male and female, admit to being positively influenced by advertisements that contain gay and lesbian imagery and say that they would most likely buy these products".[166] A Google Consumer Survey from August of 2014 found that over 45% of consumers under 34 years old say they are more likely to do repeat business with an LGBT-friendly company. Of them, more than 54% also say they would choose an equality-focused brand over a competitor. The "LGBTQ Inclusion in Advertising and Media" study conducted by GLAAD[167] and Procter & Gamble in 2020, revealed that 82% of those surveyed in the US believe marketing efforts to promote LGBTQ representation are reflective of a brand valuing all forms of diversity. The study showed that of those who were exposed to LGBTQ+ folks in the media, 48% reported being more accepting of gays and lesbians, compared with a 35% acceptance rate among those who had not.

## Sexual Orientation Biases at Work

Despite the efforts to date and the benefits for organisations, our attitudes and behaviours towards others whose sexual orientation is not heterosexual is often fraught with biases. Depending on where we grew up and our family's beliefs about sexual orientation, we are socially conditioned to have an understanding of what is and is not acceptable. Unlike racial and ethnic minorities, LGBTQ+ individuals are not always raised with other family members, teachers or communities who share their minority status. They may face biases, not just from broader society, but from their immediate family as well.

In many societies, homosexual identities and behaviours go against socialised accepted gender norms. These norms are likely to constitute heterosexuality, heterosexual marriage, and children as a result of heterosexual unions.[168] Any deviation from this is frowned upon, more severely in some communities than others. Media, religion, and government also play significant roles in the existence and propagation of these biases in society and legislatively.[169] Therefore, our biases against people's sexual orientations intersect with the ethnicity and cultural dimension of diversity, and even our beliefs and values, particularly those that stem from religious beliefs.[170] This interaction influences the way we view sexual orientation and accounts for the variations in open-mindedness and tolerance towards non-heterosexual orientations across different cultural groups. Also, these factors mean that each LGBTQ+ member has had a varied life experience in managing this dimension of diversity. It is these embedded biases, often unconscious, social, and cultural, that we take with us into our workplaces.

Studies estimate that about 5 to 10% of people are LGBT.[171] Given this, it is surprising that there were no openly LGBT chief executives on the Fortune 500 until Apple's Tim Cook publicly announced that he is gay in 2014. This tells us that there is a need to address the sexual orientation biases at work, which take many forms, from microaggressions to prejudices.

*Sexual prejudice* encompasses all negative attitudes based on sexual orientation, whether the target is homosexual, bisexual, or heterosexual,[172] but given the deeply embedded "acceptable" norms of behaviour, sexual prejudice is almost always directed at people who engage in homosexual behaviour or label themselves gay, lesbian, or bisexual.[173] Sexual prejudice is an attitude which involves a judgement or evaluation; it is directed at a social group and its members; and it is negative, involving hostility or dislike. This sexual prejudice results in a negative perception of a person's sexual identity, so much so that being gay is seen as being "bad".

The Merriam-Webster dictionary defines *homophobia*, a term coined by heterosexual psychologist George Weinberg[174] in the late 1960s, as "irrational fear of, aversion to, or discrimination against homosexuality or homosexuals". It is a combination of the Greek words for "same" and "fear" to mean "fear of the same". It is expressed as a "fear, disgust, anger, discomfort, and aversion that people experience in dealing with gay people".[175] *Transphobia* - negative attitudes, feelings, or actions towards transgender people or transness in general; and *biphobia* - aversion toward bisexuality and toward bisexual people as a social group or as individuals; are subsets of homophobia.

Homophobia can manifest as unspoken negative thoughts regarding sexual minorities, negative attitudes, stereotypes, and labels about gay men and lesbians, and in discriminatory behaviour. It can range from derogatory joke telling to denying equivalent legal rights and protections to domestic partnerships.[176] In extreme cases, it can be demonstrated as violence against gay, lesbian, bisexual, and transgendered people.[177] Other possible targets of homophobia include heterosexual people who are perceived to be non-heterosexual because of their mannerisms or behaviours, as well as the children of gay, lesbian, bisexual, or transgendered parents. While homophobia can be exhibited or experienced by anyone regardless of gender, age, or sexual orientation, it is prominent among adolescent males in our society.[178] Because of the prevalence of homophobia in adolescence, when self-identity and self-worth are taking shape, those who identify outside heterosexuality face potential shame. This shame, nurtured by parents, family members, teachers and peers, can lead to subsequent self-loathing, reinforced by cultural and religious value systems. This can result in shame, denial, self-harm, hatred or anger and even abuse of other homosexuals, affecting their self-esteem and confidence in their sexual identity well into their adulthood.[179]

*Heterosexism* is a "belief system that values heterosexuality as superior to and/or more 'natural' than homosexuality".[180] It is a term similar to sexism and racism, describing an ideological system that denies, denigrates, and stigmatizes any non-heterosexual form of behaviour, identity, relationship, or community.[181] It includes the assumption that all people are heterosexual and denies or rejects the possibility of being other than straight. It is the idea that everyone is, or should be, heterosexual or straight and can be thought of as a more subtle and pervasive form of homophobia. The difference between the two lies in the spheres of operation; heterosexism operates on the societal level, and homophobia operates at the individual level.

Much like institutional racism and sexism, heterosexism is pervasive in societal customs and institutions, and operates through a dual process of invisibility and attack.[182] Heterosexism usually remains culturally invisible and comes to light only when people who engage in homosexual behaviour, or who are identified as homosexual become visible, and results in them being subjected to attack by society or those around them.

In October 2019, Glassdoor released its 2019 Diversity and Inclusion Study in the US, UK, France and Germany.[183] When compared to the other countries in the study, the percentage of employees reporting having experienced or witnessed workplace discrimination related to LGBTQ identity was highest in the US at 33% compared to the UK (25%), France (22%) and Germany (15%). Amongst US employees, one in three (33%) have experienced or witnessed LGBTQ discrimination at work. The study also showed that in the US younger employees (43% of ages 18-34) are more likely than older employees (18% of ages 55+) to have experienced or witnessed LGBTQ discrimination. In addition, employed men (38%) are more likely than employed women (28%) to have experienced or witnessed discrimination at work. When it comes to LGBTQ discrimination among younger workers specifically, younger employed men (51% of aged 18-34) are significantly more likely than younger employed women (34% of aged 18-34) to have experienced or witnessed it.

This discrimination stems from a range of microaggressions. First, microaggressions in this dimension can take the form of derogatory heterosexist language towards LGBTQ+ colleagues that include words and phrases like "faggot", "sissy" or "that's so gay". Gay jokes are surprisingly common in the workplace. Gay men are often made fun off for walking or having gestures "like a lady". Given that one's sexual orientation is an invisible dimension of diversity, people cannot ascertain another person's sexual orientation just by looking at them. This makes LGBTQ+ members the subject of jokes without others knowing that they are being discriminatory about someone in the room or group. In fact, depending on the individual and her/his/their life experiences, they may even consciously choose to hide it by joining in with the jokes to avoid being perceived to be "different" from others to "fit in".

Second, microaggressions can take the form of endorsing gender-conforming culture or behaviours by expecting LGBTQ+ colleagues to behave in heteronormative ways. For example, telling a gay individual to "act straight" in public. In the public sector and in educational institutions collecting information about families through the use of categories like "mother" and "father" leave out a variety of family configurations, including same-sex parents. Many have now switched to more inclusive categories like "Parent/Guardian 1" and "Parent/Guardian 2.".

Third, microaggressions can center around the universalism of LGBTQ+ experiences. Many assume that someone who is transgender must be gay, without realising that one can be transgender and be gay, straight, bisexual, or asexual. Comments like "You are transgender? You don't look it." reflect underlying assumptions that being transgender is somehow associated with being unattractive. Transgender persons are often stereotyped as being sex workers; while both gay or transgender individuals are often thought to have HIV/AIDS. We also see the presence of affinity bias in micro-aggressive behaviours when heterosexual colleagues meet homosexual colleagues. "Oh, you're gay, you should meet my friend Tom. He's gay too". This assumes that just because they are both gay, they will be compatible. You wouldn't introduce a straight man to a straight woman simply because of their matching sexual orientation, would you?

Fourth, microaggressions can take the form of disrespect, discomfort, or disapproval towards LGBTQ+ experiences. For example, staring in disgust at a lesbian couple showing affection to one another. Finally, microaggressions can take the form of the very denial of sexual prejudices, homophobia, heterosexism, or transphobia by dismissing a co-worker's concerns as paranoid for thinking that someone at work is discriminating against them on the basis of their sexual orientation.

## The Impact of Sexual Orientation Biases

Sexual orientation is sometimes known as the "last acceptable and remaining prejudice" in modern societies and organisations in comparison with other dimensions of diversity.[184] LGBTQ+ employees continue to face a variety of challenges that range from being forced to remain closeted to actual job dismissal.

Sexual prejudices, homophobia and heterosexism, along with the resulting microaggressions, impact who we hire and promote, how equitably we pay them, and also have an impact on the marketing of the products and services we sell as well as products and services themselves. In June 2020, the US Supreme Court ruled that workers cannot be terminated for being gay or transgender after three cases were filed by employees who had been fired from their jobs because of their sexual orientation. High profile legal cases bring to light the prevalence of sexual orientation biases in workplaces. In 2019, a jury awarded a US police officer in St. Louis County nearly $20 million in a sexual orientation discrimination case. The police officer claimed that over six years he was turned down for promotion 23 times, despite having 15 years of experience, a clean record, and strong performance reviews. The jury agreed.

**Gay friendships**

A study that looked at data over a ten-year period from 1998 to 2008 showed that in the US, gay men earned 10% to 32% less than similarly situated heterosexual men.[185] In another study published in 2015, a meta-analysis of 31 studies published between 1995 and 2012 from the US and other developed countries, revealed that gay men earned 11% less than heterosexual men.[186] On the other hand, a large-scale study by the World Bank found that lesbians earn an average of 8% more than their heterosexual female colleagues and in some countries, like the US, lesbians were found to earn up to 20% more.[187] Why is this? Are gay men penalised in the workplace? Do lesbian women gain by not conforming to societal expectations of traditional family roles or motherhood, which, in turn, eliminate those barriers to moving ahead?

In some parts of the world and in some workplaces, people are not comfortable being open about their sexual preferences, resulting in the need to leave a part of themselves behind as they enter the glass doors of an organisation. Globally, about 40% of LGBTQ employees are closeted at work and 75% have reported experiencing negative day-to-day workplace interactions related to their LGBTQ identity in the past year.[188] 36% of employees who have come out of the closet have lied or "covered" parts of their identities at work in the past year, while 54% of employees who are out at work remain closeted to their clients and customers. When talent cannot bring their whole selves to work, it has a huge psychological impact on them, affecting their emotional and mental well-being in the workplace. A 2011 study showed that LGBTQ participants described that when they experienced microaggressions, they felt depressed, anxious, and even traumatized.[189]

LGBTQ+ employees react to the sexual orientation biases and microaggressions that they face at work in many different ways. These responses can be (1) behavioural, when employees rely on passive, confrontational or protective coping mechanisms, (2) cognitive, when employees use resilience and empowerment, or conformity or acceptance strategies, and /or (3) emotional, when employees feel uncomfortable and unsafe, anger, frustration, sadness, embarrassment, and shame.[190] Microaggressions can have a significant negative impact on the mental health of employees in the form of depression, anxiety, and post-traumatic stress disorder.[191]

Sexual orientation is a polarised dimension that is made complex by religious beliefs, social conditioning and political views. Those from the LGBTQ+ community have likely faced tremendous bias and discrimination, making them cautious in trusting others as allies. For their colleagues, interacting with someone who is from the LGBTQ+ community may feel uncomfortable as they struggle to find the right vocabulary. For example, for someone who is transgender, colleagues may struggle with pronouns, not knowing what is preferred. Similarly, it can be awkward if a colleague has undergone a sex change, identified as non-binary, or shared that moving forward, they will be someone of the opposite gender. It is awkward because we are not used to it. We are socially conditioned to believe it is unnatural or immoral or wrong. It is awkward because we do not see it as "normal". It is awkward because we do not have the know-how, vocabulary and strategies to be an active ally to normalise these workplace interactions.

## Looking Ahead

A Boston Consulting Group (BCG) LGBTQ employee survey in 2020 highlighted two main themes for the LGBTQ workforce.[192] It showed that the makeup of the LGBTQ workforce has changed dramatically and that young, straight employees are increasingly attuned to LGBTQ issues, signalling a much larger audience who cares about inclusion in this dimension. The survey showed an increasing number of younger employees, women, and people of colour identifying as members of the LGBTQ community. A recent 2020 YouGov poll of more than 4000 US adults showed that fewer than half (48%) of Gen Z respondents and Millennial respondents (48%) say they are completely heterosexual, which is less than the older generations of X (65%) and Boomers (78%).[193] Additionally, Gen Z and Millennials responded that they believed sexual orientation was more of a spectrum rather than simply heterosexual or homosexual.

In the UK, a study by Ipsos Mori showed that only 66% of young people today identify as exclusively heterosexual - which is the lowest of any generation up until this point.[194] The study has labelled Gen Z as "the liberal generation" being more tolerant and most fluid, and finds that 10% of the generation regards prejudice toward the LGBT community as one of the most pressing issues in the world today, as compared to only 2% of Millennials, Gen X, and Baby Boomers who believe the same. Other studies published by Ipsos Mori suggest that over 70% of Gen Z is comfortable with homosexual relationships, as compared to the 43% of Baby Boomers. According to the BCG survey, compared with previous generations straight employees in the US under the age of 35 are 1.6 times more likely to know LGBTQ colleagues, 3.6 times more likely to join ally programs, and 3.0 times more likely to find value in LGBTQ colleagues being out. With this generational shift in attitudes, organisations will need to ensure that their workplaces keep up by having an inclusive culture for all sexual orientations.

In inclusive workplaces where LGBTQ+ employees feel like they belong, these employees could be a great asset to provide insights or advice on marketing campaigns in order to ensure that they appeal to the LGBTQ+ community as well as their allies. This is the time for companies and advertising firms who are still sitting on the fence to show their support for the LGBTQ+ talent within their organisation and amongst their consumers. It helps to have an overarching LGBTQ+-inclusive marketing policy for all markets to guide decision making, avoiding 'gay-window' and 'gay vague' advertising. Companies should take a stand as an organisation in supporting the rights of the LGBTQ+ community across all their markets, while adapting only when absolutely necessary to extreme cultural or religious sensitivities and local legislation. Not including a gay person in a marketing campaign simply because audiences "don't like it" is not a good enough reason. This will require the leadership in organisations to take the risk. There may be a short-term loss of sales or backlash, but in the long-term, the company will be seen as standing up for inclusion and diversity, which is likely to garner greater support from the LGBTQ+ community and their ever-growing allies, particularly amongst consumers from younger generations.

So, how can you ensure inclusive workplaces where all sexual orientations feel that they are welcome, respected and appreciated?

To find out how to be an active ally as an individual, team, and organisation, turn to the chapter titled 'Active Allyship in Action'.

# TELIA COMPANY

## Dare-Care-Simplify – the Values Driving Inclusivity for (LGBTQI) Talent

Originally founded in 1853, Telia Company – Telia - is the fifth largest telecom operator in Europe and the leading Nordic media house. The Swedish multinational telecommunications company and mobile network operator is a Nordics & Baltics focused integrated digital operator and content owner on a mission to build a new digital society, empowering people, companies, and societies to stay in touch with everything that matters to them. The company is present in Sweden, Finland, Norway, Denmark, Lithuania, and Estonia, and employs close to 21,000 employees who work towards the company's purpose to 'Reinvent Better Connected Living' while living the company's values, Dare-Care-Simplify. In 2020, Telia was recognized as the most LGBTQI (Lesbian, Gay, Bisexual, Transgender, Queer, and Intersex) friendly workplace by Unionen, the largest trade union in Sweden, for its unwavering stance for LGBTQI rights, even in countries where those rights are under threat.

Chris Hovde, the Global People Movement lead and Diversity Lead Telia Norway explains: "Diversity has always been a part of our DNA for as long as we have existed. In the Tech industry, we are so reliant on needing to tap into the talent of the world, so it is important that everybody feels like they can fulfill their full potential at Telia. In our company, we try to create a culture where everybody can be their full, authentic self."

Inclusion efforts for LGBTQI talent at Telia began at the grassroots level. Telia employees have always had the autonomy and freedom to self-organize employee interest networks. A few years ago, the LGBTQI network groups requested funding to participate more actively in Pride events. The company agreed and over the next few years, these groups grew bigger, wanting to do more. This was happening even in the Baltic region where engaging on LGBTQI inclusion was considered sensitive and even political. The message from Telia management was to continue enthusiastically endorsing employees' participation in Pride parades.

Realizing the potential of these network groups, and recognizing the need to do more, Telia partnered up with their three largest telecom competitors in the Baltics in the belief that there was greater power in standing together. They collectively communicated their message to stand together for Pride, and visibly marketed this message by changing all their logos to reflect the rainbow. In countries where there was fear of repercussions, Telia used technology in creative ways, by giving employees the chance to participate in the parade anonymously through robots. Even when faced with resistance from customers, Telia's customer service agents in the Nordics and Baltics region reaffirmed their values.

In one incident, a customer asked a customer service agent to remove the company's rainbow logos. The agent responded with the simple answer: "No". The incident spread virally on social media and as a result, Telia was invited on podcasts and to events to share their inclusive vision.

Chris adds: "We see it as our responsibility to stand behind the rights of our employees for them to be able to be themselves".

Continuing in the spirit of building partnerships for change, Telia - together with 40 other companies in Norway - held a Pride forum for businesses to go beyond the colourful outfits at Pride parades and towards exchanging ideas on how to be inclusive for LGBTQI talent. Along with the big consultancy companies, legal and Tech firms, the police and the armed forces were also involved. The forum included talks by external role models, including a transgender executive boldly sharing her story. Telia believes that having internal and external role models are crucial to enabling change. Telia's internal role models are also important as they dare to speak up, wanting to make the room bigger and more welcoming for those who are walking behind.

In 2020, given the global COVID-19 pandemic, Telia organized a global virtual Pride celebration. In the same year, Telia was recognized as the most LGBTQI-friendly workplace across the footprint for their groundbreaking collaboration with their competitors in regions where supporting LGBTQI rights has the potential risk of losing market share; and for organizing a safe, inclusive way to celebrate Pride globally.

Looking ahead, Chris shares his dream: "My dream is for a male manager to be able to walk around in a dress, giving a high-five to a person in a wheelchair".

## Key Takeaways:

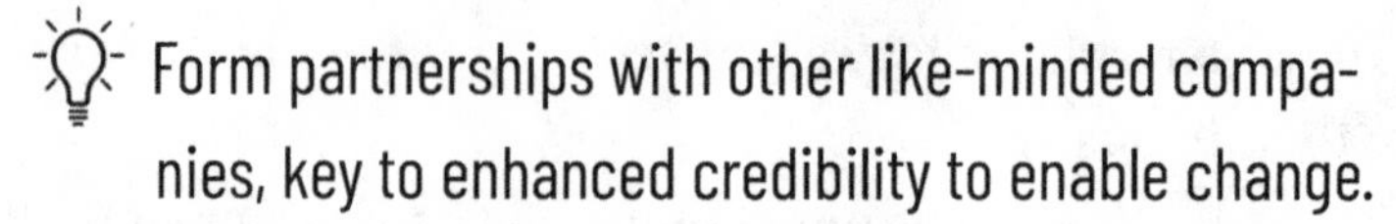

- Form partnerships with other like-minded companies, key to enhanced credibility to enable change.
- Nurture a culture of trust.
- Say yes to bottom-up initiatives to improve employee engagement and gain support from employees.
- Harness the unique power of influence of internal and external role models.
- Expose employees to topics and issues that people do not want to talk about. Bring different perspectives together to expand employees' mindsets to think differently.
- Listen to the LBGTQI-community. What matters to them?

Explore more about Telia Company at https://www.teliacompany.com/

# Age

*"Age is whatever you think it is,*
*you are as old as you think you are."*

Muhammad Ali, American professional boxer

Age. Now here is a dimension we can all connect with. We were all young once and we all age. So why and how is a natural part of life a key dimension of diversity at work? Well, it is the differences between generations that contributes to diversity in our workplaces. A generation is made up of people born over a 15 to 20-year period; and today, our workplaces comprise five generations co-existing simultaneously.

Did you know that in 2020, 41% of the global population was under the age of 24[195], 26% under the age of 15[196] and Millennials made up 35% of the global workforce?[197] As of 2020, India was home to a fifth of the world's youth with more than 50% of its population of 1.3 billion people below the age of 25, and more than 65% under 35. The average age of an Indian was 29 years, compared to 37 for China and 48 for Japan.[198] In 2020, 41% of the African population was under the age of 15.[199] In the US, Millennials were the largest generation in their labour force.[200] With increasing life expectancy, the majority of those born in the mid-1940s to 1960s are still very much part of the workforce. Glassdoor's "Job and hiring trends for 2020" indicate that Baby Boomers were the fastest-growing age category in the US and UK workforces in 2020.[201]

The co-existence of multiple generations creates opportunities for harnessing the best that each generation offers. Younger employees who are more technologically savvy, working side by side with older colleagues with a wealth of experience, have the potential to reap the synergistic benefits from their collaboration. The different perspectives and experiences of each generation contributes towards the diversity of thought and innovative ideas. Multigenerational workforces have the added advantage of being able to understand customers' diverse needs. In companies that value knowledge, experience, and skill above age or seniority, employees of all ages have the opportunity to engage in mutual mentoring to teach, share and learn from one another while ensuring that the talent pipeline continues to pass down know-how, legacy, traditions, and experiences from generation to generation. After all, age is merely a number, not a credential.

At the same time, multigenerational workforces also present challenges when navigating across generations. After all, each generation has a set of behaviours and expectations that manifest in the way they communicate, how they receive and provide feedback, what motivates them, their preferences for teamwork and their attitudes towards technology. These differences result in age-related biases or *ageism*, which can lead to miscommunication, conflict, misunderstanding, and a lack of trust between the generations, creating an "us" and "them" attitude in the workplace.

## Ageism: Is it a Real Thing?

Navigating and managing generational differences is something we do all the time – at home, in our families, at the grocery store and at work. I remember my shock and disappointment when I was told by a senior colleague that I would not be considered for the opportunity to teach a Master's level course at university until I was much older "with white hair", and that I "should not waste my time trying to do so". I was 29 at the time, with solid performance evaluations.

Two years ago, I remember driving back from just having bought my sons new shoes. In the car, my older son said to me "Mom, thank you so much for my new shoes, they're so sick". Instead of being thrilled that he actually remembered to thank me by himself, my mind got stuck on the word "sick". Who says "sick"? What does it even mean? So, I asked him why he couldn't have used other more positive adjectives like nice, cool, amazing. His reply? "Mom, that's just how my generation speaks".

I bet many of you have had similar experiences in your personal life and with people you work with. In the workplace, in spite of anti-age discrimination laws, ageism still exists. Some of you might recall the May 2013 *TIME* Magazine cover "The Me Me Me Generation", which declared "Millennials are lazy, entitled narcissists". In 2007, Mark Zuckerberg said "Young people are just smarter".[202] He must have forgotten that it was Steve Jobs and Bill Gates, both Baby Boomers, who led the information revolution that made Facebook possible. Recently, we have heard the term "Ok, Boomer"[203] – a phrase used as a retaliation or verbal eye roll against the older generation. The term was popularized as a reaction to a video on TikTok of an unidentified older man declaring, "Millennials and Generation Z have the Peter Pan syndrome…they don't ever want to grow up [and] they think that the utopian ideals that they have in their youth are somehow going to translate into adulthood".

In 2018, IBM was sued for systematically laying off older workers to build a younger talent force with claims that the company fired 20,000 employees above the age of 40 in the six years prior.[204] While the case was dismissed in court in 2020 and went to settlement, it was a high-profile case of a large organisation engaging in age discrimination at a significant scale, flaunting the US Age Discrimination in Employment Act (ADEA).[205] The ADEA not only covers discrimination in employment policies and practices, but it also addresses harassment based on a person's age.

While these age biases are blatant and obvious, there are many times when they are not. Have you been in meetings where the phrase "we have always done it this way" has been used by those who have been in the organisation for a while, as a means of continuing with the way things have always been done? During a recent D&I training session, a line manager was joking about a young Millennial's lack of patience towards career progression and commented "You know, they need to learn to walk before they can run". I am sure you have met someone who has been told "You are too young to lead a team". I met a manager who was part of the team leading a digital transformation who said, in passing, that he thought the new app being launched would be "way to techy for them". And by them, he was referring to fellow colleagues who were older. Similar phrases like "Do you even know what TikTok is?" imply that someone is too old to learn a new technological tool or computer program. HR business partners shared with me that they have on occasion preferred younger candidates on the basis "you know bad habits haven't formed yet". Candidates applying for internships get rejection letters accompanied by excuses along the lines of "there were many applicants with more years of experience".

Experience for an internship? That sounds like an oxymoron. Occasionally, a comment can even seem complimentary - "You look so young; you must be an intern".

What I have just described are age-related microaggressions. In Deloitte's 2019 State of Inclusion survey, of biases witnessed or experienced by respondents, age topped the list.[206] In the same survey, when asked "Do you feel that you have experienced bias based on age?", the oldest, Baby Boomers, and youngest, Generation Z, reported the highest perceived level of age-based bias.[207] Similarly, the 2019 Diversity and Inclusion Study by Glassdoor in the US, UK, France and Germany showed that younger employees (52% of ages 18-34) are more likely than older employees (39% of ages 55+) to have witnessed or experienced ageism.[208] This data would be much higher if subtle, age-related microaggressions were considered.

I was speaking to a manager in his late 30s who was eager to make a career switch. His plans were casually ridiculed with statements like, "Oh you must just be having a mid-life crisis – you're at that age". He did not notice that it was a microaggression until it was pointed out. We are conditioned to think that these types of microaggressions are acceptable; if we call them out we are accused of not having a sense of humour and of being over-sensitive. After a keynote speech I had given, a 31-year-old woman shared her story with me. She had recently been promoted to CEO of her company and kept facing surprised looks from employees and colleagues. To her, the underlying message was clear: How can someone so young do your job? How did you even get this position? And worst of all, the unspoken question so many women in positions of power face: did she sleep her way to the top?

## Ageism's Power

Ageism still exists because we simply are not aware of these unconscious age biases that manifest as microaggressions. Age-related biases and microaggressions have an impact on several organizational processes. Ageism affects the talent we hire or do not end up hiring. In periods of increased unemployment, organisations make choices to hire more experienced talent for entry-level roles and internships as they can certainly get more bang for their buck; discriminating against the fresh graduates who are keen to begin their careers. At the same time, hiring managers tend to be weary of hiring candidates who are older – who may have the wealth of experience – but assumed to lack the flexible and nimble mindset for a rapidly changing environment.

The language used in job advertisements can also contain biases that prevent certain age groups from applying for the jobs. Using words like "extensive experience" or "demonstrates deep understanding" all suggest that older and more experienced candidates will be considered rather than someone younger with fresh ideas. Conversely, using phrases like "we are looking for high-energy individuals" or "contemporary ways of thinking" seem to suggest a preference for younger candidates, making assumptions that those who are older cannot be high-energy or have innovative ideas.

When promoting talent, top performers who are young are often disregarded with excuses about the need for more experience. To address this, there has been a recent movement to include shadow boards. Made up of younger generations to guide the organisation's strategy, shadow boards keep the organisation more attuned with the changing demographics of their customers. Unless organisations have adequate representation of the various generations, products, services, as well as the marketing of them, they run the risk of being misaligned with the reality. Internal representation of the customer base helps improve the understanding of spending habits, attitudes to money and brands, alongside the role of sustainability, climate impact and fair trade on customers choices.

In my conversations with managers and leaders, managing the different generations in organisations is a key concern. Yet, according to PWC's 2015 Global CEO Survey, only 8% of CEOs surveyed included age inclusiveness in their company's D&I strategy.[209] So, what can we do to reduce ageism? In comes GQ.

## Generational Intelligence (GQ)

No, this is not referring to the men's magazine. We have heard about IQ (Intelligence Quotient), EQ (Emotional intelligence), CQ (Cultural intelligence), but what about GQ? The more recent Q to join the HR block is Generational Intelligence.

> *Generational intelligence (GQ)* is the capability to relate and work effectively in a multi-generational workforce in order to embrace micro-generations and minimise micro-aggressions. GQ can be nurtured and cultivated both at the individual, team, and organisational level.

At the individual level, by developing our GQ, we become conscious of microaggressions in ourselves and those around us. We are better able to empathize and rationalise someone's behaviours and expectations to which generation they are from. This increased understanding reduces conflicts, misunderstandings, and the transactional costs of working across generational differences.

Within teams, the co-existence of multiple generations means that we have to use mindful communication and customised feedback to navigate across the generational differences. It is helpful to adapt the medium of communication and speed of communication as we interact with different micro-generations. At a large pharmaceutical company that was keen to improve the communication between their micro-generations, everyone was encouraged to experiment with different modes of communication. What they found was that when communicating with a young millennial, using WhatsApp or messenger to engage in instantaneous communication or feedback was appreciated, and even preferred. Older employees were trained in the use of these tools, much to their delight as they could now communicate instantaneously with their own grandkids – and became the "cool" grandparents. Mutual mentoring opportunities are a great way to enhance a deeper respect between the micro-generations. Ensuring that teams and project groups have age-diverse talent helps generate a wider range of thoughts and ideas, while developing respect between the generations.

Collectively, by nurturing GQ, we create workplaces where both the young and those older, and those in between, all feel that they are valued and respected. A workplace where ageism is minimised. We become allies in creating organisations where we invite both the young and old in, and where everyone is comfortable to dance. Imagine for a moment a family wedding, in which all the micro-generations are happy, feel respected and are engaged on the dance floor - the young bride dancing with her father and a little seven-year-old boy dancing with his mother. That is the feeling of inclusion we want to recreate at work.

One of the main reasons for generational conflict is that older and younger employees misinterpret behaviour.[210] Understanding why someone from another generation behaves the way they do reduces biases and is crucial to better generational harmony. This begins with identifying which generation your employees belong to and understanding their work-related values and behaviours. So, who are the generations in our workplaces, and how are they indeed different from each other?

## Generations and Micro-generations

Generational research has traditionally defined a generation as being made up of people born over a 15 to 20-year period with common formative life experiences, and similar work-related values, attitudes, and behaviours. These formative life experiences are known as a "Generation Defining Moment" by the Centre for Generational Kinetics.[211] Such Generation Defining Moments usually take place in the late childhood and teenage years when the members of the generation are mature enough to deeply experience the event in such a way that it would significantly impact their value, attitudes, and behaviours. With the ever-increasing pace of change in world events, politics, parenting styles, education and technology, the way we look at generations as comprising people born over 15- to 20-year periods needs to change. This is where we need to start paying more attention to the existence of micro-generations.

Micro-generations comprise people born during the cusp of two generations, displaying a mix of qualities of each of the generations that they straddle. If you - like me - have looked at the generational stereotypes out there and wondered, which generation am I? I don't seem to fit in completely with the generation I am supposed to be from, Gen Y/Millenial. I have some qualities of Generation X. I also enjoy having increased flexibility, more frequent feedback and am pretty comfortable with technology. I am an Xennial, sitting on the cusp on the 2 generations, X and Millennials.

**Generations at a wedding**

The micro-generations in today's workplace are the Xennials and YZennials. With Generation X, Y/Millennials and Z making up about 65% of the global population in 2020,[212] these micro-generations of the Xennials and YZennials are not small population sizes.

---

**Generations**

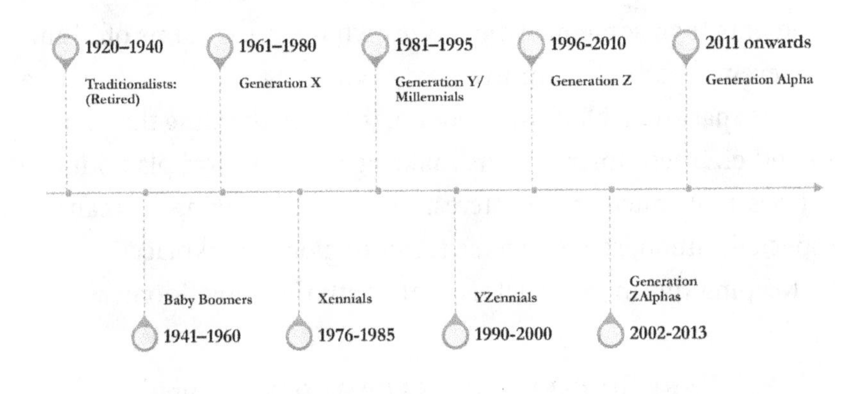


---

Companies that can map and understand the generations and micro-generations in their workplaces are better able to address the needs of their generations. In 2012, BMW Group launched its *Today for Tomorrow* program to prepare itself for an ageing workforce. As part of this, the company redesigned their workplaces to reduce the physical strain for their ageing workforce. What they found was that these changes were not just benefiting their older workers, but benefiting workers from all generations.[213] Now that is a win-win.

As we look more closely at each generation, it is important to bear in mind the intersection between the generational dimension of diversity with the ethnic and socio-economic dimensions that cause variations from the generalisations of each generation. Someone from the Boomer generation growing up in America would have had very different Generation Defining Moments that have shaped their values, attitudes, and behaviours compared to someone from the same generation who has grown up in Africa. Someone who has grown up in an upper-middle class family in Mumbai, India will have had very different Generation Defining Moments than someone who has grown up in the slums of Mumbai; even if both of them live next door to each other – one in a private apartment block overlooking the slum dwelling that houses the other. These intersections make age related workplaces interactions that much more interesting and challenging to manage, especially amongst age-diverse talent in global workplaces.

Keeping this in mind, let us begin with the Baby Boomers.

### Baby Boomers (born from 1941 to 1960)

This generation was the largest cohort of babies born in the period right after WWII. Soldiers returning home to their wives and girlfriends, coupled with medical advances that reduced infant mortality rates, gave rise to more people having children. This was a time of great optimism, growth, and expansion. The baby boomers born in this time were cherished by their parents and grew up in nuclear families. With this large population growth, baby boomers learnt to work in teams very early on in life at home with more siblings and in over-crowded schools.

Boomers were influenced greatly by the civil rights movement led by Martin Luther King, the election and assassination of

President Kennedy, the Vietnam war and the first landing on the moon. With the invention of the contraceptive pill, the younger of the boomers saw an increase in women in the workplace as they delayed having children; accompanied by rises in divorce rates as boomers pursued personal gratification.

With the sheer numbers entering colleges and the workforce, baby boomers faced high levels of competition and experienced the recession of the 1970s and 1990s in which many lost jobs. Their life experiences at home and in school resulted in them adopting a more collegial and consensual style of leadership as they progressed into the workplace. In fact, it is this generation that advocated removing corporate hierarchies. The boomers are *extremely hard-working, fiercely loyal to the organisation and motivated by flexibility, position, perks, and prestige.*

### Generation X (born from 1961 to 1980)

This is the generation sandwiched between the large groups of the baby boomers and the generation Y/Millennials; often viewed as the middle child. Generation X were born to parents who put off having children until later in their life with the invention of the contraceptive pill. Economic growth made it difficult for families to sustain on a single income, resulting in more women entering the workforce, leaving latchkey children of this generation to fend for themselves. Many returned home from school to empty houses, watching television until parents returned home from work. This generation became known as the MTV generation, influenced by popular music and culture. This generation lived through great social change with the end of the cold war, the fall of the Berlin wall and soaring divorce rates. They are a generation with a *survivor mentality that preferred individual work and are more loyal to the profession than to the organisation.*

With the invention of the personal computer, Internet and early mobile technology, technologically savvy Generation X was the first generation to truly integrate computer technology into their daily work processes and life. While Generation X has been viewed as the forgotten middle child, this generation holds middle to senior management positions in today's workplace, has the largest number of start-up founders and entrepreneurs of any generation to date, and is proving that they can work hard and play hard. They are using their positions of power to make a difference in the world.

### Xennials (born from 1976 to 1985)

The Xennials, straddling both Generation X and Generation Y/ Millennials, were born between 1976 and 1985. Unlike Generation Y, Xennials have had a childhood without computers or the Internet and have come of age during the dot com bubble. They can recall a time without the Internet, but have spent their adulthood on emails, instant messaging and Yahoo. Xennials have had the unique experience of being the early adopters of the first iPhone that was released in 2007. Their adulthood was spent using the PC and PowerPoint along with tablets and smartphones, but without the prevalence of social media. They combine the *strong desire for work-life balance* of Generation X with the *optimism and desire for more open relationships with authority* and flatter organisational structures of Generation Y. While Generation X prefers more individual work, the Xennials see the value in harnessing collective power to achieve goals and are comfortable both working *individually and in teams.* They demand more feedback than Generation X, but are content with weekly feedback rather than the on-demand feedback desired by Generation Y.

### Generation Y/ Millennials (born from to 1981 to 1995)

Generation Y, also known as the Millennials, are a large generation and sometimes referred to as the echo boom generation. They were raised with a kinder, gentler, and more involved parenting style. Having helicopter parents constantly hovering over them, and teachers constantly micro-managing them, this busy generation has a very open relationship with and a great deal of *trust in authority* figures, including parents and teachers, and values their continuous feedback. They were encouraged to speak up and not be fearful of authority, and view education as being "cool" and parents as role models. The Millennials have constantly been told that they are special and can follow their dreams and do anything they set their mind to. While this has created a heightened sense of *confidence*, it has also created a "trophy" or entitled generation that does not know what failure is, let alone how to handle it. This generation has faced its share of biases often being referred to as the "strawberry generation" – a generation that crushes easily upon pressure or "snowflake generation" – a generation that is less resilient and more prone to taking offence than previous generations.

Growing up in a time with global economic prosperity, the Millennials are a very optimistic generation and the first generation to be *truly global citizens* who are cross-cultural, having had significant interaction with and awareness of other ethnicities through travel, education, and the media. They are motivated by work that is meaningful and that allows them to make contributions to the greater good. They crave constant micro-feedback from approachable managers and opportunities for continuous learning, while demanding flexibility and *freedom* in how and where they work. As digital natives they are *technology-dependent*. The pervasiveness of social media channels such as Facebook and YouTube have created a generation that looks to collective power and collaboration as means to solve problems.

### YZennials (born from 1990 to 2000)

Emerging research that studies the behaviours of those in their early 20s are in fact looking at the unique YZennials. YZennials were young children when 9/11 happened, and have, in America, grown up accepting that school shootings and the corresponding lockdown drills are a part of their childhood. This "Google it" *technoholic* generation has grown up without the high-speed Internet and ubiquitous Wi-Fi connectivity that Generation Z has been born into, but have had access to more sophisticated social media apps including Instagram, Twitter, WhatsApp, mobile banking apps and Spotify. The self-identity and self-worth of this "selfie generation" is intrinsically tied to their *online identity*. This is perhaps the first generation that looks at the world as a union connected by technology and has seen the hope of being able to truly embrace diversity with the election of the first Black President of the USA. Like Generation Y, they look to *harness collective power to solve problems* and take on social causes, along with *demanding authenticity* in their leaders. At the same time, like Generation Z, the work that the YZennials undertake needs to align with their own individual *life-purpose*.

### Generation Z (born from 1996 to 2010)

Generation Z or Gen Z has grown up in a globalized world with access to advanced technology that no previous generation has ever seen. This *mobile-first-technologically-saturated* generation, or what we call, "the YouTube generation," is one where Instagram is the most popular app amongst them. 58% of them own a tablet computer, 57% of them own a desktop computer and on average, Generation-Z spends three hours a day on social media.[214] FOBA (Fear of Being Alone) and FOMO (Fear Of Missing Out) define this generation's view of technology and the role of social media. Apps like Instant Messenger and WhatsApp have created a generation that demands and expects *instant communication* and feedback from parents, from educators, and they will likely also demand this from their future employers.

In some parts of the world, Gen Z has grown up accustomed to terrorism or even gun violence. This is also a generation, inspired by Greta Thunberg, that sees the power in *collective effort to solve the world's biggest challenges* - climate change, mental health, and racial and social justice. During job interviews, the top two areas that young people ask questions in are sustainability and D&I. Common questions include "What is the purpose of the organisation and which of the UN sustainable goals do you address?" and "What is your policy on diversity and inclusion?" showing just how important these issues are for younger candidates.

Generational research shows that significant events in youth or childhood can define a generations' values, attitudes, and behaviours as well as future actions. Due to the COVID-19 pandemic these students, the classes of 2020, have completed their degrees having written and submitted their final dissertations and exams under lockdown and completed oral defences online, all with an uncertain future waiting for them. While graduates received encouragement, empathy, and valuable words of advice from virtual commencement speeches by President Obama, Malala Yousafzai, Oprah Winfrey, David Chang and Bill Gates, 2020 was certainly no normal year for these graduates, the impact of which will define the values, attitudes and behaviours of this generation.

### Generation ZAlphas (born from 2002 to 2013)

This is a micro-generation that also has been significantly impacted by the COVID-19 pandemic of 2020. At its peak in April 2020, UNESCO's data shows that about 1.5 billion students worldwide, corresponding to 90% of the world's learners, were not going to school.[215] In more developed nations students had the opportunity to access remote or emergency learning, and continued their education, albeit in a very different format, with considerable modifications in terms of content and delivery. In developing and underdeveloped countries, the picture was very different. COVID-19 highlighted the digital, gender and access divide across the world in education. While educators, educational institutions and parents have found innovative and creative ways to deal with education through a pandemic, utilising whatever resources they can – televisions, radios, laptops, and phones, the impact on this generation will be significant and long-term. This micro-generation will also likely develop a new relationship with technology, moving away from over-dependency and reaching a more balanced relationship, understanding the value it adds as well as what it is unable to replace – the human connection.

Across the developed and developing world, the micro-generation ZAlpha has seen their parents forced to Work From Home (WFH) through lockdowns. For those who have had positive remote learning experiences, and seen their parents working effectively through virtual means, they are likely to question the need for large, physical office spaces and the need to be physically present. This could define a new way of achieving work-life-balance, one which allows employees to work virtually, meeting face-to-face when needed, allowing for more time with their children and loved ones.

The oldest students of this micro-generation have had to give up their higher, secondary graduations and celebrating important milestones with friends to protect the health and well-being of others. They were told by the adults in their life that they need to think of the collective good and act accordingly. This experience may strengthen the view that Generation Z has about the need for collective action to solve the world's biggest challenges, inspired by the work of young Millennials like Greta Thunberg. They have seen that the halting of air travel and other modes of transportation, along with factories being shut, can have a positive impact on reducing carbon emissions and pollution levels. They have seen the Himalayan mountain ranges become visible after decades of pollution rendered them invisible, wildlife emerging and multiplying, and cleaner skies. This is not something this micro-generation will forget and will likely lead to their greater sense of agency and purpose-driven action. They will likely seek out opportunities to work for *purpose-driven* organisations.

### Generation Alpha (2011 onwards)

What about Generation Alpha – the youngest generation, and the generation we know least about?

The VUCA (volatile-uncertain-complex-ambiguous) world they are growing up in will certainly shape their values, attitudes, and behaviours when they hit the workplace in about ten to fifteen years' time. As a result of the COVID-19 pandemic, kindergartners, and nursery children in many parts of the world are beginning their entire school education virtually, and are missing out on vital early childhood education to meet their developmental needs.[216] The long-term impact of this on defining this generation remains to be seen.

To this generation, diversity and inclusion will be a big part of who they are. Alpha is the most racially diverse generation across the world with the most non-traditional family structures. They are growing up in a world where diversity and inclusion, as well as sustainability, are integrated into educational curriculum as well as in the way in which they are parented. This generation may be known as Generation Hope, for bringing about a desire in older generations to change things towards a better, more just and sustainable world for their children and grand-children.

## Are Generations Really that Different?

> *"I see no hope for the future of our people if they are dependent on the frivolous youth of today, for certainly all youth are reckless beyond words. When I was a boy, we were taught to be discrete and respectful of elders, but the present youth are exceedingly wise and impatient of restraint."*
>
> Greek Poet Hesiod

The above quotation was written over 3000 years ago, yet seems to be reflective of the perceptions of today. While the differences between each of the generations are significant, there is a school of thought that suggests the generations are actually very similar to each other. There are certain core values and expectations of the workplace that all the generations have. Everyone wants to be respected, and have their contributions to the organisation valued, regardless of which generation they are from. Flexibility is also one of these core values that all the generations hold as very important, whether it is to take care of aged parents, young children, or to pursue hobbies and interests outside the workplace. Other commonalities amongst the generations include the demand for trustworthy leaders, a desire for opportunities to learn and get feedback, as well as money as a key motivator.

You may be asking yourself: why is ageism something we need to address now? After all, we have always had generations in workplaces: young, old and those in the middle; so age-related biases must have always existed. Just because ageism is normalized, does not make it right.

We need to build our Generational Intelligence (GQ) so we move a few steps closer to truly inclusive workplaces for all ages. So, how can we all build GQ in ourselves, within our teams and in our organisations?

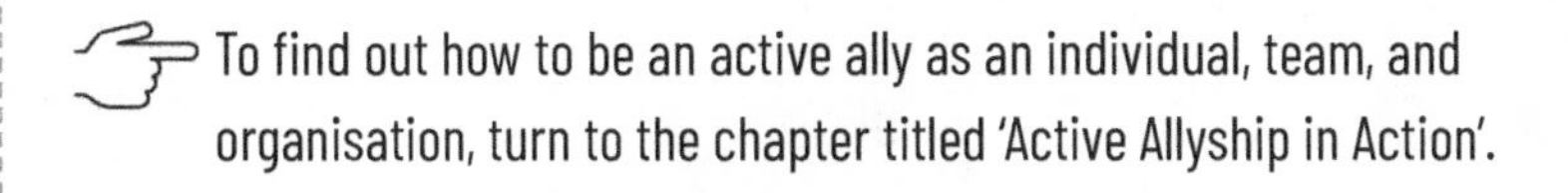

To find out how to be an active ally as an individual, team, and organisation, turn to the chapter titled 'Active Allyship in Action'.

# Physical Abilities and Appearances

*"There is no greater disability in society, than the inability to see the person as more."*

Robert M. Hensel, born with Spina bifida and Guinness World Record holder for the longest non-stop wheelie in a wheelchair

Imagine working in an office where you are not judged or discriminated for being in a wheelchair. Imagine a workplace where the way your appearance, your weight, your height, your natural hair and what you wear do not determine if you are hired, promoted or how much you earn. Unfortunately, that is not the world we live in. The world we live in is an ableist and image-conscious one.

Did you know that 15% of the world's population - that is over a billion people - live with a disability, making this the largest minority group?[217] At least 785 million of them are of working age. Yet, according to the United Nations, 80% to 90% of persons with disabilities of working age in developing countries are unemployed. In industrialized countries the figure is between 50% and 70%.[218] In most developed countries, the official unemployment rate for persons with disabilities of working age is at least twice as high as for those who do not have a disability. Did you also know that people who are more attractive are, on average, more likely to be employed and have a higher salary than those who are viewed as being "average" looking?[219] As you look around your workplace, what do you notice? Do you get the feeling that the workplaces of today have been created by and for able-bodied people who conform to a certain prescribed standard of physical appearances?

A few years ago, I stumbled upon a powerful campaign run by Coca-Cola in the Middle East.[220] The video opens by reminding us that it takes just seven seconds to form a prejudice based on someone's appearance.[221] Six strangers, all men, were brought together in the dark and were asked to tell each other about themselves. There was an extreme sports athlete who skydives and participates in other high-risk activities. When the lights came on, this man was in a wheelchair. Another man played heavy metal in a band; those around him said he must have long hair and body piercings. When the lights came on, he was a man in a dark grey formal suit. One of the other men around the table was a Ted Talk speaker who enjoyed reading books on cognitive psychology and behavioural science; those around him said he must look nerdy. When the lights came on, he was a well-built man with many tattoos across his arms.

We make assumptions about what someone can or cannot do based on their abilities or disabilities. We have biases that affect what we think about how someone looks or how they should look. How many times have you got the feeling that people you meet have false assumptions about who you are based solely on your physical appearance? How often have you assumed what someone else is capable of doing based on their physical disabilities or appearances? Have you been to a meeting or a networking event where you felt someone was "sizing you up" and trying to determine whether it was worth speaking to, or addressing you directly? I am sure many of you have had moments where you have felt like you did not belong because of the way you looked or a physical disability that you may have. That feeling is the feeling of non-inclusion. That feeling is exactly the feeling we want to avoid in our workplaces.

## Ableism

Physical disabilities are impairments or limitations in the body that make it difficult for the person to perform certain activities and interact with people around them. Physical disabilities can take many forms such as movement, vision, and hearing; they can be temporary like a broken leg or can be permanent; they can be mild or severe; they can be from birth or developed due to injury or disease. In their most severe form, physical disabilities include spinal cord injuries, cerebral palsy, epilepsy, multiple sclerosis, muscular dystrophy, and Tourette syndrome. Other forms of physical disabilities include missing or broken limbs, hearing impairment, visual impairment and blindness, dwarfism, cystic fibrosis, and spina bifida. While these latter forms of physical disabilities certainly affect a person's ability to engage in activities and interact with others, people can, within reason, be gainfully employed.[222] It is these forms of physical disabilities that we are referring to in this section, where people can - with some support - be effective contributors to a workplace environment.

What is unfortunate is that our physical abilities are a dimension of diversity that is still the cause of bias and discrimination – what is known as *ableism. Disabled World* defines ableism as "discrimination action against people based on the physical ability of their body, especially against people with disabilities in favour of people who are not disabled". [223] We live in an ableist society where those of us who do not have disabilities determine what are considered "normal ways of living". The rise of the civil rights movement led many countries in the late 20th and early 21st centuries to pass anti-discrimination laws to also protect those that are disabled. Thanks to the UN Convention on the Rights of Persons with disabilities (CRPD), many countries around the world have national legislation that makes discrimination on the basis of disabilities unlawful.[224] In some of these countries, this aspect of discrimination is part of broader anti-discrimination or equality laws. In others, it is a separate law in itself. In the UK, the Equality Act of 2010 covers disabilities and states that no one should be discriminated against because of a disability. The Americans with Disabilities Act (ADA) prohibits discrimination against people with disabilities in several areas, including employment, transportation, public accommodations, communications and access to state and local government' programs and services.

A group of talent in our society who are often discriminated against on the assumption of physical disabilities are veterans. Veterans, also known as ex-service men and women, are those who have served as part of the Armed Forces of a country, usually for an extended period, and who have been discharged from their duties under conditions that were not dishonourable. Veterans often face discrimination in hiring processes by employers who may be concerned about their physical or even mental abilities. This could be because a significant number of veterans experience Post Traumatic Stress Syndrome (PTSD) due to the traumatic nature of their service in hostile conditions. Some may even be concerned about possible insurance claims that may arise in the future. There are laws that protect veterans, making discrimination against them illegal. In the US, the Uniformed Employment and Reemployment Rights Act of 1994 (USERRA) is designed to protect those who have served in the armed forces from discrimination based on their military service.

While the law seems to be on the side of people who are physically disabled, they remain an underrepresented group in our workplaces. In 2018, only 29% of working age Americans with disabilities (between ages 16 and 64) participated in the workforce, compared with 75% of Americans without a disability. In 2018, there were 15.1 million people of working age living with disabilities in the US and a report by Accenture suggested that if companies embrace disability inclusion, they would have access to a new talent pool of more than 10.7 million people.[225]

We have seen some progress in the UK. In 2019, over 4.2 million disabled people were employed, an increase from 2013 when the number employed was just 2.9 million.[226] Also encouraging? The employment rate gap between disabled men and disabled women has reduced, with more disabled women being employed, and the overall unemployment rate for disabled people has roughly halved between 2013 and 2019.

So, what is standing in the way from employing someone with a physical disability? The reasons cited by managers and leaders are many. Fears about the added risk, additional healthcare costs, accommodation costs of accessibility features and training, as well as legal issues form part of the list. While numerous studies show that these fears are not substantiated,[227] one of the biggest barriers to hiring and retaining people with physical disabilities are attitudinal barriers stemming from people's biases.[228] These biases towards those with physical disabilities affect the entry and progression of people with disabilities.[229] At the same time, there is a clear lack of support and prioritisation from organisational leadership at the top. According to the 2018 annual global CEO survey, disability was addressed by only 7.2% of the CEOs surveyed in their D&I strategies.[230]

Disabilities are a sensitive and somewhat uncomfortable topic for many people to talk about in workplaces and even society. In fact, very few people openly acknowledge that they have biases against people with disabilities because of the guilt experienced for even having these biases; making it easier to not talk or think about it. While we may not openly acknowledge it, many of us have biases against those who are physically disabled. A 2019 study conducted using data from 300,000 participants, gathered over 13 years, showed that even though people were positive towards others with disabilities, their unconscious or implicit biases grew over time and with age.[231]

People with physical disabilities face bias and discrimination every day. Over one in three people show an unconscious bias against those with a disability, making this higher than levels of bias on the basis of gender or race.[232] People with disabilities may face bias when they go to a grocery store or movie hall, with store employees actively ignoring or avoiding communicating with them, and perhaps in some instances, even making assumptions about their intelligence. They may face bias if taxis do not stop for them because of the extra effort needed and not seeing them as an equal customer. People with certain types of physical disabilities face architecture and construction discrimination every time they are confronted with stairs to enter a café or an office building. Wheelchair quotas at concert venues, public buses, and airplanes act as another source of discrimination with limited capacity for those in a wheelchair. They face bias every time strangers walk by them avoiding eye contact or when people take their parking spots.

**Why is my disability the topic of conversation?**

At work, people with physical disabilities face biases from fellow colleagues who avoid eye contact, who talk over them, or even ignore their presence in meetings. It does not stop there. When we think of someone with a disability, we tend to focus on what they cannot do rather than what they can do. We associate people with disabilities working in certain types of jobs. We feel a sense of sympathy or even pity for someone with a disability. When we meet someone for the first time, we notice their disability first, before anything else. We use the terms "able-bodied" or "normal" to describe those without a physical disability, suggesting that those who are physically disabled are incapable and abnormal. We may even see those with physical disabilities as less competent or productive than others. In fact, over a third (36%) of people tend to think of disabled people as not as productive as everyone else.[233] We may think of someone who is physically disabled as a costly hire. We assess people with physical disabilities differently from others. We give allowances or special treatment to those with physical disabilities. We may even make someone with a physical disability feel that they have been hired because they fulfilled a "tick-box" exercise to get someone with a disability into the organisation. We may engage in microaggressions by saying "I am so inspired by the way you have overcome your disability", reflecting our shock and surprise that someone with a disability is able to achieve as much as, if not more than, someone without it.

Encouragingly, a 2010 study showed that both employees with physical disabilities as well as their employers have a strong desire to want to treat people with disabilities as 'regular' employees and take attention away from their disability.[234] However, this sometimes results in hesitancy on the part of the disabled employee to ask for help. At the same time, employers do not offer additional support unless asked, not wanting to highlight the disability, fearing stigmatisation. The research concludes that given this reluctance from both employees and employers, it is possible that people with disabilities continue to remain an underrepresented talent pool.

What does this mean for organisations? These biases result in over half (51%) of people with a physical disability saying that they had taken pains to hide their condition from employers when applying for a job.[235] 60% of UK employees with a disability have experienced bias in the workplace, in comparison to just 35% of those without a disability. What is concerning is that 45% of those with a physical disability believe that their organisation does not offer an inclusive environment. Unsurprisingly, the research further revealed that around half (48%) of disabled candidates have either left a job or not applied for a role or promotion due to workplace bias, in comparison with just 20% of those without a disability.

Beyond being the right thing to do, is there a business case for this dimension of diversity? A young girl named Jordan made the answer to that question very clear to me. A few weeks ago, my children and I began watching The Marvel Hero Project[236] on Disney+; a series about real kids making a real difference. In one episode, 13-year-old Jordan, who was born with no left forearm, was featured. This young girl had faced a life full of stares and whispers, and assumptions by those around her of the things she could not do. Instead of feeling defeated by the disability, Jordan was inspired to get innovative by designing and creating products for people with physical disabilities like herself. This young lady highlighted that the product design process often does not include people with physical disabilities, resulting in many day-to-day household essentials like toilet roll holders designed for people with two hands. In trying to tie shoelaces with only one full arm, Jordan showed us that people with physical disabilities find ways to navigate a world created by and for able-bodied persons. They problem-solve unlike those without disabilities, and it is these diverse perspectives that drive innovation.

Did you know that two of the most used technological tools in our lives today – the keyboard and email – followed from inventions of people with physical disabilities? In 19th century Italy, lovers Pellegrino Turri, who was sighted, and Countess Carolina Fantoni da Fivizzano, who was blind, struggled to find a way to send each other secret love letters. This led them to create the first working typewriters and sparked the 'printing by touch' phenomenon that we all use today. Hearing-impaired Vint Cerf led the creation of the first commercial email service in the 1980s to enable him to communicate with family members and colleagues without straining to hear.

In 2013, Haben Girma, a Black, disabled woman and the daughter of refugees, was the first deaf-blind person to graduate from Harvard Law School. Since then, she has worked as a human rights lawyer advancing justice for those with disabilities, and has received the Helen Keller Achievement Award, as well as a spot on the Forbes 30 Under 30 list and TIME100 Talks. She has spoken at Apple, GE, Lenovo, Microsoft, the New York Times, Oxford Law, Pearson Education, and Stanford about accessible design. In an article published in the *Financial Times* titled 'People with disabilities drive innovation', Girma says: "Disability creates a constraint, and embracing constraints spurs inventive solutions… Hiring people with disabilities leads to a more innovative workforce. Old myths allege that people with disabilities are a burden on society, and stem from unfounded fears of those who are different. Contrary to those myths, we now know that difference drives innovation."

In 2012, the International Labour Organisation's (ILO[237]) Bureau for Employers' Activities held a special session to increase awareness of the business case for hiring people with disabilities as part of the International Labour Conference. In that session, it was shared that hiring and retaining a qualified person with a physical disability brings greater benefits to the organisation than just filling a head count. Organisations generally employ people with disabilities as part of their Corporate Social Responsibility (CSR) efforts and to improve the diversity within the organisation. However, in addition to the diverse perspectives that they bring to the company, people with physical disabilities help build empathy in the organisational culture and are extremely loyal to the employers who are willing to hire them, display high morale that contributes towards improved productivity levels and lowered job turnover rates.

A 2018 study[238] by Accenture, in partnership with the American Association of People with Disabilities and Disability:IN, reports that businesses that actively seek to employ people with disabilities outperform businesses that do not. Their revenues were 28% higher, net income was two times more, and profit margins were higher by 30%. Additionally, the US Department of Labour[239] found that employers who embraced disability saw a 90% increase in employee retention.[240] Companies across various industries in India have seen that employing people with disabilities makes sound business sense given the low attrition rates, high productivity, loyalty, and low absenteeism.[241]

A few years ago, it came to Microsoft's attention that children with certain physical disabilities or missing limbs were having difficulty playing video games with traditional controllers. The company began working on an alternative controller which included touchpads instead of buttons and bright colours for the visually impaired. The company then launched the commercial titled "We All Win" which showed just how far the technology giant will go to help customers and prospects with all different abilities. Since then, organisations like Microsoft have realised that hiring talent with physical disabilities will help them to better understand their diverse group of customers, some of whom are physically disabled and therefore design inclusive products and services, as well as target their marketing campaigns to the physically disabled customer segment. Nike's FlyEase[242] lace-less shoes were inspired by a man with cerebral palsy and have been purchased not just by disabled customers, but able-bodied customers too. ANKHGER's MagZip[243] is a system that enables zipping with one hand for people with different abilities, and is being used by brands like Tommy Hilfiger, Moncler and Under Armour.

The 2018 report by Accenture shows that companies that have successfully hired people with disabilities did so by (1) enabling their employees to perform their job to their fullest abilities, (2) engaging with awareness building, disability education programs and grassroots efforts for employees, and (3) empowering their disabled talent by offering mentor and mentee opportunities, implementing skill-building programs, and making space for diverse talent to hold roles at all levels.[244]

In addition, companies need to make conscious efforts to make their physical spaces inclusive. These may include lift access to all parts of the buildings, ramps, special parking lots and having larger toilets to accommodate those in a wheelchair. Bloomberg's Chairman, Peter Grauer said on the stage of the World Economic Forum's summit in Davos in 2020 that its 4.5 million square feet of real estate is fully accessible to those with disabilities. The company has also rolled out disability awareness training and expanded that to 6000 team leaders and managers by the end of 2020. What is interesting is seeing an increasing number of toilets in workplaces being re-labelled from "handicapped" to "differently abled", or better still, having a sign with a person in a wheelchair rather than assigning a label to them. Perhaps we need a term to replace "differently abled" as even that seems to hold an underlying assumption that there is a preferred way of being abled emphasizing those that do not "fit" with that.

IBM is a company that is well known for its inclusionary policies in many dimensions of diversity including its efforts to be a workplace that is inclusive to those with physical disabilities. IBM was well ahead of its time and did not wait for the Americans with Disability Act of 1990 to make accommodations acceptable for those with physical disabilities. These accommodations have included interpreters for those who are deaf; curb cuts, accessible buildings, and access to wheelchair accessible transport as well as physical accommodations inside buildings.

IBM India created a business resource group called EnAblers India to increase employee awareness, networking, mentoring, and learning opportunities. Why are they doing this? "At IBM, our most important asset is our people. We are proud of our long-standing commitment to diversity and inclusion - not only because it is morally right, but because workplaces are smarter, more creative and more successful when they include people with a wide range of diverse abilities, preferences and backgrounds. Accommodating diversity also makes sense for our business in other ways. We can ensure that technology innovation is focused on being adaptive to everyone's abilities. Having many employees with diverse abilities means we get smarter feedback on products and services, increasing innovation in this important area".[245]

In 2017, after facing growing criticism about not addressing the needs of disabled customers adequately enough, Airbnb acquired

Accomable, a London-based start-up that sought and listed wheelchair accessible peer-to-peer rentals to address the needs of a wider range of customers, particularly those with physical disabilities. Accomable was set up in 2015 by avid travellers and friends Srin Madipalli and Martyn Sibley, who both have Spinal Muscular Atrophy and use wheelchairs. Their own frustrations when planning their travels led them to set up their company.

A 2011 census report states that India had 26.8 million people with some form of disability. This is out of a population of over 1 billion people and a 450 million workforce. Estimates by the World Bank and the World Health Organisation (WHO) put the figure upwards of 70 million. Given the country's jobless economic growth and the fact that almost one million people are added to the country's workforce every month, people with disabilities are often denied employment opportunities.[246] To address this, the 2016 Rights of Persons with Disabilities, and the 2017 Rights of Persons with Disabilities Rules, have contributed to companies not only ensuring that at least 3% of the workforce is differently abled, but also providing assistive technology, tailor-made training, and support systems to ensure that people with disabilities learn and grow in their jobs. Flipkart, India's biggest online store, has made sincere efforts by hiring talent who are primarily speech or hearing impaired, and a smaller group with physical disabilities. The organisation works with sign language interpreters and helps convince families to let their family members with a disability come to work.

For some organisations, it is about leading from the top. At Dell-EMC India, Deepa Narasimhan, the head of diversity and inclusion is herself tetraplegic, paralysed from the neck down. Narasimhan leads by example to ensure that inclusion is not restricted to a recruitment initiative and is internalised by the company top-down.

The company assesses the needs of all employees to enable them to be independent and empowered and provides technological or infrastructure support as needed. Through this, the company has hired over a hundred differently abled individuals, including ones with multiple disabilities like deaf-blindness and paralysis, in addition to autism and cerebral palsy.[247]

## The -isms of Appearance

It is hard to believe that the way we look or what we wear can be the source of bias and discrimination at work – *physical appearance bias.* Are we really that shallow? It turns out that many of us are. When it comes to physical appearances within workplaces, we have been conditioned as to what kind of "look" we associate with leaders or how women should dress for success. We live in an image-focused society. "Good looking people", however that is defined in different parts of the world, seem to have it all. They have a wide group of friends, get all the dates, and even get all the jobs. Studies have shown that physical appearance biases begin very early on in life, with children discriminating against other children based solely on the way they look or dress.

These same biases carry through adulthood and into our workplaces. Unlike physical disabilities, discrimination based on physical appearances is not covered explicitly in anti-discrimination or equality legislation. For the most part, physical attractiveness bias is largely unconscious, but has an impact on who we hire, and who gets promotions and better career opportunities. While other dimensions of diversity seem to get much more attention, this very subtle dimension is very often overlooked. Studies have shown that workplace decisions that are based on non-job-related factors are detrimental to organisational performance. Physical appearance biases in workplaces manifest through lookism, weightism, heightism and hairism. Never heard of these -isms? Let us take a look at them.

## Lookism: Beauty and Dressing Bias

If you always thought beauty lies in the eye of the beholder, you may want to think again. While very few companies will admit to hiring people for their attractiveness, there is evidence to show that this bias indeed exists. Did you know that it is an official requirement to have "good looks" to join the Chinese Navy?[248] Until 2015, Abercrombie and Fitch hired only attractive people. Abercrombie's former CEO Mike Jeffries said in 2006 that sex appeal was core to the Abercrombie DNA: "That's why we hire good-looking people in our stores. Because good-looking people attract other good-looking people, and we want to market to cool, good-looking people. We don't market to anyone other than that".[249] The Danish juice bar, Joe & the Juice, which is now in 300 locations around the world, may not openly admit that it primarily hires attractive young men, but it is obvious when you walk into any Joe & the Juice store[250] that employees represent an idealized view of attractiveness.

At work, many of us draw on physical appearance stereotypes that we hold when we interact with others and apply the *halo effect* to assume that physically attractive people also possess other socially desirable traits.[251] It gets more complicated; there is a cultural element to consider. In more Western cultures, studies have shown that people believe and listen to those who are more physically attractive[252] and in more collectivist societies, physical attractiveness is associated with concern for others, loyalty, and integrity.[253]

In Korea, university students associated being beautiful with being trustworthy and showing a greater degree of concern for others, but did not share the North American association that physically attractive people are more dominant and assertive than those who are not.[254] This stereotype acts as a self-fulfilling prophecy. Being more attractive is perceived to be of more value to society, leading them to receive greater benefits and preferential treatment.[255] As a result of the halo effect, research shows a correlation between physical attractiveness and higher income, social skills, and even self-confidence.[256]. This contributes towards attractive jobseekers standing out to employers.[257]

In more recent research, it was found that it is not just those who are very attractive who seem to be reaping the fruits, "very ugly" people also do well and may even have an advantage. While "ugliness" is absolutely subjective, it was found that the least attractive 3% of the population earned more than 50% of the population who were considered to be average looking or sort of ugly.[258] Peggy Drexler, in her opinion piece written for CNN,[259] paints a more sinister reason, which lies in intra-gender sexism and female misogyny. She suggests that women hold other women back in an effort of self-preservation, fighting for the few spots at the top of the corporate ladder. Supporting and rewarding the "very ugly" is an unthreatening way to keep the threatening women, who are more attractive, smarter, or wealthier, down.

Feeling uncomfortable? Are you thinking, how does one even define "attractiveness" or "ugliness"?

It seems like the beauty bias is more complex than we think. While the "what is beautiful is good" heuristic seems to have plenty of support, a 2018 study published in the *Journal of Personality and Social Psychology* showed that perceptions that attractive individuals have a greater sense of entitlement can result in negative treatment of attractive people.[260] This study supports other research which suggests a "beauty is beastly" effect.[261] For example, when applying for less desirable jobs, good looking people could be disadvantaged because we feel the need to reward people based on how good-looking they are. It might be a person's lifelong ambition to be a rubbish collector. However, if they are good-looking, our subconscious will tell us it is 'beneath' them to be doing that job. Margaret Lee, co-author of the study, says we "perceive attractive individuals to feel more entitled to good outcomes than unattractive individuals".[262] A study looking at situations where attractiveness can be detrimental for women found that attractive women, when applying for masculine jobs where physical appearance is not as important (think Director of Security), are discriminated against.[263]

While it is not surprising that how we dress contributes towards people's perceptions of whether we are "good looking" or not, dress codes can be a source of workplace discrimination in and of themselves. In a study published in 2009,[264] subjects rated women on competence, work comfort, and sociability, and found that models dressed in attractive clothing were perceived more positively than models dressed in unattractive clothing. These results provide some support for a clothing attractiveness stereotype. While we do have some control over the clothes we wear, workplace dress codes can be discriminatory for both men and women.

The Tech industry and start-up culture may allow for more casual dress codes, like the jeans, T-shirt and sneakers "uniform" made popular by Mark Zuckerberg, but women in the corporate sector are often expected, even if not officially mandated, to wear dresses or skirts, heels, and makeup. This sends a subtle message that women are expected to dress 'femininely' and men 'masculinely'. This can be hugely discriminatory towards the range of employees' gender identities. At the same time, almost ironically, women who make their way up to leadership are expected to dress like "men" in pantsuits in order to "fit in". Some of you may remember the shoulder pad trend of the 1980s, which broadened women's shoulders, giving them a more masculine silhouette. Men too face discrimination when it comes to dressing. Women can wear open toed sandals, but men cannot; women can wear cropped trousers but men have to wear full length ones; women can wear earrings but men cannot; men are expected to keep their hair short while women are not. It doesn't seem fair, does it?

## Weightism: Weight Bias

In the US, 70% of adults are overweight, and 40% of those are obese,[265] while the number is one in four for UK adults.[266] In urban areas of China, obesity rates are over 20%.[267] India has seen a surge in obesity, with 135 million individuals affected by obesity.[268] In developing countries, unhealthy food habits, sedentary lifestyle, lack of health care services and financial support have all led to escalating rates of obesity.[269]

While obesity is prevalent in many societies, employees who are obese or overweight seem to be less accepted and more discriminated against. This is known as *weightism* or *weight bias.* In my training sessions in the Nordics, when asked to describe the character "White male business leader", very often people use the words "fit" and even "athletic". As one of my trainees explained: "In Denmark and Norway, if you can't get your weight in order, people wonder how you can lead an organisation". This stems from a workplace prejudice that obese workers are lazy, less intelligent, lacking in self-discipline, sloppy in appearance, and less healthy.[270]

**Run as fast as you can to get to the top**

In addition, personality stereotypes suggest that obese individuals are less conscientious, less agreeable, less emotionally stable, and less extroverted than average-weight individuals.[271]

A review of research in this area shows that overweight individuals face negative perceptions and stigmatization in the workplace at every stage of the employment cycle, from selection, placement, compensation, assignments, promotions, assessments, discipline and termination.[272] Obesity is a key factor in unequal treatment at work and can be seen in inequity in pay, unequal treatment by superiors, and lower social acceptance in the workplace. It is found to be a barrier to professional success and results in fewer prospects for promotions.[273]

In a study conducted in 2015, research assistants wore "fat suits" when applying for jobs at retail stores.[274] These job applicants observed more discrimination in the form of subtle interpersonal behaviours such as less nodding and smiling, more interpersonal distance, and shorter interactions when they were wearing the suits than when they were not. This discrimination is also experienced once the person is hired as an employee. Studies show that people have lower expectations from trainees who are obese.[275] There seems to be an added gender bias: weight gain for women is significantly related to lower salaries, but only affects the salaries for men when they are formally obese.[276] Research also shows that senior leaders, CEOs, senior Vice-Presidents, and board members are not spared from weight bias. Supervisors, subordinates, and peers of senior executives rated obese leaders more negatively, both in terms of task and interpersonal performance than thin leaders.[277]

## Heightism: Height Bias

Malcolm Gladwell, in his bestselling book *Blink*, writes: "I polled about half of the companies on the Fortune 500 list, asking each company questions about its CEO. In my sample, I found that on average CEOs were just a shade under six feet. Given that the average American male is 5'9" that means that CEOs, as a group, have about three inches on the rest of their sex. But this statistic actually understates matters. In the U.S. population, about 14.5% of all men are six feet or over. Among CEOs of Fortune 500 companies, that number is 58%. Even more strikingly, in the general American population, 3.9% of adult men are 6'2" or taller. Among my CEO sample, 30% were 6'2" or taller."

Are you wondering if this is merely a coincidence? Surely, we don't favour tall people for leadership positions - or do we? It may be hard to believe, but a study published in 2004 in the *Journal of Applied Psychology* shows that every inch above average in height may be worth $789 more per year in earnings.[278] The study also found that someone who is 6' tall earns, on average, nearly $166,000 more during a 30-year career than someone who is 5'5" - even when controlling for gender, age, and weight. Height bias is deeply unconscious. While no one is consciously keeping the short people out, it is likely that we perceive that people who are taller are likely to have greater self-esteem and social confidence than shorter people; we may even perceive them as more leader-like and authoritative. This height bias may be a product of old patterns of thinking where taller humans were thought to be better able to protect others. What is interesting to note is that heightism seems to be harsher for men than women; shorter men experience greater height bias in the workplace than shorter women.

## Hairism: Hair Bias

It is hard to imagine that a person's hair can be a source of discrimination and bias. But it is. A person's hair, and often its intersection with ethnicity, has been found to be a source of bias in the workplace. African women and women of colour who have hair that has a different texture to what is considered "acceptable" face considerable discrimination, solely on the basis of their hair. Hairism is the "belief that one hair type is superior to another and can sometimes be affiliated with discrimination against a person because of their hair style and type".[279] What is this superior hair type that is acceptable at work? In many Western countries, standards of professional appearance have been based on White people with straight hair. As a woman of colour with curly, frizzy hair myself, I know this discrimination all too well. It is embarrassing how much time and money I have spent on straightening my hair to conform to what I thought was an acceptable hair texture.

Recent research published in August 2020 in *Social Psychology and Personality Science* showed that the hair-related bias in recruitment against Black women with natural hairstyles is very real.[280] In the study, participants from various diasporas evaluated the profiles of Black and White female job applicants across a variety of hairstyles. The study found that Black women with natural hairstyles were perceived to be less professional, less competent, and less likely to be recommended for a job interview than Black women with straightened hairstyles and White women with either curly or straight hairstyles. In industries with conservative dressing norms, Black women with natural hairstyles received more negative evaluations when applying for jobs in those industries. In one of the experiments as part of the study, participants reviewed Black women with natural hairstyles and Black women with straightened hair for the same employment opportunity. The Black women with straightened hair were consistently reported to be more professional, with professionalism being defined as "refined, polished, and respectable", leading to more positive recommendations for an interview for those women.

This puts an immense pressure on Black women to spend large amounts of money straightening their hair, exposing themselves to danger from the harsh chemicals used, and having to bear the psychological impact of needing to change the way one looks to conform with others' standards of professionalism. Black women also spend a greater amount of time and money on hair products to help them manage their hair in a way that conforms to other peoples' standards of appropriateness. These were part of the findings from a "good hair" survey conducted by Perception Institute in 2016,[281] which also found that White women show explicit bias against Black women's textured hair. This bias resulted in one in five Black women feeling a social pressure to straighten their hair for work - twice as many as White women.

If you had never imagined that someone's disabilities and how they look could have such a significant impact on their prospects for being hired or promoted, the salary and feedback they receive, and the kind of interactions they have at work, think again and be an ally to address this dimension of diversity. Wondering how?

☞ To find out how to be an active ally as an individual, team, and organisation, turn to the chapter titled 'Active Allyship in Action'.

# Be My Eyes

## Accessible Support Made Simple

Be My Eyes is a free mobile accessibility app with one main goal: to make the world a more accessible and inclusive place for individuals living with vision challenges. After six years of operation, Be My Eyes has become the largest online community of blind and visually impaired people and one of the world's largest micro-volunteering platforms. The app works by connecting those experiencing vision challenges with a sighted volunteer or company representative through a free one-way live video stream. The app is dedicated to making everyday life, wherever that may be, more accessible and inclusive.

The Be My Eyes journey for a more accessible future began in Denmark in 2012, when Hans Jørgen Wiberg, through his work at the Danish Association for the Blind, realized that individuals with low-vision could benefit from additional visual support from time to time. Being visually impaired himself, Hans Jørgen understood the importance of reaching out for help while still maintaining personal autonomy. Through the discussion with a visually-impaired friend who would call his friends and family over Facetime to solve small daily problems, Hans Jørgen came up with Be My Eyes. The immediate goal was to provide a free assistive technology that could provide independence, regardless of socio-economic status, to the over 2.2 billion individuals living with vision impairments worldwide.

But a challenge arose when considering how and where to find assistance. Many assistive technologies are unaffordable to individuals with a lower income. Hans decided to provide the service at no additional cost to the user. To do this, volunteers would join the service to keep costs at zero for those visually impaired individuals using the app. In terms of design, the app has been optimized for use with a screen-reader and can be used by any form of vision impairment. Be My Eyes launched in 2015 with a small team that has quickly grown to twenty full-time employees. Since 2015, over four million volunteers worldwide have signed up to offer free assistance to a community of hundreds of thousands of blind and visually impaired users.

By adopting a profit-and-purpose model, Be My Eyes has seen a steady increase in support from companies worldwide who want to make their solutions accessible for their visually impaired customers. In 2018, Be My Eyes partnered with Microsoft to offer Specialized Help for Be My Eyes users, a service allowing users to receive visual technical support for free.

This solution quickly solved a problem that has pervaded the blind and visually impaired community for decades. Prior to this, when an individual would call customer support with a technical question, the customer support agent would ask them for visual cues. With Specialized Help, customer support agents can see the issue directly from the camera of the user's phone, greatly enhancing the customer support experience for visually impaired individuals. Additionally, Microsoft realized that they could gain unique user insights into the accessibility of their products by providing this Specialized Help service. Since partnering with Microsoft, Be My Eyes has also partnered with industry leaders like Google, P&G, ClearBlue, Accessible Pharmacy, and more to create an accessible customer experience. These companies' support ensures that Be My Eyes remain sustainable and free to its blind and visually impaired community.

The result of adopting an approach that puts the user first has had a positive result in terms of growth. Almost all the marketing and growth has occurred organically through Social Media and Digital Media Outlets. Most notably, volunteers share their positive experiences and how much joy the app provides them by being able to assist someone. Many volunteers consider the app to be helping them just as much as they help blind and visually impaired users. In this way, the Be My Eyes app can proudly state that it helps over four million individuals daily on both ends of the call.

One of the app's long-term goals is to reduce the current unemployment rate of over 70% amongst individuals with vision impairments by providing them with a free resource that gets them through the day more independently. A dream for the app would be to become an essential part of the daily life of consumers. The ability to provide quick, live visual support to every consumer, not just those with vision impairments, would be a dream goal for the future.

## Key Takeaways:

- Accessible design does not have to be complicated. Products designed with accessibility in mind from the start save time down the line.
- Have a conversation with disabled employees and prospective job-seekers about what accommodations they need to succeed.
- Embracing accessibility and inclusivity makes a positive statement about a company and enhances its brand image.
- Providing an inclusive environment helps employees with disabilities and allows all employees to have greater empathy to work better as a team.
- Tapping into the voice of your community is the most effective way to drive content and engagement with your solution.

Explore more about Be My Eyes at https://www.bemyeyes.com/

# Cognitive Dimensions of Diversity

# Education

*"Education is the most powerful weapon which you can use to change the world."*

Nelson Mandela, South African anti-apartheid revolutionary, political leader and philanthropist

UNESCO states that education "is a human right for all throughout life".[282] While it may be a fundamental human right, access to and quality of education varies significantly across the world, and across genders. Education becomes a basis of discrimination when there are differences (1) between those who have (had) access to education and those who do not; (2) between those who have (had) access to better quality education and those who do not; and (3) between those who are educated in higher-ranked institutions and those who are not. Discrimination in all these three areas leads to a lack of diverse representation in workplaces as well as a lack of diversity in the talent pipeline into organisations.

A report in 2019 by UNESCO Institute for Statistics (UIS) on the world's out-of-school children reveals that very little or no progress has been made in over a decade. About 258 million children were out of school in 2018, corresponding to around one sixth of the global population of school-age children between the ages of 6 to 17 years old.[283] Even amongst those who have access to education, there are great disparities in the quality of education, often tied to availability of funding. A report by UNICEF titled "An Unfair Start" states that "in the world's richest countries, some children do worse at school than others because of circumstances beyond their control, such as where they were born, the language they speak or their parents' occupations." Poorer students in the UK are almost three full years behind their wealthier peers academically. 46% of disadvantaged students do worse than their peers in affluent schools. Where poorer students attend advantaged schools, they were two and a half years ahead of those at disadvantaged schools, a study by the Organisation for Economic Co-operation and Development (OECD) found.[284]

In the US, public school districts are run by local cities and towns that are funded by local property taxes. High-poverty areas have lower home values and therefore collect less taxes, which means less funding for schools to invest in guidance counsellors, school psychologists, personal laptops, and up-to-date textbooks.[285] Yet these are the areas that need it the most. While education is meant to be a great equalizer, that is far from reality. In 2015, the richest 25% of school districts spent, on average, $1,500 more per student than the poorest 25% of school districts. To make matters worse, there is a relationship between race and poverty. In 2016-17, one-third of all Black children under 18 were living in poverty in the US, compared with a quarter of Hispanic children. In comparison, White and Asian children had a poverty rate of 11% and 10% respectively.[286] This means that Black and Latinx children are more likely to attend schools with less funding because they likely live in poorer areas. This results in less access to better education, and therefore fewer opportunities for higher education. Black students are much less likely to graduate from high school and attend college than White students with the same family income,[287] making social mobility a distant possibility.

## "We Only Hire From the Ivy League"

In workplaces, where you have been educated is another dimension of diversity and source of discrimination. Thanks to school and university league tables, we have created a hierarchy of institutions of learning, ranking some higher than others. Educational institutions certainly do more than just providing book knowledge; they nurture how we learn, think, and behave. Where we study impacts our opportunities for internships, and the jobs that we are offered.

The higher education system in the US, which many other universities around the world are modelled on, has been referred to as the caste-system of the US.[288] In the US, tertiary education can range between $5000 and $50,000, while in the UK it is about $11,000. An Ivy League education will set a student and their parents back a substantial amount, making it available to few: those who have such resources available, those fortunate or talented enough to obtain a scholarship, or those who are eligible for bursary funding. This caste-system in education is not unique to the US. We find this caste system in other countries as well; between state and private schools, elite and non-elite state schools, and Ivy League and non-Ivy League universities.

Having grown up in Singapore, where it is all about where you go - or don't go - to school, I am acutely aware the impact of ranking educational institutions has in creating distinctions between those who are perceived to be more "intelligent" and those who are not. Parents buy apartments, sometimes in very expensive parts of the country, to be in the one to two kilometer range needed for priority at higher-ranked primary educational institutions. Some parents spend copious amounts of money on additional after-school tuition in the hope their children do exceptionally well in their exams, increasing their chances of admission to a prestigious secondary school. Students from more prestigious institutions enjoy the perception of being more "intelligent", and have access to better opportunities in school and at work. The reverse is also true. Those from what are known in Singapore as "neighbourhood schools", are perceived negatively. This attitude is not unique to Singapore. We see similar attitudes across Asia in India, China, Hong Kong, and South Korea as well as in the UK and US.

The bigger problem is that these attitudes towards education are so prevalent and deeply embedded in our minds that they impact our behaviours and actions as adults.

Biases based on a person's education have implications for the talent we recruit. Companies have a '*university bias*' in recruitment, preferring people who are from esteemed institutions, based on the assumption that students from these educational institutions are smarter, have undergone better training, are more hard-working or even innovative.[289] As HR and line managers look through piles of job applications and the details blur, they may default to selecting candidates based on the "prestige and rank of the university" from which graduates come from.

The finance industry and business consulting firms are notorious for hiring only from top pedigree business schools around the world, creating a non-inclusive - in fact *ex*clusive culture - in these organisations. This recruitment practice perpetuates the elite status of the industry as being only for those who can afford to go to elite high schools which, in turn, help them get into "esteemed" educational institutions. In the very first episode of the acclaimed

Netflix Series *Suits*, a firm partner tells a prospective junior hire "we only hire from Harvard". That is not far from reality.

This university bias is further supported by *affinity bias*, whereby line managers demonstrate a preference for hiring candidates from the educational institutions that they themselves are from, or from educational institutions like theirs: "Oh this candidate is from Stanford, he will be a good hire for the team (like me)". The *halo effect* comes into effect in justifying the hiring decision. By playing up the university the person is from as a positive attribute, it compensates for things the candidate is lacking in other areas. The *horns effect* helps line managers justify why they did not choose another candidate, by emphasizing that someone from a non-elite institution is likely not to be a good hire, even if the candidate was strong in other areas.

It is not just in hiring but also in pay scales that we see discrimination. Students from elite universities receive a higher starting pay than those who are not from these institutions.[290] This higher starting pay seems to continue into mid-career as well. If we compare data from the top ten and the bottom ten colleges ranked by US News,[291] at the start of their career, the median salary for graduates of the top ten colleges is 31% higher than the median salary for the bottom ten colleges. By the sixth year, this gap has nearly doubled to 58%.[292] This discrepancy is much higher when looking at colleges below the top 100. In the UK, a graduate from London School of Economics earns a median salary of £38,000 while one from Cambridge or Oxford earns about £35,000. This is almost double that of graduates from universities at the bottom of the list.[293] It is also worth noting that graduates earned about £10,000 more than non-graduates.[294] Bias does not just surround where you attended college or university, but if you did in the first place.

Is there any basis for this 'university bias'? Are students from elite universities really better hires that justify the higher pay? Do university degrees predict job performance? One of the assumptions underlying this bias is that through their selection processes, higher-ranked universities choose students who are likely to be better at performing their jobs. However, this is untrue and universities' criteria for selecting students are very different from companies' criteria for hiring talent. Additionally, the former set of criteria are shown not to be a great predictor of employees' success.[295] A 2020 study published of 28,339 students across 294 universities in 79 countries, showed that graduates of better ranked universities performed better, but only nominally, after controlling for age, gender, and years of study.[296] While the difference in performance between top and average graduates from universities that are further apart in rank (think 10,000 ranking positions apart) seems significant at 19%, this becomes less relevant for organisations hiring within a much narrower ranking range of universities, when the difference in performance is only about 1%.

## Expanding the Pool

It is encouraging to see Apple, Google and IBM making efforts to hire people without college degrees.[297] This is a positive step in changing the way we think about college education and hopefully will give companies an opportunity to tap into a wider and more diverse pool of talent. 15% of IBM's US hires do not have a four-year degree and the company looks for candidates who have had hands-on experience.[298] These companies are not on their own. Glassdoor found that 12 other companies, including EY, Costco, Hilton, Starbucks and Bank of America, all hire candidates without college degrees.

**The apparent value of a piece of paper**

Why should companies follow suit and look outside the universities they normally hire candidates from? The top reason would be to stop supporting systemic biases. With ethnic minorities underrepresented at top schools, focusing only on top ranked institutions means that companies implicitly support systemic biases. Expanding the universities from which companies hire means they have access to a much wider talent pool that is more diverse in terms of ethnicity and gender as well as skills, perspectives, and experiences.

This richness of diversity of thought adds far more value to the company than the higher ranking of the university that the candidate is from. In fact, candidates from elite universities tend to have lower interpersonal skills, appear less friendly, be more prone to conflict and less able to identify with their team, leading to an erosion of team dynamics.[299] Numerous studies have shown that interpersonal relationships are crucial to employee motivation, job satisfaction and an employees' performance and career success. Employees from elite institutions tend to be perceived as arrogant and snobbish, and as seeing themselves and their role in the company as superior. This creates a divide between themselves and others.

This us-and-them divide is further exacerbated by the pay differences for students from higher-ranked universities. It is certainly more costly for companies to initially hire students from these universities and continues to be more costly even mid-way through their careers. Given that this higher pay does not correspond with a significant difference in job performance, companies could save some money by hiring from outside the higher-ranked university group, and benefit from the added diversity of experiences, skills, and ways of thinking and learning.

# Project Access International

## Making Top University Education Inclusive

Project Access International is a global charity headquartered in London working to boost social mobility and increase diversity amongst global elites. They do this specifically by increasing access to top universities for students from less privileged backgrounds through a tech-enabled mentorship program powered by thousands of student volunteers. The mix of tech and volunteers is employed to ensure the scalability and cost-efficiency of the program. Project Access was founded at Oxford in 2016 by co-founders Emil Bender Lassen, Rune Kvist, and Anna Gross.

Formed on a belief that learning potential is equally distributed, but recognising that access to top universities is not, the charity began analysing the reasons behind the stark inequalities. They found that three barriers are keeping students from less privileged backgrounds from accessing top universities today, namely:

**A lack of role models and inspiration:** Students from less privileged backgrounds – be that students with refugee backgrounds, low-income students, first-generation university applicants or students facing other barriers – are less likely to have role models that inspire them to pursue their academic potential. Project Access has tackled this challenge by mobilising a team of more than 250 trained volunteers and 2,000+ mentors who function as ambassadors for the charity. These volunteers lead outreach activities across the world in partnership with schools, foundations, ministries of education, companies and others with the goal of reaching as many high potential students from less privileged backgrounds as possible and plant the dream in their heads.

**A lack of high-quality application support:** Students from more privileged backgrounds are likely to encounter application support from early on – from guidance on selecting extracurricular activities to private tuition and higher quality schooling more generally, yielding highly competitive university applications. In contrast, students from less privileged backgrounds are often left on their own to figure out the rigorous application processes, yielding less competitive applications. Project Access tackles this challenge with their 100% free tech-enabled mentorship program in which students are matched with a peer-mentor from their own country studying their dream degree at their dream university. The mentor helps the applicant circle in on aspirations and navigate the application process, while supporting the applicant on making the most use of the materials offered on the program.

**A lack of supportive community:** alongside being less likely to gain admission to a top university, a student from a less privileged background is also twice as likely to drop out. The charity found that this challenge is centred around the notion that less privileged students rarely feel like they "belong" at top universities. Project

Access tackles this challenge by forming a community around their mentorship programs in which applicants connect with other applicants and mentors both during the application process and after they receive offers. In addition, Project Access operates Campus Communities at all the universities they target – from Cambridge to Harvard to Bocconi – where the organisation brings successful applicants and mentors together for events and opportunities.

The charity funds its work through a combination of philanthropic donations, with previous donors including WeWork, the Hempel Foundation and the Tuborg Foundation, university partnerships, with partners including Cambridge University, and corporate partners including McKinsey & Company, Boston Consulting Group and Gorrissen Federspiel.

Emil Bender Lassen, who today is chairing the charity's Board of Trustees, remembers a meeting with a UK based tech company that later became a partner: "We met the Chief HR Officer of the company, who – rather embarrassed – shared that she had run an analysis on the schooling backgrounds of recent hires and found that every single one had gone to a private school before attending university. She had not considered this when hiring them, as the company simply focused on hiring from top universities. But the correlation between private education and top university admissions really manifested itself in her analysis and made her realise why working with organisations like ours can help diversify the talent pipeline early on that she will choose her next hires from 3-4 years down the line".

## Key Takeaways:

- Barriers manifest themselves in many ways: Project Access supported students from over 70 countries in their 2020 program cohorts. With such a wide reach – ranging from Denmark to India – the barriers faced by the individual students differ a lot. Companies need to consider that when developing diversity strategies.
- Authentic perspectives matter: Project Access realised early that to have a successful outreach strategy in Peru, they needed Peruvians at the table. Similarly, the team that is best suited to tackle inequalities will often be made up of members who have experienced these inequalities themselves. Bringing authentic perspectives to the table is key.
- Diversity, Equity and Inclusion (DE&I) must be integrated in the core fabric of organisations: considering DE&I as a project running in parallel with company operations will constrain its impact. Instead, DE&I should be considered in the core of a company's operations – from how you hire and onboard, to how you run meetings and strategy sessions to ensure that all perspectives are heard.

Partnerships can be strong impact drivers: the increasing focus on DE&I has led to the formation of organisations and companies like Project Access that have grown to be experts in tackling specific challenges for specific groups. Instead of reinventing the wheel, companies should consider partnering with organisations in a more focused way.

Companies serious about tackling diversity challenges are talent magnets: Project Access has itself had much success attracting strong team members and advisors, and have also found that corporate partners opt to work with them because they see that the best candidates increasingly expect DE&I to be a top priority in the companies they wish to work for.

Explore more about Project Access at https://projectaccess.org/

# Experiences & Skills

*"Be brave. Take risks.*
*Nothing can substitute experience."*

Paulo Coelho, Brazilian lyricist and novelist

I am an educator at heart and for me, one of the great joys of teaching university graduate degree programs is being able to draw on the diverse experiences and skills of my students in the lecture theatre. The greater the diversity of the students, in terms of industries and functional roles that they are from, the richer the discussions and sharing of experiences; with each of us in the classroom learning vicariously through the experiences of others. For those of you who have done a graduate, executive or leadership course, I hope you would agree that you were most engaged, learnt the most and felt inspired from sessions where there was a mix of experience and skills of fellow learners.

Despite knowing the immense value diverse experiences and skills would add, and as much as it makes sense in a university context, we seem to struggle to replicate this indirect learning in our workplaces. Companies prefer to hire talent with similar work experiences and skills to teams and functional groups. Why is that? What is standing in the way of companies hiring talent with a different range of experiences and skills, compared to others in the team? Risk. There is a risk-aversion to hiring people from outside of the industry and/or functional role. We tend to consciously and unconsciously prefer candidates who we see as "safer" and more predictable.

In 2019, one of my Fast-Moving Consumer Good (FMCG) sector clients was undergoing a digital marketing transformation with the goal of reaching out more effectively to their younger customers. During one of my inclusive marketing training sessions, an employee suggested that the company should be hiring talent with different experiences and skills, possibly from the Tech industry. Others snapped back that this was "too risky", and it would be a real shift in hiring practices without certainty of positive benefits. There certainly was resistance in the room that day to deviate from what had always been done, which was hiring talent from other FMCGs who had been successful in order to replicate that success for their new employer. However, what this does is create 'cookie-cutter' solutions, where employees move from company A to company B and implement tried and tested solutions. They bring what worked in company A to company B, perhaps with a different product line or context. This is not innovation. To be able to harness the true benefits of digital transformation requires new and innovative ways of thinking, which requires a range of experiences and skills to draw on.

## Hiring for Similarity

We have an *affinity bias* to hire people who have similar experiences and skills as ourselves or others in the team. We assume that they are more likely to "fit in", perform well on the job and work well with their colleagues in the team. We presume that anyone with a different set of experiences and skills will not be able to make the jump and transition to "fit in", and therefore, assume that they would not be as successful at their jobs and within their teams. We rely on stereotypes that a particular person, with a certain range of experiences and skills, will be better suited for a job.

This way of thinking needs to change. Homogeneity of experiences and skills is not good for business. In a business world that is faced with constant disruption and change, being able to innovate is crucial to survival. This requires talent who are able to think differently from the way the company and industry has been done before. To be able to differentiate themselves from competitors, companies need talent who are looking at their product lines and services in novel ways. If innovation is needed, diversity of experiences and skills is key.

For the past 40 to 50 years, we have been conditioned to think that deep expertise will lead to increased credibility, better job prospects and even higher incomes. But that is changing. Vikram Mansharamani, a Lecturer at Harvard University and author of the book *Think for yourself: Restoring Common Sense in an Age of Experts and Artificial Intelligence,*[300] suggests that in a world fraught with uncertainty and change, breadth of perspectives and "connecting the proverbial dots" (the domain of generalists) is just as important as depth of expertise and the ability to "generate dots" (the domain of specialists).[301]

In fact, there is evidence to suggest that diversity of experience has the most positive impact on company performance in sectors characterised by greater dynamism and frequent change, particularly in Tech.[302] We have been inspired by leaders like Jeff Bezos who, with no prior retail experience, became hugely successful in creating Amazon. Forward thinking companies like Google openly share that they actively hire for multi-functional experience. They value candidates who are problem solvers with more general cognitive ability rather than role-specific knowledge.

**You are not supposed to be here**

While the technology sector comes to mind, what if you are from a more stable industry, one which does not change as frequently? Are you wondering why then the need for diversity of skills and experience? The short answer is that the world is constantly changing. A stable industry today is likely to be one confronted by change in the future. In a recent Fintech panel debate that I was a part of, this was evident. As more banks look into expanding into the Fintech sector, they could certainly benefit from hiring talent outside of the usual banking and consulting circles and draw on talent with experience from other relevant industries.

Indirect learning from others' experiences and skills has the potential to add value to a company's growth in new markets. Research published in 2015 compared 116 Indian (emerging-market) firms with 160 UK (developed-market) firms and found that emerging-market firms without prior experience in developed markets used indirect learning - learning from the experience of others, to achieve the growth in those markets.[303]

When we think of innovation, we often associate it with dreaming up a novel way of doing something or even a new product or service. We need to think of innovation more broadly than that. *Innovation is Being Inspired – Learning – Modifying – Adapting.* It is about being inspired by others, learning from what others have done before, modifying it, and then adapting it to a different concept. How can we be inspired by and learn from others? We can certainly look outside the organisation through indirect learning, but we can also draw on the diverse experiences and skills of our own talent within our teams and workplaces.

Dr. Vishal Sikka, Chief Executive Officer & Managing Director, Infosys, India shares that "design thinking teaches us that great products and solutions come when there is a synthesis of lots of different kinds of perspectives, and when we are diverse we create the opportunity for that rich synthesis of great perspectives. The more diverse we are, the better we will all be".[304] Having talent with diverse experiences and skills enables teams to be able to approach challenges and problems from different perspectives and find inspiration to do things differently from what has been done before. This enhances the creativity and innovativeness of the outcome. Teams that have a homogeneity of experiences and skills limit their ability to do this.

> *"If you have a broad range of experience beyond your own sector, company and region, you will be able to walk in the shoes of others more easily because you've effectively been there before. Some of us may be able to more naturally take the perspectives of others but we can all nurture that skill by seeking diverse experiences – whether we're in the C-suite or running our own tiny business."*
>
> Rajesh Chandy, Professor of Marketing at London Business School[305]

Given the strong case for talent with diverse experiences and skills, companies must make concrete efforts to actively hire this diverse talent. In PWC's 2015 annual CEO survey, 78% of CEOs expressed that their business used multiple channels to find talent, including online platforms and social networks. 71% said their business actively searches for talent in different geographies, industries, and demographic segments. Tapping into the labour pool in emerging markets is particularly important; by 2020, it is estimated that more than half of graduates aged 24 to 35 years will be found in these countries. Developing the skills of the existing workforce is also high on CEOs' list of priorities. Most (81%) say that their business always looks to equip employees with new skills, through continuous learning or mobility programmes. Nurturing an adaptable talent pool can have real value for the business; research indicates that this could unlock up to $130 billion in additional productivity globally.

Another hiring strategy that is increasingly becoming a mantra amongst recruiters and talent acquisition experts is to "hire for potential, not experience"; implying that teams should be hiring beyond relevant experiences and skills that are directly related to the job itself. The underlying belief here is that companies should be hiring for attitude, and training for job-related hard skills that can be taught. Hiring for potential involves taking a risk on candidates with the faith that they have the capacity to develop into someone who will add value to the company. Hiring for potential involves identifying five critical traits in candidates - curiosity, determination, engagement, insight, and motivation.[306] Companies adopting this way of thinking about their hiring decisions benefit from an expanded candidate pool as well as the diverse perspectives that the hired talent bring to the workplace.

## Hiring an Ex-convict: Would You Do It?

Let us challenge ourselves further to think even more broadly about what constitutes diverse experiences. Would you hire someone who was an ex-convict, someone who has served time in prison? Would you hire someone who had been convicted multiple times? Some of you may be thinking "no" or "probably not". Others may be thinking "Why not, they should be given a second chance".

27% of those who have served a prison term in the US are unemployed.[307] In the UK, only 17% of ex-offenders manage to get a job within a year after release from prison.[308] The main barrier is discrimination and the resulting lack of opportunities.[309]

When unemployment levels are low, companies need to look more broadly for sources of candidates to fill talent shortages. In the UK, a third of businesses state that they are unable to address skills gaps in their workforce.[310] This is pushing companies to be more willing to take the risk and hire ex-offenders.[311]

Greyston, a New York bakery that makes brownies for Unilever's Ben & Jerry's Ice Cream unit, Amazon's Whole Foods grocery chain and Delta Air Lines, adopts an "Open-Hiring" human capital model.[312] This means that anyone who applies for a production job will get an opportunity when it becomes available. The catch? Every potential hire must undergo an apprentice program where they test and build workplace aptitudes. The company makes efforts to make sure they are set up for success. While nearly half do not make it through the program, enough do. Some of those who do are ex-offenders. This model shifts the focus from spending time and money on screening people to training, learning and development as well as employee support. This not only saves recruitment costs but expands the potential pool of talent to hire from, while creating value in organisations and "fostering equality, respect and growth in communities".[313]

Globally, it is encouraging to see a growing number of companies that hire ex-offenders. These include Starbucks, Sainsbury's, Tesco, Walmart, Unilever, Marks & Spencer, Sony, Flipkart, and Google. Of these companies, those that are based in the US have signed the Fair Chance Pledge, which was brought into effect by President Obama with the hope of giving ex-offenders a fair chance to find employment by having fair chance hiring practices, eliminating barriers to re-entry into the workforce, and providing meaningful opportunities for employment.

While a criminal conviction is not a skill or job-related experience that companies may consciously look for in a potential hire, there is growing support for the positive benefits to companies that do hire ex-offenders. In a report published by the Society for Human Resource Management in May 2018, about two-thirds of HR professionals say their company has hired workers with criminal records. More than 80% of managers and two-thirds of HR professionals feel that the value these workers bring to the organisation is as high as or higher than that of workers without records. The study was based on data collected from 2,000 corporate managers and HR executives in the US on their attitudes about ex-offenders. In the UK, evidence from employers such as Marks and Spencer suggest that hiring ex-offenders reduces initial recruitment and job advertising costs, helps resolve skill shortages, reduced staff absences and increased retention. Ex-offenders are found to be very loyal as they are grateful for being given the opportunity, leading to greater long-term job commitment.[314]

For people who have been in prison, the traumatic experience itself leads to the development of life skills that include mental resilience, emotional strength and valuable interpersonal skills including negotiation and effective communication. Many prison inmates also receive formal vocational training and even participate in certification for college degrees. This training, in addition to the life skills, can be transferable and in fact valuable to our workplaces.[315] Data from the UK shows that 81% of people think that businesses employing ex-offenders are making a positive contribution to society, 86% of employers of ex-offenders rate them as good at their job and 92% of employers say diverse recruitment has enhanced their reputation, helping them win new contracts.[316]

Over two-fifths of employers in the UK say that hiring ex-offenders has increased the diversity of their workplaces and contributes towards their Corporate Social Responsibility efforts, which has improved their employer branding and reputation as an equal opportunity employer. As it turns out, it may not be as "risky" a hiring decision as one may think.

**Go on, hire someone different**

# Personality & Ways of Working

*"I want freedom for the full expression of my personality."*

Mahatma Gandhi, Indian lawyer, anti-colonial nationalist, and political ethicist

While everyone has a personality, our personalities are different. No two people - even identical twins[317] - have the same personality. Our workplaces are made up of individuals, each of us with our own personalities - characteristics that define how we think, feel, and behave - some of which are genetic and others environmental. Our personality influences how we view and experience the world. It shapes the actions we take and affects how we interact with others.

It is the differences in personality that form the basis of bias and discrimination in what is called "*personality bias*". Are you wondering why we would have biases based on personality? After all, we all have this dimension; it is not like some have a personality and some don't. We also know and accept that people are different. The reason personality bias exists is because of *affinity bias* and *ingroup favouritism*. We prefer to work with people who are similar to us in personality so that we get along better and our workplace interactions are smoother. We also experience *trait ascription bias* which is the tendency for people to view themselves as relatively variable in terms of personality, behaviour and mood while viewing others as much more predictable in their personal traits across different situations.

The range of personalities that can exist in our workplaces and in teams makes it extremely challenging to "manage". We try to "manage" personality differences by hiring and promoting people who "fit" with the personality profile complementary to others within the team. In doing so, we miss out on the value we can gain from having diversity in the personality types that make up our workplaces. Having people who are similar to each other in personality limits the range of perspectives, ideas and ways of working that we are drawing on, and may contribute to groupthink. It is in this spirit of trying to make sense and "manage" the various personalities in our workplaces that personality tests were developed.

Personality testing really began in 1917, with the Woodworth's Personal Data Sheet which was developed to identify soldiers prone to nervous breakdowns during enemy bombardment in World War I. This test was later adapted for industry-use and focused on screening for employees with maladjustments who may create workplace disturbances. With the publishing of Carl Jung's book *Psychological Types* in 1921, personality tests, and their role in organisations, have certainly evolved and have become more comprehensive in their supposed ability to measure our personality and categorise it accordingly. In today's workplaces, commonly used personality tests include the Myers-Briggs Type Indicator, Big 5, DISC assessment, The Caliper profile, and Hogan Personality Inventory.

How and why do companies use these tests? Well, they may use a personality test to determine whether a job candidate is a good fit for a specific role or the culture of the company, gain insights into a person's working style, or easily compare different candidates. For example, for customer-facing roles, employees who are extroverted are more likely to perform better at engaging with the customer and translating that engagement into sales than someone who is more introverted. Sometimes companies also use personality testing to assess their current employees to better understand and manage them, and leverage their individual strengths. A study found that employees who "fit in" with the company, team and their supervisors are more satisfied, more successful and more likely to stay within the business.[318] Personality tests are often justified by the premise that employees who fit with the culture of the business are important because those employees are better able to get along with each other, which, in turn, leads to greater job satisfaction and team success. Personality tests also help HR and recruiters in making decisions between otherwise well-qualified and capable candidates.

These benefits mean that there has been a surge in the use of online personality tests by employers like Facebook and Google in the past decade as companies try to streamline their hiring process. The Institute of Student Employers in the UK reported that in 2019, 92% of employers that they surveyed used some form of personality testing when in the process of hiring potential employees.[319] Personality tests are used to assess the personality, skills, cognitive abilities and other traits of 60% to 70% of prospective workers in the US, up from 30% to 40% about five years ago.[320] Workplace personality testing has become a two-billion-dollar industry[321] and is growing by 10% to 15% a year, estimates Hogan Assessment Systems Inc.

The rise of personality tests has sparked growing concerns about how effective and fair they really are, and whether hiring for "personality fit" is really the right thing for organisations in their efforts to be innovative and creative. While the use of personality tests may be legal, there are some questions we need to ask ourselves as we think about whether we, from an ethical perspective, should be using personality testing in the first place: Are people of different personalities treated equally? Do we hire certain personality-types, and not others? Once talent comes through our doors, do we support some personalities more than others in their progression and growth in our organisations? What are we missing out on by limiting the kind of personality-types we have on our teams? On a more practical level, these tests ask for personal information. If people answer questions honestly, it could reveal mental health problems or emotional instability, which employers could use as a reason not to hire someone. Given these concerns, some companies have scaled back, changed, or eliminated their use of such tests.[322] Many critics and civil-rights groups have long claimed that the data-driven algorithms which power the tests could make it much harder for people who do not "fit" with the personality profile to get jobs.

## Personality Bias

One of the key problems with personality tests is that it forces people into a set category that may be too generalised and broad. For example, people are forced into extremes: extrovert or introvert, conscientious or not, neurotic or not, open-minded or not, feeler or a thinker. The categories go on. Except our personalities are not binary. Yes, we may lean one way more than another, but our personality characteristics lie on a scale, and are very much contextual. In a particular context, the same person may exhibit different personality traits than in another. The spectrum of our personality is not captured in personality tests, and when we base decisions on these tests, we stand to miss out on hiring talent that may actually be an asset to our organisation.

The underlying reason for the usage of personality tests is to hire people who will compliment and fit well with the existing personality types in teams and functional groups. We also tend to hire people with a personality profile that has been shown through previous experience to be "successful" in a particular role.

It turns out that our success in our workplaces, across a range of dimensions, seems to be very much correlated with our personality. A study done in 2015 looked at how our personality influences our careers - whether certain kinds of people make more money, why certain kinds of personalities tend to end up in that nice corner office, and so on.[323] The study looked at the 16 Myers-Briggs personality types and found the following results:

- Extrovert, Sensor, Thinker and Judger (ESTJ) made more money than other personality types.
- Extrovert, Sensor, Feeler and Judger (ESFJs) were more satisfied at work.
- Extroverts tend to manage larger teams as do Thinkers and Judgers.

The study supported previous work that showed that personality types that are especially ambitious and inclined to leadership are the ENTJ. Those who are ESTJ and ENTPs (Extroverts, Intuitive, Thinker and Perceiving) tend to be more entrepreneurial, while ESFJs are nurturing and focused on the task of parenting. I am sure you can imagine how biased hiring and promotion decisions can be if based solely on such personality tests. I hope you also noticed that introverts do not seem to feature very much at all. Perhaps we need to question how we define success.

I am reminded of the powerful words of Susan Cain in her 2012 TED talk titled "The Power of Introverts", in which she says: "It is the world's loss. Because when it comes to creativity and leadership, we need introverts doing what they do best. A third to half of the population are introverts". [324] Through her books *Quiet: The Power of Introverts in a World That Can't Stop Talking* and *Quiet Power: The Secret Strengths of Introverts*, Susan Cain shows us the real power that lies in introverts. In our workplaces, we celebrate extroverted behaviour – people who are outgoing, confident, assertive, and expressive. In doing so, we lose out on the talent within our organisations and in talent pools outside who do not "fit in" with this personality prototype but who, if given the opportunity, are able to add such value. This expectation to conform to a certain personality prototype forces introverts to be more extroverted to "fit in" with what is expected of them to succeed. Cain says she became a Wall Street lawyer to prove to herself that she could also, like everyone else, be bold and assertive, rather than become the writer that she always longed to be.

We live in a society and work in workplaces that glorify and celebrate extroverts. In doing so, we ask the talent in our organisations to be someone who they are not. We ask them to leave their introverted personality outside the revolving doors of the building and miraculously become extroverted in the workplace. Except this is not authentically who they are, and it is mentally and emotionally exhausting being someone who you are not. Organisations need to recognise the power of different personalities and enable everyone to be themselves, their whole selves, at work; just as they are when they are at home with the ones who are closest to them. In doing so, we open our workplaces to a diversity of thoughts and ways of working that add value to innovation and creative ideas; we have talent that are engaged and energised from being themselves; and we open up our workplace as a place of work to a talent pool that we may not have considered before. This is why personality tests should never be the primary basis of a hiring or promotion decision. It can be helpful once someone has been hired or promoted to adjust communication styles, feedback methods and even motivators to ensure that each and every person in the organisation is being recognised for their individual personality and has a talent development plan that is unique to them. But it should never be used as a tool for inclusion or exclusion of talent.

In our workplaces, consciously or unconsciously, we engage in biases and microaggressions that demonstrate that we value certain personalities over others. These biases and microaggressions tend to focus on labelling people, giving the impression that the way they are, their personality traits, are not desirable and will not lead to success. "Oh, you're so quiet, you should speak up more"; "You're so disorganised, how can you work like that?"; "Oh, you need to be more logical, we can't follow your way of thinking"; "Come on, you have to be more of a team player to succeed". Our workplaces reward and value certain personality traits. The reality is that for our organisations to be a place where there is creativity and innovation, we need a range of personalities who force us to think about problems and situations in different ways. We need to be as inclusive to the person who is pragmatic as much as someone who is a dreamer. Think about your own workplace or team. Do you see a pattern in the personalities in your team? Might it be time to perhaps shake up the personality jar and see the magic unfold?

# Ways of Thinking and Learning

*"The things that make me different are the things that make me ME."*

PIGLET from *Winnie the Pooh* created by English author A. A. Milne and English illustrator E. H. Shepard

## The Power of Neurodiversity

We are all different in the ways in which we think and learn. Yet our societies, educational systems and workplaces seem to propagate the belief that there is a preferred way to think and learn. *Neurodiversity* - the diversity of the human brain and mind - is an essential dimension of cognitive diversity. Neurodiversity is very common, with one in seven people being neurodiverse.

*Neurodiversity* refers to the infinite variety of cognitive styles of thinking and learning because our brains all work differently. The term neurodiversity itself was only developed in 1998, and is an umbrella term that is often used to refer to people who have dyslexia, dyspraxia, autism, Asperger's and attention deficit hyperactivity disorder (ADHD), and refers to people whose brain may function, process and learn information in a different way from someone who is neurotypical.

The challenge we face is that less than 50% of those who are neurodiverse know it.[325] In fact, we could say that we are all neurodiverse – we all think and learn differently. Dr. Nick Walker is a queer, autistic, transdisciplinary scholar, author, and educator who says: "The idea that there is one 'normal' or 'healthy' type of brain or mind or one 'right' style of neurocognitive functioning, is no more valid than the idea that there is one 'normal' or 'right' gender, race or culture."[326] He suggests that the classification of neurodivergence of those with autism or dyslexia or ADHD as a medical or psychiatric condition has no scientific support but rather is a product of biases, particularly prejudice.

The British Dyslexia Association estimates that 4% of the population is severely dyslexic while a further 6% have mild to moderate dyslexia. Dyslexia International[327] estimates that 10% of the global population experience dyslexia, which equates to around 700 million people worldwide, with other studies estimating it higher at 17%.[328] According to the WHO, one in 160 children have autism.[329] In the US, 1 in every 42 boys and 1 in every 189 girls born are autistic.[330] About 15% of the UK population, or 1 in every 7 people,[331] are neurodiverse. This represents a significant proportion of existing staff, job applicants and customers, yet statistics published in 2017 show that just 16% of autistic adults are in full-time employment in the UK, even though 77% of unemployed autistic adults want to work.[332] Other estimates show that unemployment of neurodiverse talent is even higher at 80% (this includes those with more serious conditions of neurodiversity who are not candidates for neurodiversity employment programs).[333]

We have been conditioned to believe that there is a "normal" or a "neurotypical" way to think and learn, and that anyone who deviates from this "normal" is seen to be ill and somehow unwell. Our workplaces have been created for neurotypical ways of thinking and learning. We expect people to "fit in" with the prototype of being neurotypical. Given how many people in our population are neurodiverse, the question that we have to ask ourselves is why haven't our workplaces made adequate space for neurodiversity?

Thanks to greater research and knowledge, we have certainly made progress with increased awareness of the neurodiversity within our populations since 1998, when the term was first developed. This greater awareness has meant that there is greater acceptance in society of the idea that people are neurodiverse, resulting in more people getting diagnosed and diagnosed earlier in life. There has also been a real shift in people's mindset away from neurodiversity as something to be "cured" to something that is to be celebrated.

It certainly helps when famous personalities like Greta Thunberg and Richard Branson speak openly about their neurodiversity. Richard Branson wrote on his blog: "dyslexic people can be hugely creative in identifying solutions to problems, and to coming up with new ways to tackle challenges…From my own experience, I know that dyslexic people can achieve great things when they focus on their strengths and get the right support in school."

Why should companies hire neurodiverse talent? Well for one, there is a skill shortage in many parts of the world. Some estimate that 40% of global employers are struggling to find the talent they need.[334] With about 10-17% of the global population having some form of neurodiversity, this is a talent pool that could be vital in filling in those gaps. SAP[335] found that applicants who applied to their Autism at Work program included Master's degree holders in engineering, anthropology, economic statistics; Bachelor degrees holders in computer science and engineering; some even had dual degrees.

For companies who are looking for ways to be more innovative and relying on this innovation as a basis for their competitive advantage, having talent who think and learn in different ways is crucial to making that happen. What better way to do this than by hiring neurodiverse talent? Many people with dyspraxia, dyslexia, ADHD, Asperger's, social anxiety disorders, and autism have higher-than-average abilities and often have extraordinary skills, including superior problem-solving skills,[336] pattern recognition, memory, and mathematics, as well as bringing different perspectives to the workplace.[337] Research suggests that autistic employees are as much as 140% more productive than their neuro-typical colleagues because of their increased ability to focus on certain tasks and ability to concentrate for an extended period of time.[338] Finally, from an inclusive workplace culture viewpoint, having talent who are neurodiverse helps develop empathy amongst talent by requiring people to accommodate the needs of this valuable talent pool.[339]

## Fighting the Neurotypical Bias

So, what is preventing such well-educated talent from finding jobs? What is holding companies back from hiring neurodiverse talent? The answer is bias; and our preference for talent who fit with the neurotypical prototype. Those who are neurodiverse are stereotyped in a negative way by those who are neurotypical. But who decides what is neurotypical? For example, people with autism are assumed to be anti-social, socially awkward, rely heavily on structure and routines, are either high functioning or low functioning, or just good at technical jobs. Our workplaces have been created by and for people who fit into the neurotypical ways of thinking and learning. Neurodiverse talent struggle to fit the profiles sought by employers; profiles that include being a good communicator, team player, have high emotional intelligence, persuasiveness, extroverted personalities, and the ability to build relationships and networks. This automatically screens out talent who are neurodiverse and do not fit with the prototype. We also, individually and collectively, express our view of neurodiversity as a disorder through the usage of discriminatory phrases like "she suffers from autism". Unfortunately, our workplaces seem to assess neurodiverse talent based on how neurotypical they can behave.

What is certainly encouraging is seeing a growing number of companies - SAP, Hewlett-Packard Enterprise, Ford, EY, Dell Technologies, Google, and Microsoft - that have made efforts to redesign their recruitment processes in order to embrace neurodiverse talent. What these companies are seeing are productivity gains, quality improvement, boosts in innovative capabilities, and increased employee engagement as a result, making having neurodiverse talent a competitive advantage for these companies.[340]

The prevalence of neurodiversity in our workplaces may be much higher than we imagine. In his book *NeuroTribes,* Steve Silberman points out that autism is particularly high in the Tech sector. Walt Disney, and Donald Winkler, former CEO of Ford Credit, are examples of very successful people with learning disabilities. A study found that self-made millionaires are four times more likely to be dyslexic than the rest of the population, and 40% of the 300 millionaires studied were, in fact, diagnosed as dyslexic.[341] The study emphasized that those with dyslexia may not be good at focusing on details but excel at focusing on the big picture and producing creative ideas.

While expectations are growing for organisations to report on, act on, and advocate for neurodiversity in their workplaces, there remains little practical advice or real-world experience on how to go about it. Many organisations want to 'get it right', or to leverage the strengths of neurodiverse talent. But they are not sure where to get started or they invest significant resources with mediocre results at best. What organisations need to think about are the accommodations that they may need to make to make workplaces inclusive to neurodiverse talent. To begin, companies need to redesign their recruitment practices to be open and accommodating to all, starting with the job descriptions themselves. Using language that is structured, clear and concise while avoiding the use of complicated, metaphorical language can make job descriptions much easier to understand. It also helps to split descriptions into 'essential' and 'desirable' skill sets. Job interviews are nerve-wrecking even for neurotypical talent, and can be even more stress-inducing for those who are neurodiverse.

Rethinking the interview process itself is certainly needed. Specialisterne,[342] founded in Denmark, is a socially innovative company that works both with neurodiverse talent and employers to help secure meaningful employment for both parties. Specialisterne recommends to their clients to have half-day hangouts, which are comfortable gatherings during which job candidates can interact with managers. During these hangout sessions, some candidates are selected for further assessments. The consulting firm recommends that further assessments be project based. This could include assessment using Lego Mindstorm robotic construction and programming kits to work on assigned projects.[343]

Next, accommodations need to be made in the physical workplace environment, especially workplaces that adopt an open office layout. Talent who are neurodiverse tend to be sensitive to stimulation from their environment. To help neurodiverse talent thrive and concentrate, companies may need to create independent workspaces, provide headphones to prevent auditory overstimulation and blue light glasses to help with limiting visual stimulation. In addition, neurodiverse talent prefer to receive clear guidance and support, so it helps to provide them with a clear point of contact or mentor if they need extra support, who can work with them to understand their working style and how best to communicate. On a more practical level, it also helps to have flexible working hours to reduce the stress of peak periods of transportation and getting to work. Finally, to have a workplace environment where neurodiverse talent are able to feel included to bring their whole selves to work and function productively requires their neurotypical managers and colleague to receive training on how to work effectively with neurodiverse talent, and to be open-minded to different ways of thinking and learning.

So, if you are struggling to find new ideas and creative energy, perhaps you have neurotypical people in your teams who think and learn in similar ways leading to conformity bias and groupthink. What you may need is to take a chance on someone with ADHD or dyslexia or autism: we can learn from the efforts of companies who have taken these chances with great results and outcomes. We need to stop making the talent that come into our workplaces fit in with prescribed ways of thinking and learning, but rather embrace the diversity in talent out there so that we can all bring our whole selves to work. Given that about 1 in 7 of us are neurodiverse, is your workplace ready for neurodiversity?

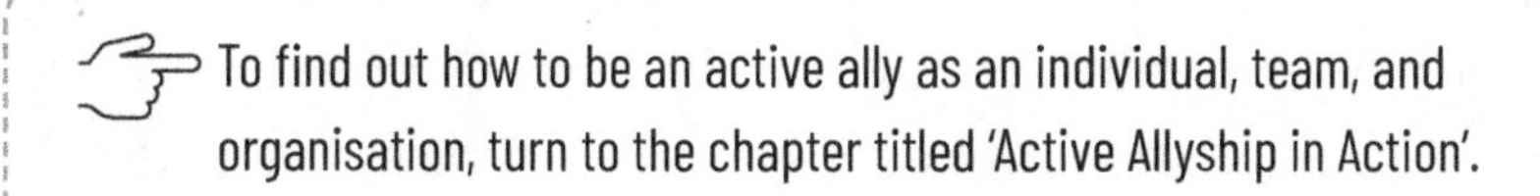
To find out how to be an active ally as an individual, team, and organisation, turn to the chapter titled 'Active Allyship in Action'.

# Stack Recruitment

## Helping Employers Attract, Recruit and Integrate Neurodiverse Talent

Stack Recruitment is a social enterprise based in London that operates as a specialised recruitment agency with the primary mission of helping corporates attract, recruit and integrate neurodiverse talent. The company realised that employing those with a neurodiversity, especially autism, was seen as an 'unknown' grey area for employers given the ambiguity associated with neurodiversity compared to those with physical disabilities, where accommodations are much more clear cut and practical.

Emily Banks, the founder of Stack Recruitment explains the company's vision "We aim to improve the employment landscape for neurodiverse individuals. We do this through three main areas: 1) recruitment, 2) training and 3) consultancy, with the aim to help corporates at every stage of their neurodiversity journey."

Stack Recruitment's recruitment services help corporate organisations attract, recruit and integrate neurodiverse talent by providing advice on how to make their recruitment processes accessible, and in turn providing them access to a large talent pool. They support their corporate clients at every stage of the process, from assisting them to adapt their job adverts to implementing adjustments during interviews. This enables their clients to start recruiting neurodiverse employees while providing them the space to ask any questions to Stack Recruitment's experts.

Secondly, the company delivers training to employees on neurodiversity to help reduce the stigma and increase awareness. This helps bust the biases that many people have. Many associate neurodiversity with young males who code, create websites and struggle to socialise. In reality, neurodiverse individuals have a wide range of skills, passions and talents just like anyone else.

Finally, their consultancy services enable employers to get expert feedback on their neurodiversity strategies and processes, which enables them to build a solid foundation and create neurodiversity initiatives that fit with their wider mission and values.

Looking ahead, Emily shares her hopes: "Although we have made significant progress so far, there is still a lot to be done to really give the neurodiversity movement the momentum it needs to change peoples lives. Going forward we aim to work with more corporate organisations on a global scale to really help them to catapult neurodiversity to receive the same attention as other areas of diversity such as ethnic and sexual orientation. It is estimated that 15% of the world is neurodiverse, so addressing neurodiversity needs to be prioritised to give these individuals the opportunities they deserve.

"Our hope is that neurodiversity will stop being seen as a charitable cause and something 'nice to do', and be seen as bringing tangible benefits to corporate organisations. We really want to focus on the fact that neurodiversity should not be something to just add to your CSR portfolio, but instead an intrinsic part of a corporates values and mission.

"Stack Recruitment has experienced great success so far, but we realise we're only just getting started. We've learnt a lot and have had the opportunity to work with some fantastic individuals every single day."

## Key Takeaways:

- There really is no 'one size fits all' approach when it comes to neurodiversity. Everyone is different and cannot be put into groups.
- Work as a team. Neurodiversity is a movement that requires collaboration and the sharing of ideas to truly make a difference.
- Small steps really are better than no steps. The underemployment of neurodiverse individuals has not changed in decades. It is important to realise that even the smallest progress is progress and that it is difficult to change such a multi faceted problem in a short span of time.
- Just start. A common question is 'where do we begin?'. There is no right and wrong answer to this, as it really does depend on your organisation. Doing something no matter how small it is will start your neurodiversity journey and move you in the right direction.
- Talk about it. The best progress is made by starting a conversation, talking to people and learning. One of the biggest ways we learn is from each other. Talking helps reduce the stigma associated with neurodiversity and pushes the movement forward.

Explore more about Stack Recruitment at https://www.stackrecruitment.org

# Social and Lifestyle Dimensions of Diversity

# Ethnicity & Culture

*"I believe there is only one race – the human race."*

Rosa Parks, American activist in the civil rights movement

What comes to your mind when you think of ethnicity and culture within the context of diversity? Racism? Xenophobia? Throughout history, ethnicity is the most recognizable dimension of diversity upon which human beings have judged, exerted prejudice and stereotypes upon, and discriminated against others.

Ethnicity comprises so many aspects of our identity - our culture, heritage, language, traditions, and values. It makes up an important part of each and every human being's identity, and is close to our hearts. Our ethnicity arouses strong emotions in us as it paints a picture about who we are and where we come from; and when we think of ethnicity, we cannot help but think of culture.

Culture is made up of artifacts, values, and assumptions,[344] and forms an integral part of ethnicity. Culture can be metaphorically likened to an iceberg, where what we see and experience when interacting with someone from a different ethnic group is only about 20% of the whole. We experience the visible aspects of culture, like language and non-verbal communication, as well as rituals and symbols. What lies underneath the surface, the parts we don't see, includes communication and listening styles, beliefs about formality, hierarchy, and silence. At the deepest part of the iceberg lies values and basic truths. When we interact with colleagues from a different ethnic group and culture, or when we travel to different countries and cities, we are only experiencing the part of the iceberg that lies above the water and maybe - if we are lucky - a little bit just under the surface. To truly understand an ethnicity's culture requires us to go deeper into the water and explore the depths.

Ethnicity is also closely related to the terms nationality and race, and these terms are used somewhat interchangeably. When you ask someone to describe their identity to you, it is likely to be a combination of these terms. *Nationality* is a legal construct, and refers to a person's citizenship or relationship with the political state they belong to. *Race* is a term that has no scientific definition and is a social construct. It refers to biological, physical traits that are deemed socially significant by groups and cultures. This may include skin colour, facial features, and even hair texture. Despite the term race lacking a scientific definition, it holds significant meaning and importance for people.

*Ethnicity* is also a social construct and is thought to be acquired and influenced by culture, language, religion and where we live. Ethnicity is more self-chosen, and one can choose to identify with multiple ethnicities. For example, being Asian American or British Nigerian, or like me Singaporean Indian. Nina Jablonski,[345] an anthropologist and paleobiologist at The Pennsylvania State University, who is known for her research into the evolution of human skin colour, suggests that "race is understood by most people as a mixture of physical, behavioural and cultural attributes. Ethnicity recognizes differences between people mostly on the basis of language and shared culture." For most of us, these aspects of our identity are deeply intertwined and we don't see them as necessarily separate. Given this, I adopt a more integrative view of ethnicity to encompass our culture, nationality and race.

## The History of Racism

History plays a significant role in the evolution of issues around race and ethnicity. The idea of race was created by anthropologists and philosophers in the 18th century as a basis to geographically group people based on their skin colour and physical traits. These groupings laid the foundation for the notion that some races are superior to others, which benefited White Europeans in slave trade, colonisation and accumulation of wealth while also promoting capitalism. Ethnicity has also been used as a basis of oppression during the Holocaust, the interethnic conflict in Rwanda and in recent times, the Rohingya genocide. In modern times, ethnic conflict and tensions exist not just between different countries, or as a result of one ethnic group having control over another, but can be prevalent even amongst those that have the same nationality and race. India, across its many states, has significant ethnic differences based on history, language, cultural and religious practices that give rise to ethnic biases between the citizens of a single country.

Ethnic bias, much like gender bias, has existed in our societies for centuries and is often used interchangeably with the term racism. According to the Merriam-Webster dictionary, *racism* is "a belief that race is the primary determinant of human traits and capacities and that racial differences produce an inherent superiority of a particular race". *Xenophobia* is the dislike of or prejudice against people from other countries and *colourism* is a form of discrimination based on skin tone. It is important to note that ethnic bias includes racism but goes beyond that to include microaggressions and systemic ethnic biases.

In spite of the tremendous efforts of leaders like Mahatma Gandhi, Nelson Mandela, Rosa Parks, and Martin Luther King, Jr., we are still nowhere near the kind of equality that should exist for all human beings regardless of their ethnic backgrounds. Has progress been made? Sure it has - chattel slavery in the US has been abolished; African-Americans have voting rights; and segregation and apartheid have been abolished. White supremacy - the belief that White people constitute a superior race and should therefore dominate society, typically to the exclusion or detriment of other racial and ethnic groups - has been and continues to be challenged.

While this is certainly progress, a conversation I had with my then eight year-old son at bedtime emphasized how much more progress is needed. My son brought home a book about Mahatma Gandhi related to the theme 'Heroes' that they were exploring in school. I was, needless to say, delighted to see that he had picked a book about a hero from our Indian heritage. At bedtime we snuggled up to read. That day, one of the chapters we read was about Gandhi's experiences in South Africa. The story described a situation in the late 1800s where Gandhi was told he could not sit inside the carriage of the horse-driven carriage, and was made to sit on the footstep instead. The carriage was only meant for those who were White. Upon listening to this, my eight year-old son said to me "Mama, will that happen to me? I am the same skin colour as Mahatma Gandhi." My heart broke. Not only because he asked me THAT question but more so because in 2020, I could not tell my son that he would not experience racism. So, I plucked up enough courage, held the tears in, cuddled him and said "Sweetheart, you will likely not experience exactly that, but yes, you will likely experience racism. Mama and Dada are here to help you learn how to deal with those situations." I tucked him in, gave him a long reassuring hug and kissed him good night. Once I had shut the door to the room, the tears came. It is in that moment that I empathised with every Black and Brown mother who has had to have a difficult conversation with her son or daughter about the racism they will face.

The world we live in today is very different from the 18th century, or even the world of Mahatma Gandhi. We are more interconnected in terms of both the movement of people and our awareness about different cultures and ethnicities. Media and travel have enabled these things to happen. This is a positive consequence of globalisation. One would think that this greater awareness of different cultures would increase tolerance and open-mindedness, but we are not as inclusive as we should be. The most recent cases of police brutality in the US against members of the African American community has spearheaded discussion and action in workplaces around the world to address the prevalence and impact of racial discrimination against minority ethnic groups.

Have you heard of the term 'hygge', pronounced 'hooga'? Hygge is a Danish word that is difficult to translate but broadly refers to cosiness. The term hygge gained popularity in 2017 when Meik Wiking's New York Times bestselling book *The Little Book of Hygge: Danish Secrets to Happy Living* put hygge on the map. The book introduced the Danish concept of cosiness to an international audience. Since then, restaurants, cafes and even co-working spaces around the world have tried to re-create hygge in their settings with blankets, fireplaces, mulled wine, and candles. In reality, hygge goes beyond just the loosely translated equivalent of 'cosiness'. It is much more and goes much deeper into the culture of the region. Helen Russell, in her book *The Year of*

*Living Danishly*, defines hygge as a "complete absence of anything annoying or emotionally overwhelming." The feeling of hygge does not have conflict and there is no sense of discomfort with opposing viewpoints. Charlotte Abrahams, author of *Hygge: A Celebration of Simple Pleasures, Living the Danish Way* says: "Hygge is very gentle. There is no discussion of politics or anything controversial that makes you feel uptight".

If you are wondering why we are talking about this wonderful cosiness, there is a dark side to hygge - "*Hyggeracisme*" or hygge racism. It is an interesting behaviour that is found not just in Denmark but across the region. Hygge racism was coined by a bachelor student at Lund University, Sweden in her dissertation and is defined as "well-intentioned racism".[346] Hygge racism is often defended as harmless and is less overt as it is often communicated through humour and sarcasm. What *hyggeracisme* shows us is that even in the most well-intentioned, tolerant and open-minded cultures of the world, discrimination based on ethnicity is present and desperately needs to be addressed.

## Racism and Intersectionality

What is worth noting is that ethnic bias and racism are experienced differently and to varying degrees by ethnic groups across the world, and even within a single societal context. The intersection between ethnicity and education, socio-economic backgrounds and gender play a role in this varying experience.

In the US, recently there has been a light shone on the differences in experiences between people of colour, more specifically between Asian Americans and Black Americans. This is known as the Model Minority Myth,[347] where a minority group is perceived as more successful compared to other minority groups. This myth has been exacerbated by the economic success that Asian Americans have achieved. Asians in the US have an annual median household income of $105,000 while Whites, Hispanic and Blacks all have median household incomes below $80,000.[348] Indians are the highest-earning ethnic group in the US, with a median income of $100,000, and approximately 72% having earned at least a bachelor's degree. This has led to a view that Asian Americans have internalized and perpetuated White supremacy, adapting their behaviour to "fit in" with the majority.

The Model Minority Myth serves to drive a wedge between minority groups by focusing on superficial analysis without understanding the depth of a proper investigation. While the above data does seem rosy on the surface, a little digging will show that Asian Americans have the highest income disparity.[349] Asian Americans are a very diverse group in itself, and the broad categorisation ignores the complexities and diversity within. This viewpoint also ignores the bias and discrimination that this minority group has undergone in the past, and continues to endure in the present.

A piece from *New York Magazin*e by Andrew Sullivan[350] in 2017 sheds light on this: "Asian-Americans, like Jews, are indeed a problem for the "social-justice" brigade. I mean, how on earth have both ethnic groups done so well in such a profoundly racist society? How have bigoted White people allowed these minorities to do so well - even to the point of earning more, on average, than Whites? Asian-Americans, for example, have been subject to some of the most brutal oppression, racial hatred, and open discrimination over the years. In the late 19th century, as most worked in hard labour, they were subject to lynching and violence across the American West and laws that prohibited their employment. They were banned from immigrating to the U.S. in 1924. Japanese-

American citizens were forced into internment camps during the Second World War, and subjected to hideous, racist propaganda after Pearl Harbour. Yet, today, Asian-Americans are among the most prosperous, well-educated, and successful ethnic groups in America. What gives? It couldn't possibly be that they maintained solid two-parent family structures, had social networks that looked after one another, placed enormous emphasis on education and hard work, and thereby turned false, negative stereotypes into true, positive ones, could it? It couldn't be that all Whites are not racists or that the American dream still lives?"

Ethnic bias and discrimination are no doubt complicated, but making an effort to understand history and backgrounds is important to get a complete picture and develop empathy towards the behaviours of others; rather than fighting discrimination with further discrimination.

What about women of colour? How does this group experience ethnic bias? Women of colour face additional stereotypes and societal biases – within the often patriarchal societies that they are from - that define their role in their families and restrict their rights to education or opportunities. It does not stop there. Women of colour face added discrimination at work in terms of access to employment, wage disparities, sexual abuse and harassment and prejudices and stereotypes about the role women of colour should play at work.[351]

In the United Kingdom, the unemployment rates of Black, Pakistani, and Bangladeshi heritage women have consistently remained higher than those of White women since the early 1980s. When the 2017 gender pay gap issue in the BBC came to light, few commentators showed outrage at the equally blatant racial pay gap, with not a single ethnic minority person making it to the top 24.

In Europe, the evidence of discrimination of women of colour can be most clearly seen in the stratification of the labour market, where women of colour are reportedly siphoned into domestic work, seen most visibly in Greece, Cyprus, Czech Republic, Italy, Ireland, Poland, and Slovenia. Domestic work is where the intersectionality of race, gender, class, and nationality - and the matrix of oppression - is most visible. Across the EU, migrant women face difficulties at work with pregnancy and motherhood. Roma women in Italy are more likely to take care of the home full time, whereas the labour participation of men is higher. Women with an African background in France have the lowest activity rates (74%) in the French labour market. While the unemployment rates of White women has dramatically decreased in the past 25 years, women of colour often face different challenges in the labour market. A report commissioned by the Women and Equalities Committee in the United Kingdom found that Muslim women are the most economically disadvantaged group in British society and that Muslim women are three times more likely to be unemployed than women generally. The report pointed to a 'triple penalty' impacting their job prospects: being women, being from an ethnic minority group and being Muslim.

## Ethnic Diversity at Work

The case for having ethnic diversity in our workplaces is solid. According to leading consulting firm McKinsey & Company, companies in the top quartile for racial and ethnic diversity are 36% more likely to have financial returns above their respective national industry medians.[352] At the other end of the spectrum, companies in the bottom quartile for ethnic diversity were 27% less likely to experience profitability (measured by average EBIT margins) above the industry average.[353] In the United States, the report found that for every 10% increase in racial and ethnic diversity on the senior-executive team, Earnings Before Interest and Taxes (EBIT) increases by 0.8%. Another study found that teams that shared the same ethnicity experienced a lower success rate for investments of 26.4%, compared to 32.2% for diverse teams.[354]

Given this, what does ethnic representation in workplaces look like in today's world? Let us take a look at the data of one of the most ethnically diverse countries – the US. Data from the US Bureau of Labor Statistics[355] shows that in the US, Whites made up the majority of the labour force at 78%. Blacks and Asians constituted an additional 13% and 6%, respectively. Indigenous groups including American Indians, Alaska Natives, Native Hawaiians and Other Pacific Islanders accounted for less than 2%. Among Asians participating in the labour force, the largest group was Indian, making up 24% of all Asians while the Chinese made up 22%. 54% of employed Asians worked in management, professional, and related occupations which constitute the highest paying major occupational category, compared with 41% of employed Whites, 31% of employed Blacks, and 22% of employed Hispanics. In the UK,[356] 85.6% of working age people were from White ethnic groups, 8.1% Asian, 3.4% Black, 1.8% had mixed ethnicity, and 1.1% were from another ethnic group.

In 2020, according to the World Economic Forum, there were an estimated 272 million international migrants accounting for 3.5% of the world's population. This was up from 150 million in 2000. While most people leave their home countries for work, millions have been driven away due to conflict, violence, and climate change.

This data shows us that globally, we have much more diversity than ever before. This is great. The question is: are we where we want to be in 2021, compared to the 18th century? Certainly not. Sadly, ethnic bias and racism are still widely prevalent in our societies and therefore in our workplaces. In the United Kingdom, Finland and several other European countries, job offers, training or progression opportunities rely on opaque, informal processes to which minorities do not have access. In Denmark, the United Kingdom and Spain, there are high rates of overqualification among immigrants and ethnic minorities. They are underrepresented in management positions and many of them find it hard to use their education in high-quality jobs. In Germany, people of African descent are disproportionately represented in the lowest rungs of society. Their monthly income is almost 25% less than the national mean monthly net income. In Portugal, people of African descent are overrepresented in the secondary sector of the labour market, consisting of low skilled jobs, low salaries, few promotion opportunities, and job insecurity. In Spain, 28% of migrant women hold a university degree, compared to 28.3% of Spanish women, but they are still overrepresented in low-skilled jobs.

Racial discrimination and racial prejudice in the workplace have led to difficult and even violent experiences for migrant and ethnic minorities. There have been several cases of severe exploitation of migrants and a widespread acceptance of a cheap workforce.[357] In Estonia, refugees from African countries who can be identified as Muslims have experienced direct racism and exploitation by their employers, colleagues, and clients, more so than other groups. In Hungary, one in five Roma surveyed in 2015 said they had experienced discrimination in the workplace. In Ireland, a large proportion of racist incidents reported are in the workplace (31%). In 40% of the cases reported, the victim's ethnic background was Muslim, followed by African (33%).[358]

When it comes to pay, did you know that Black men earn significantly less than White men - even when they were raised in families making the same amount? Black boys who grew up in poverty tend to stay poor as adults, and wealthy Black boys are more likely to be poor as adults than to stay wealthy. "Black men raised in the top 1% - by millionaires - were as likely to be incarcerated as White men raised in households earning about $36,000".[359]

We find ethnic biases deeply embedded in certain industries like education. 80% of public-school teachers in the US are White[360] while 50% of students are persons of colour. Similarly, in the UK, 85.9% of state-funded school teachers are White British while only 78.5% of the working-age population was White British.[361] This lack of diversity amongst educators means that we see greater racial bias in classrooms. Black children make up a smaller percentage of the classroom population but are suspended more frequently, showing that the severity of punishment increased when the race of the teacher did not match that of the child.[362] Students of colour are significantly more likely to be concentrated in low-income schools with less qualified teachers, fewer material resources, larger classes sizes, and lower long-term expectations for their students, affecting their ability to go to college even when their test scores and grades are up to the mark.[363]

A 2018 study found that pre-service teachers "graded the performance of a student who appeared to have a migrant background statistically significantly worse than that of a student without a migrant background".[364] Research from 2017 demonstrates that if a Black, male student has at least one Black teacher in the third, fourth, or fifth grade, he is significantly less likely to drop out of high school and more likely to aspire to attend a four-year college.[365]

What about in STEM industries? A study conducted in 2017 in the US based on census data shows that while Black, Latinx and

Native Americans constituted 31% of the US population, these groups [366] represented only 21% of the total bachelor's degree recipients in science and engineering, and 13% of the total recipients of doctoral degrees. In the US, there are some interesting data to look at. While the US White population stood at 60% in 2019, White employees in the US technology industry was 68%. Similarly, the US Asian population was 6% but the proportion in the technology industry was 14%. The US does not stand alone here.

According to data from the UK's Royal Academy of Engineering, only 7.8% of engineering professionals were from Black Asian and Minority Ethnic (BAME) backgrounds, whereas 12% of the UK working age population are from BAME backgrounds.[367] The Royal Society in the UK recognises that with diversity comes a mix of ideas, skills and approaches and that if the UK's scientific workforce is not diverse, they will be missing out on some great talent.[368] This lack of adequate representation contributes to the lack of role models from minority ethnic groups for young people thus impacting their decisions on whether or not to pursue education in these areas. This affects the diversity of the talent pipeline in the STEM industry.

Why do we see this lack of ethnic representation and imbalances in our workplaces and industries? The answer lies again in bias.

## Ethnic Biases at Work

In the workplaces of today, we have moved past engaging in deeply offensive name calling - names like Paki or Chinki or the N-word - but do not be mistaken; ethnic biases are very much a part of our workplaces in ways that you may not be aware of - not yet at least.

**The race is not fair**

While we may no longer experience or witness open racism at work, ethnic biases are very much still deeply embedded in hiring, recruitment and promotion practices, and are present in interactions amongst colleagues as well as in how we think about products, services and marketing to customers.

### Hiring, Recruitment and Promotion Practices

A 2017 study published by S. Michael Gaddis, a sociology professor at UCLA titled "How Black Are Lakisha and Jamal? Racial Perceptions from Names Used in Correspondence Audit Studies",[369] showed that when names like Lakisha and Jamal are used, they send signs about a person's social class and race. This study supports the findings of a 2004 study titled "Are Emily and Greg More Employable than Lakisha and Jamal?",[370] in which fictitious resumes were sent out in response to help-wanted ads in Chicago and Boston newspapers. The resumes were identical except for their names. The answer to the question in the title of the study is, unfortunately, a resounding 'yes', with those resumes with African American sounding names needing to be sent out 50% more than those with American/ European sounding names before getting a call-back. A similar study conducted in the University of Copenhagen in 2015 showed that applicants with Middle Eastern names like Mohammed had to apply for 52% more positions to be called for an interview than someone with a Danish sounding name like Mads.[371]

These studies show that name-discrimination plays a significant part in the ethnic biases at work and in recruitment processes. In Belgium, job applicants with foreign sounding names have 30% less chances of being invited to a job interview compared to applicants with a similar profile but Flemish sounding names.[372] I recall a story that a Black Scottish man had shared with me about his experience with his name in Denmark. He had a name that many would automatically assume was a White Scottish name, and this worked against him during interviews. While his name meant he would get called in for an interview, the reactions once interviewers met him were very different. He told me of the time he interviewed in a Danish organisation, and as he was led to the meeting room, he noticed people looking at him as he walked by. He noticed that they were all White. When the door to the meeting room opened, he was met with a shocked look from the interviewer, who asked repeatedly if he was indeed who he said he was. His first interview question? "How do you see yourself fitting in with our organisation?". You might have guessed he did not get the job, and the response he received from the company was "we did not see you fitting in with our organisation". When we hire for ethnic "fit", we lose the ability to benefit from the diversity of thought, ideas, and experiences that someone from a different ethnic background brings with them, along with the ability to understand the diversity of customers.

A 2016 study showed that minority job applicants who "Whiten" their resumes by altering any information that indicates their ethnicity are more than twice as likely to receive a call back than those who do not.[373] During the two-year study, 1,600 fictitious resumes were sent to 16 different metropolitan areas in the US. Some resumes were left as is, whereas others were "Whitened". The results were very interesting. When African American names and experiences were unaltered, 10% of them received a call-back. However, when African American candidates' resumes were "Whitened", that number jumped to 25.5%. For Asian applicants, 21% heard back if they changed their resume, and only 11.5% of candidates did if their resumes were not "Whitened". The researchers of the study also interviewed 59 Asian and African American candidates between the ages of 18 and 25. 36% said they "Whiten" their resumes, and two-thirds reported knowing someone who does.

Some of you reading this might be wondering what "Whitening a resume" means and possibly feeling uncomfortable with the term itself. In the study, "Whitening a resume" involved altering the presentation of the name, either by changing the first name (for example from a Chinese name to "Sarah") or using an additional name (for example, a Korean name and English name). In some cases, the presentation of experience was altered, either by omission (for example when the candidate worked in an organisation for ethnic minorities like the National Society for Black engineers) or changing the description by leaving out any words that might suggest the experience involved work with ethnic minorities, or even adding experiences that are strongly associated with "White" communities. If you were not feeling uncomfortable before, I am sure you are now.

The data does not look good as we look at talent progressing through the organisation. 2018 data from the US Equal Employment Opportunity Commission shows that Black professionals held just 3.3% of all executive or senior leadership roles, which are defined as within two reporting levels of the CEO.[374] Among Fortune 500 companies, less than 1% of CEOs are Black. In 2020, there were only four, down from a high of six in 2012. Over the past two decades, there have only been 17 Black CEOs in total, of which there has been only one Black woman -- Ursula Burns, who ran Xerox from 2009 to 2016. Among Fortune 100 companies in 2020, Black professionals account for just 3% of CEOs, 1% of CFOs and 3% of profit leaders like division presidents.[375] Only 52 out of Britain's top 1,099 roles are held by ethnic minorities, up from 37 in 2017 and corresponding with just 4.7% of the total number compared to the 13% proportion of the UK population.[376]

Why is this the case? The answer lies in *affinity bias*. The presence of affinity bias means that we tend to prefer hiring and promoting people with whom we have a greater similarity of culture and experiences, and with whom we assume we can get along better. At more senior levels of organisations and on boards, there is a risk aversion to recruiting diversely with decisions being made to hire people who are more similar and who ethnically "fit" with the rest of the leadership team members. This is how we have landed with all White leadership teams or boards in Europe or the US; all Indian leadership teams in India; or all Chinese boards in China - board compositions that do not reflect the composition of the working age population or consumer markets.

Our perceptions about certain ethnic groups are deeply influenced by embedded cultural stereotypes, and this means that we are making decisions that are heavily biased. A 2017 study found that people tended to perceive young Black men as taller, heavier, and more muscular than similarly sized White men, and hence more physically threatening.[377] Persistent notions that Black-Indigenous-People of Colour (BIPOC) candidates are inherently less qualified than White candidates can limit efforts to increase diverse representation in companies because such candidates are more likely to be negatively evaluated and ultimately not selected.[378]

## Workplace Interactions

What do microaggressions in workplace interactions look like? They are comments or questions that demonstrate an inability to see each individual beyond their ethnicity. "Oh sorry, wrong person", is a common microaggression and happens when a majority person confuses the name of the one of two people belonging to the same underrepresented community, even when they do not look alike. "Is that really your natural hair?" is another example, which might be a reason why one in five Black women feel pressure to straighten their hair for work. That is twice the rate of White women.[379] Ethnicity related microaggressions can take the form of assuming someone's skills or job scope simply because of where they are from. South Asian men from the Indian subcontinent are assumed to be the IT folk, or women from East Asia are assumed to be good at math and computer science.

One of my pet peeves is when someone says to me: "I don't see colour, I am colour blind". This way of thinking shows a lack of understanding of the discrimination and systemic biases that a minority person faces and has faced. It serves as a way to make a person from the majority ethnic group feel better about themselves, without realising the bias which underlies the statement. I especially like South African comedian and host of *The Daily Show*, Trevor Noah's response to that - "Then you don't see me".

The way someone speaks - their accent - can be a source of workplace bias in what is known as *accentism* or linguistic discrimination. Our accent forms an integral part of who we are, our identity. Research has shown that most of us have a hierarchical sorting of accents based on what we perceive to be more socially and culturally acceptable.[380] This is done somewhat unconsciously, but creates prejudices in us which cause snap judgements about others - perhaps that someone with a particular accent is not as smart or clever. This linguistic discrimination means that those with accents different from the majority feel ashamed of their accents and feel pressure at work to change the way they speak to "fit in". This can be mentally and emotionally exhausting, creating identity issues in people, along with anger and bitterness, as it forces people to change who they are.[381]

A trainee of mine from the North of England was sharing a joke that whenever he hears the voice of an aircraft pilot with the same accent as his, he thinks "Oh dear, I really hope this plane doesn't crash". While he may have been joking, we do make assumptions about someone's competence based on their accent. In fact, it takes us less than 30 seconds to linguistically profile a speaker, and make quick decisions about their ethnic origin, socio-economic class, and their backgrounds.[382]

A few months ago, I asked a group of trainees what stereotypes they had drawn on before they met me in person, based on a short description that they had received along with my photo. Some said they assumed I would speak with a "thick Indian accent". Others said they assumed I would dress "differently". This got me thinking. I am a brown woman who is ethnically Indian, but I speak with a "western accent" and wear western business clothes. What if I spoke with a South Asian accent, how would people react to me? If I wore traditional clothes - a salwar kameez or saree - how would they perceive me? I occasionally wonder, would I have more opportunities at work if I had had a more European or American sounding name?

Code-switching is a technique used to help those in minority groups manage their workplace interactions. Code-switching "involves adjusting one's style of speech, appearance, behaviour, and expression in ways that will optimize the comfort of others in exchange for fair treatment, quality service, and employment opportunities".[383] The term code-switching was originally created to refer specifically to linguistics when the speaker alternates between two or more languages, language varieties, accents or informal mixtures of language within a single conversation. This happens often in multicultural workplace environments. However, code-switching involves much more than just speech, including any behaviour in an effort to "fit in". Altering one's name is one aspect of code-switching.

An American study in 2019 found that Black and Hispanic people are more likely than their White counterparts to say they 'feel the need to change the way they express themselves when they are around people with different racial and ethnic backgrounds'.[384] In 2012, a video of President Obama in a locker room of the U.S. men's Olympic basketball team went viral. In the clip, viewers can see that there is a clear difference between how President Obama greets a White assistant coach and how he greets the Black NBA player Kevin Durant. That's right, even the President of the United States code-switches.

Why do people of minority ethnic groups engage in code-switching? Firstly, it helps to increase the perception of professionalism and increase the likelihood of being hired by downplaying membership in a stigmatized racial group. Secondly, its helps minority races to be seen as leaders when they avoid being associated with negative stereotypes about the particular racial identity they are from (e.g. being late, incompetent or lazy). Finally, expressing shared interests with members of the majority ethnic groups helps to raise the chance of promotion by being seen as similar to key decision makers.[385] On the flip side, code-switching can put tremendous psychological, emotional, and social strain on employees to be someone they are authentically not, leading to a depletion of productivity and burnout. The need to code-switch is evidence of the presence of non-inclusive workplace environments in which minority talent are unable to bring their whole diverse selves to work.

### Name-based Discrimination

Biases related to names goes beyond recruitment processes. When we meet someone for the first time, a person's name is the first identifier that enables us to connect with them but also, consciously or unconsciously, it can lead to stereotyping, *in-group favouritism*, and at times discrimination based on our biases.

> *"What's in a name? That which we call a rose by any other name would smell as sweet."*
>
> WILLIAM SHAKESPEARE (from Romeo and Juliet)

It turns out that Shakespeare may have got that supposition wrong. Research shows that *name-based discrimination* runs deep and has significant implications on the diversity we see in organisations. Microaggressions related to a person's name are so commonplace that those with "different" sounding names sometimes do not even notice them – it is so normalised in our world. You might be surprised how often someone with a "different" sounding name gets asked: "That's a difficult sounding name, can I just call you Kate?". I have Chinese friends with supposedly difficult-to-pronounce names who have informally taken on western names like 'Angela' and 'Peter' just to be able to fit in. I have had numerous instances where friends and colleagues have asked if there was a shorter form of my name – Poornima - that would make it easier for them. Other micro-aggressive questions include "That is a very unusual name, you obviously aren't from here - where are you actually from?". The reality is that a name is so much more than just an identifier.

In 2020, LinkedIn introduced a new feature to enable users to record how to pronounce their name. Given that I have a difficult name to pronounce, this is indeed a welcome feature. My name is certainly 'foreign sounding' in some contexts - I get that. It has been distorted in so many ways by those outside the global Indian diaspora - I have stopped counting. I went through high school actively choosing to cut it down to 'Nima' because it saved me from constantly cringing at hearing the mispronunciation of my name. As a teenager, I used to wonder why my parents picked that name for me of all names and chose to spell it that way - it could have been spelt Purnima, which would have made things easier.

When I moved to Copenhagen from my multicultural home of Singapore, my name became more than just a name. It became very much a part of my identity and defined who I was. Of course, it always was my identity - but in Denmark where I am clearly a minority - my name says so much about who I am. It tells the people I meet and interact with that I am ethnically Indian. For those who know a little bit more about India, the way it is spelt tells them that I am from the South of India. My name sparks conversations about the meaning behind names. Poornima means full moon - I was born on a full moon day and my paternal Grandmother suggested the name. For those wondering why a full moon would be special - in Indian mythology and culture, a full moon is regarded as being an auspicious day, a day where there is positive energy and vibrancy. Over time, I have come to accept the sound of my name in many intonations. As long as it is said with respect, it does not bother me. In fact, I really appreciate those who have asked me how to pronounce my name, even if it is for the third or fourth time. I am more than happy to engage with someone curious enough to ask me what my name means or where it originates from. My name is a reminder to me and those around me of my rich heritage, the colour of my skin, my culture, my background, my family, and in all this – my identity.

This makes for a good story about my name but what does a name have to do with diversity and inclusion? In fact, it has a lot to do with the diversity we see in organisations, and more importantly

**My name is my identity, respect it!**

how inclusive our organisations are to those who are different from the majority. How many "different" sounding names do you notice in your team? Are they pronounced fully and accurately? While having employees from a variety of backgrounds is an opportunity to leverage the benefits of an ethnically diverse workforce, we need to ensure that our organisations are being inclusive in creating a sense of belonging where every employee can bring their whole selves to work - including difficult-to-pronounce names - and feel fully accepted.

### Is My Voice Heard? - Beliefs of Silence

One of the key indicators of inclusion is whether everyone's voices are adequately heard. Our varied *beliefs of silence* across ethnic cultures have an impact on the extent to which ethnically diverse employees' voices are heard. Beliefs of silence refer to the role that silence plays in personal interactions and manifests itself during meetings and discussions in workplace scenarios. In some ethnic cultures, people speak in turn. One person speaks, they finish, and the next person begins. In other cultures, communication is more fluid, and people frequently interrupt one another. In yet another category, there are gaps in communication – silence between people speaking. These moments of silence can range from thirty seconds to even minutes. For many of us used to more constant communication, such moments of silence can be very uncomfortable. In fact, to avoid uncomfortable silence, those afraid of ending conversations use 'interruption endings' to end our sentences like 'and' or 'so' making it necessary for someone to continue the conversation – giving people an easy chance to interrupt and avoid having moments of silence. Have you noticed that in yourself or perhaps in the people you work with? Finally, there are ethnic cultures where everyone speaks at the same time.

In many companies, it is often said that 80% of the conversations during meetings happen from 20% of the people in the room. This gap could be even wider in ethnically diverse groups that include people from cultures where silence is valued. Knowing these differences in beliefs about silence can really help ensure that employees' voices are adequately heard, so that they feel included.

---

**Shhhhh...the beliefs of silence and how we communicate**

A

B

C

D

---

## Products, Services, and Marketing to Customers

In 2020, the term 'cultural appropriation' saw a surge in interest on Google's search engine, primarily in the White majority societies of Canada, US, Australia, New Zealand and the UK.[386] Cultural appropriation involves borrowing elements of a culture that is not one's own. Cultural appropriation has a negative connotation and

**Take a moment**

occurs when there is a lack of respect or complete understanding about the cultural element in its usage. It contrasts with cultural appreciation or cultural celebration where there is a deep respect and understanding about the cultural practice that is being adopted, often in consultation with members of the culture. Saurav Dutt, the author *The Butterfly Room* which explores racism and interracial relationships within Indian society, explains that enjoying something and being fascinated by it doesn't mean you are appropriating it. He says "cultural appropriation arises when people, anyone, takes aspects of another culture specifically to mock or disrespect them".[387]

In workplaces and across industries, cultural appropriation occurs when elements of another culture - usually a minority culture - are taken and used by companies to generate profit or use objects or designs in the wrong context. In these cases, there is no reciprocity, nothing is given back to the culture being mined. Asma Khan, Chef at the famous London restaurant Darjeeling Express and star of Netflix's *Chef's Table,* shared her take on cultural appropriation in the food industry in *The Guardian*: [388] "A lot of countries take the food and don't respect the culture. But you cannot have my food if you don't have me. It is a connection and if you take that away, you disrespect me…You can be from any culture, be any colour, you can cook our food but you must respect our traditions and our people." This was in response to UK's Marks & Spencer being accused of cultural appropriation by having a vegan biryani sweet potato wrap in its food outlets. Biryani is a traditional Indian rice dish and Khan likened the appropriation to calling a rocket salad a "toad in the hole" (a traditional English dish consisting of sausages in Yorkshire pudding batter, usually served with onion gravy and vegetables) – using words that have certain connotations associated with them.

These are not isolated incidents. Gordon Ramsay's London restaurant, Lucky Cat, was criticised for selling itself as an "authentic Asian Eating House"- despite not having an Asian chef. Chef Shaun Beagley (aka 'Boring Thai Chef') was fired from the restaurant Som Saa in London for faking an Asian accent in some of the racist videos he posted on social media. His supper club, called The Boring Thai, claimed to cook classic simple Thai dishes the traditional way. Yet, he was found mocking the very culture he was profiting from.

Lingerie designer Victoria's Secret found itself in hot water with the native American community for sending their bikini-clad model down the runway in a floor-length feathered headdress which has spiritual and ceremonial significance. In 2019, Gucci used Sikh headgear in a Milan fashion show, on White models. Designer Marc Jacobs received backlash for its use of dreadlocks on White models. In 2017, the New York Times faced criticism for showing a picture of an Asian-inspired restaurant's dishes with chopsticks vertically sticking out of a dish, which symbolises death and is a sign of funeral offerings in Japanese culture. Avoiding cultural appropriation is very much on the mind of marketing experts, learning from the many instances of cultural appropriation errors by companies.

Occasionally, companies can get it badly wrong. Ad agency Ogilvy & Mather India created an illustration for Indian mattress company Kurl-On. It featured a sequence of cartoon images depicting Pakistani activist and Nobel Peace Prize winner Malala Yousafzai getting shot in the face point-blank then tumbling downward onto a mattress, and then bouncing back up to win the Nobel Peace Prize with the slogan "Bounce Back". [389] This is based on the horrific incident in young Malala's life when she was shot in the head by Taliban gunmen for speaking up about the rights of girls to receive an education. She recovered and went on to be a champion for the rights of girls' education. The ad, which was posted on the 'Ads of the World' website, sparked international outrage on Twitter and elsewhere for its cultural insensitivity. Ogilvy did apologise,[390] surely regretting the incident, but it should never have been made to start with. Turns out, the graphic was created by a South American illustration firm who lacked the cultural know-how to understand the insensitivity. Having ethnic representation in companies reduces the chances for misunderstanding from producing what may be an offensive message.

What is hugely encouraging is seeing organisations take strong stands in the past decade - and more so in 2020 following the resurgence of the Black Lives Matter movement - to address racial inequalities. Walmart said it would end the practice of storing "multicultural cosmetic products" in locked cases in its stores. You can draw your own conclusions as to why products marketed to one ethnic group were kept under lock and key while products for others were not. HBOMax, owned by WarnerMedia has temporarily removed the movie *Gone with the Wind* from its library acknowledging the painful stereotypical portrayal of African Americans. YouTube, the Google owned platform will invest $100 million to fund and support the work of Black creators and artists.

Internally, organisations are making efforts to improve ethnic representation. Adidas has made a commitment to fill 30% of open positions with Black and Latinx candidates. Amazon and IBM both will stop the use of facial recognition technology for mass surveillance or racial profiling. Facial recognition algorithms were found to be far less accurate at identifying African-American and Asian faces compared to Caucasian faces, which has led to the increased skepticism in the use of the technology in law enforcement.[391] The cosmetics brand Estee Lauder said that it would mirror the percentage of Black people in the US in its employees over the next five years. Tech giants like Facebook have committed to increase the number of Black people in leadership positions by 30% over the next five years. In August 2020, Microsoft added its ninth Employee Resource Group (ERG) called Indigenous at Microsoft, with Dan Te Whenua Walker, the company's only Maori executive, tasked with bringing more indigenous people into the company. The first group that Microsoft set up was called Blacks at Microsoft, and was initiated in 1989. Other groups that followed include Asians at Microsoft and Hispanic and Latinx at Microsoft. Fitbit, the company behind the fitness app, has pledged to offer more workouts from Black fitness influencers and feature them on its app and social media channels, along with supporting research to address health conditions that disproportionately affect Black people. PepsiCo said it would increase Black managers by 30% and promote a minimum of 100 Black employees to executive ranks.

Increased representation of minority ethnic groups enables greater diversity of thought, skills, and experiences. Diverse talent means more culturally sensitive marketing and better understanding of the diversity of customers. This will lead to products and services that meet the needs of diverse customers.

## Your Cultural Thumbprint™

While there are many benefits to gain from a multi-ethnic workforce, there are many challenges with managing multiple ethnicities. Individuals, managers and leaders need to make conscious efforts to manage these potential challenges in order to gain the advantages of having an ethnically diverse talent pool.

The reality is that in the face of biases, microaggressions, prejudices, or negative cultural stereotypes which affect how we hire, manage or engage with other people, integration across ethnically diverse teams can be difficult. Very often, ethnically diverse teams are not functioning at their optimal levels of collaboration, productivity, and efficiency because of a lack of understanding of why others communicate or behave the way they do. Varied communication forms, different working styles and different understandings of professional etiquette can be misinterpreted or difficult to understand across languages and cultural differences, increasing conflict and eroding trust between ethnic groups. How do we address this? By knowing your and others' cultural thumbprints.

Geert Hofstede was a Dutch social psychologist whose pivotal work on understanding national culture using data from IBM in the 1970s has formed the basis of our understanding of national culture differences.[392] Hofstede's work has since been supplemented by the work of Edward Hall,[393] and most recently, by Erin Meyer in her book *The Culture Map*.[394] The work done by these researchers offers generalised descriptions of the national cultures of various countries across a set of dimensions.

When exploring the influence of national culture on individual behaviours, many of my trainees and university students struggle to identify with generalisations about the countries they are from. Curious, I wanted to delve into why this was the case. What I found was that my trainees and students' cultural identity went beyond their nationality. They identified with some aspects of their national culture, but certainly not all. Thanks to media, travel, cross-border education and employment opportunities, as well as interracial marriages, many of them saw their cultural identity as more multicultural and global in nature. They also viewed their cultural identity as more dynamic in nature as they gained new life experiences, rather than being static.

In 2016, the BBC conducted a poll together with Pollsters GlobeScan in which they asked 20,000 people in 18 countries if they identified themselves as global rather than national citizens.[395] While about half of the populations in the UK and US identified as global citizens, more than half of those (56%) in emerging economies with large populations saw themselves first and foremost as global citizens rather than national citizens. The data is particularly significant in Nigeria (73%), China (71%), Peru (70%) and India (67%). With this growing group of these global individuals,[396] it is more relevant for us to understand our own cultural thumbprint.

Your *Cultural Thumbprint* is your individual cultural identity. It defines who you are across a set of cultural elements. It is a reflection of your life's influences and experiences; and is some combination of the cultural backgrounds of your parents, the national culture you grew up in, the education systems you were educated in, your personality, your religious or spiritual beliefs and values, the cultural background of your partner or spouse, which countries you have lived in, the culture of the companies you have worked for, and so on.

Your cultural thumbprint is complex and absolutely unique to yourself. No one else in your workplace has the same cultural thumbprint because no one else has had the same life influences and experiences. Even within the same family, no two people have exactly the same cultural thumbprint; we all internalise our life experiences differently. Your cultural thumbprint evolves over time as you acquire new experiences. By creating our own cultural thumbprint, the hope is to be able to know your cultural identity better and to also reduce th.e biases and microaggressions we have towards others - recognising that everyone is indeed culturally unique.

**Elements of the Cultural Thumbprint™**

*How do I communicate with others? Low context or High context*

In low context communication, communication is simple, precise, and clear. Things are understood at face value and paraphrasing, or clarifications are encouraged.

In high context communication, communication is subtle, nuanced and often made up of many layers.

*What is my attitude to time? Monochronic or polychronic*

In monochronic attitudes to time, scheduling and sequential planning of events and meetings are preferred. Last minute changes to planned actions are not preferred and even frowned upon. Deadlines and milestones are strictly adhered to. Punctuality is valued.

In polychronic attitude to time, timelines are more fluid and flexible. Events, deadlines, and milestones are approximate and subject to change.

*How do I build trust with others? Assumed or socialised*

In assumed trust building, trust is presumed because of the working relationship between colleagues regardless of hierarchical positions. "I work with you, I trust you."

In socialised trust building, trust is built over time through frequent and consistent interactions.

*How do I manage disagreement? Confrontational or Non-confrontational*

When managing disagreement, those that are confrontational are comfortable in engaging in debate and disagreement, and in fact view the rich exchange as a means of building trust in the relationship. Within this confrontational approach to disagreement, those who are more emotionally expressive tend to use a louder tone, stronger language and even large hand gestures to get their view across to the other party. In contrast, those who are more emotionally inexpressive, may use strong language but in a calmer tone with less hand gestures.

When managing disagreement, those that are non-confrontational do their best to avoid situations where conflict and disagreement may arise.

*How do I provide negative feedback? Direct or Indirect*

When providing direct negative feedback, the feedback is communicated upfront and clearly highlights the areas of improvement needed.

When providing indirect negative feedback, the feedback is packaged and hidden in between more positive feedback and requires the receiver of the feedback to unpack the layers and sift through it to get to the negative feedback.

*How do I persuade others? Why-first or How-first*

When using the why-first approach to persuading others, the reason and rationale is explained first before presenting the suggestion, recommendation, or plan of action.

When using the how-first approach to persuading others, the suggestion, recommendation, or plan of action is presented first before the reasons behind it are explained.

*How do I lead others? Egalitarian or Hierarchical*

In egalitarian leadership, the power distance between a line manager and team member is very low, and communication across the flatter structures can skip hierarchical lines.

In hierarchical leadership, the power distance between a line manager and team members is very high, and communication needs to follow strict hierarchical lines.

*What motivates me? Individual goals or Group goals*

Those motivated by individual goals are motivated by personal rewards and benefits, seeking opportunities to fulfil those individual aspirations.

Those motivated by group goals are motivated by common goals, seeking opportunities to work collectively to achieve community aspirations for the collective good.

*How do I make decisions? Consensual or Top down*

In consensual decision making, input from all relevant team members are sought and agreement has to be reached before actions are taken.

In top down decision making, leaders or managers take decisions and inform relevant team members of the decision and the next steps of action to be taken. There is little or no input from team members in the decision-making process.

Note: The elements of the cultural thumbprint are based on the work of Erin Meyer, Geert Hofstede and Edward Hall as well as my own work with thousands of university students and corporate trainees.

To create your own cultural thumbprint involves three stages:

**Stage 1: Create a cultural thumbprint for yourself.**

Carefully read the descriptions for each of the elements of the cultural thumbprint. For each of the questions on the template, indicate with a dot where you lie along the continuum. When all 8 questions have been answered, join the dots to complete your own unique cultural thumbprint.

**My Cultural Thumbprint™**

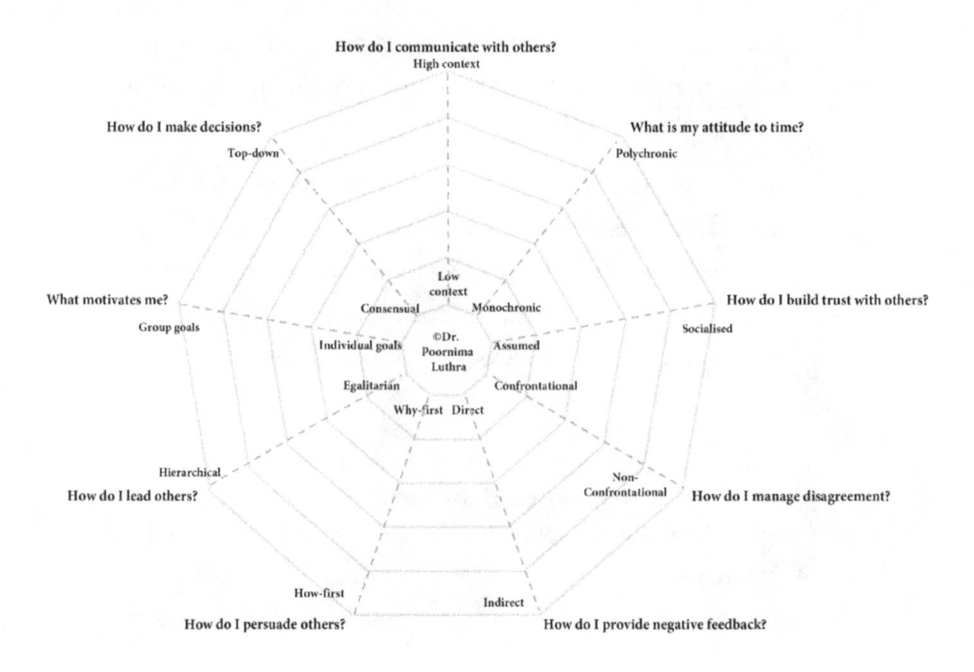


When creating your cultural thumbprint, keep the following in mind:

- This cultural thumbprint is for yourself at work. For some dimensions, we may place ourselves differently on the continuum in our personal lives.
- Ask yourself: "What represents me best and most frequently at work"? While we all adapt continuously to the people we work with and situations, we also have a dominant way

of behaving. Place yourself on the continuum where you would prefer to act.

- Be honest with yourself. This is an opportunity to reflect upon your own cultural identity without judgement. There are no rights and wrongs here.

**Stage 2: Ask for anonymised cultural thumbprints of you.**

Request the people that you work closely with to do an anonymised cultural thumbprint of you. This can be helpful in providing insight into how others view you.

---

**My Cultural Thumbprint™ by others**

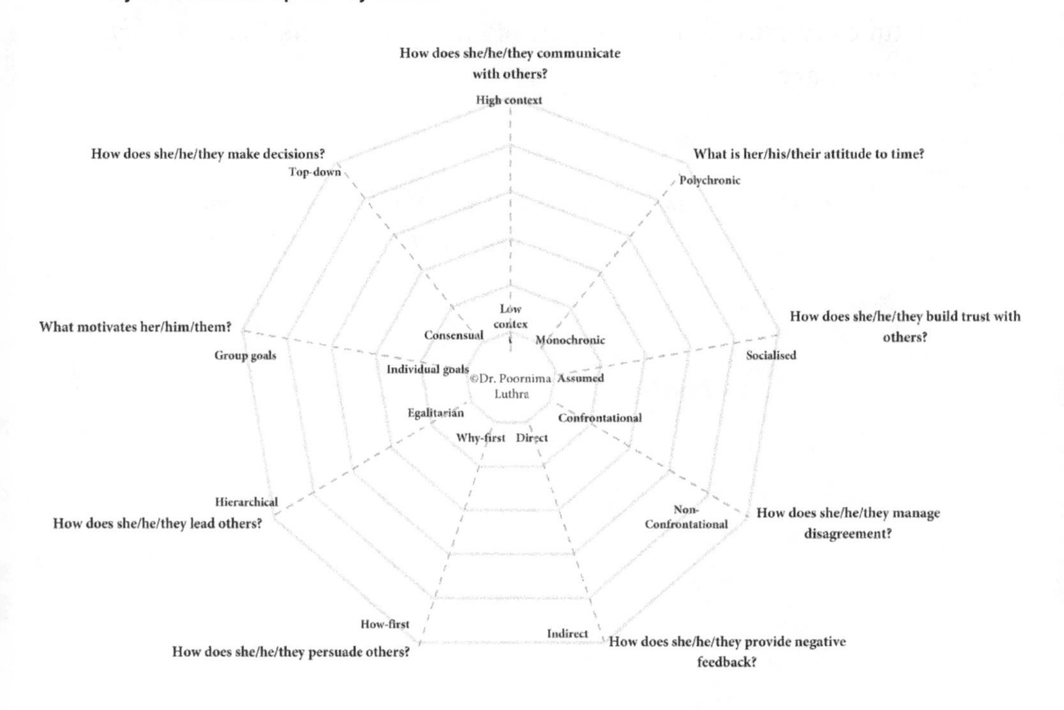


---

**Stage 3: Compare your cultural thumbprint with team members and colleagues.**

The cultural thumbprint provides an opportunity for teams to create their own individual thumbprint, and then engage in a positive and constructive team session to understand each other's cultural identities. The focus should be on the relative position of yourself with your colleagues, rather than the absolute position. This exercise can be very powerful to unpack the differences and similarities, as well as provide insight into the dynamics within the team and between colleagues.

A 2019 Pew Research Centre report highlighted that Generation Z is the most racially and ethnically diverse generation.[397] As we see more Generation Z talent entering our workplaces, making ethnic diversity an integral part of an organisation's D&I strategy is necessary.

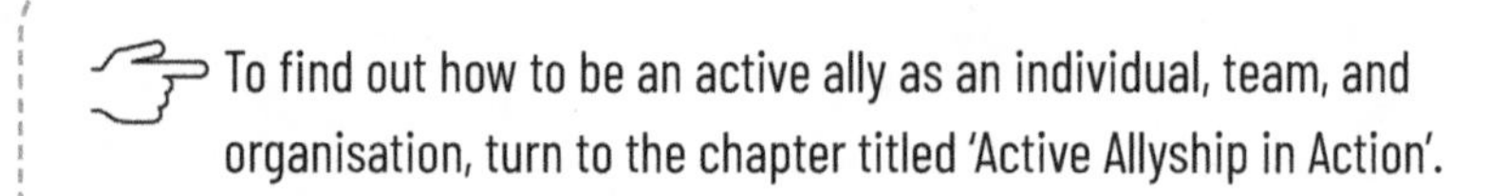

# Beliefs and Practices

*"Your beliefs become your thoughts, your thoughts become your words, your words become your actions, your actions become your habits, your habits become your values, your values become your destiny."*

Mahatma Gandhi, Indian lawyer, anti-colonial nationalist, and political ethicist

We all have beliefs; and our beliefs differ. Our beliefs are our brain's way of making sense of and navigating the complexity of the world we live in. Beliefs are really the mental representations of the ways in which our brains expect things in our environment to behave, and how things should be related to each other - the patterns that our brain expects the world to conform to. You may recall reading earlier on in the book that our brain receives 11 million bits of information every second.[398] To help us process this vast amount of information, we use algorithms and heuristics, or mental shortcuts. As human beings, we experience the world through our five sense organs, and we find it hard to accept that the world experienced through these five sense organs is somehow incomplete or even inaccurate. In fact, to conserve our energy, we use mental shortcuts that can take the form of connecting dots, filling in gaps, extrapolating and making assumptions based on the limited and incomplete information we have or receive. Beliefs can be thought of as energy-saving shortcuts in modelling and predicting the environment around us.

Beliefs are formed very early on in life through our interactions with close family members, particularly parents and even grandparents, as well as other authority figures, such as teachers. Our trust and faith in these adults make us accept beliefs and ways of thinking as accurate representations of the world around us. These beliefs then become the assumptions that we hold to be true. Beliefs can also be formed through our life experiences and evolve throughout life. Our beliefs help us to navigate the world around us; our beliefs provide us a foundation to stand on as we face the challenges thrown at us; our beliefs provide us a safety net to walk through life. As human beings, the beliefs we hold affect the quality of our life, our work, and our relationships.

## The Hijab, Turban and Bindi

When we refer to beliefs, many of us refer to a person's religious beliefs. While religious beliefs are not the only beliefs one holds, it seems like a good place to begin. Whether we are religious or not, we would all probably agree that our workplaces should be a place where people feel that they are not being discriminated against based on their religious beliefs; where hiring and promotion decisions are not biased for or against a particular religion; and where employees are not expected to behave or dress against their own religious beliefs to conform with what others are comfortable with.

*Religious biases* can be very deeply rooted and are often consciously held. These biases can take the form of extreme views about a specific religion, implying that everyone practising that religion must be inherently bad. These views can be reflected in casual comments about people of a religious faith and go on to make stereotypical assumptions based on religious affiliation.

Following the events of September 11th 2001 - the deadliest co-ordinated terrorist attacks conducted by the Islamist terrorist group Al-Qaeda against the United States - there has been a huge surge in the discrimination and biases against Muslims and those from Muslim countries. With the rise in terrorist attacks in the past two decades, we have seen an uptick in Islamophobia - the fear, hatred of, or prejudice against the Islamic religion or Muslims - in politics and in our workplace environments. The US Equal Employment Opportunity Commission (EEOC) reported that in the aftermath of September 11th 2001, discrimination against those who identify as Muslim, Sikh, Arab, Middle Eastern and South Asian, or those perceived as a member of these groups, has risen. The EEOC indicates that this type of discrimination is typically related to national origin, religion, or both.[399]

While in the UK, US, and many other parts of the world, it is illegal to discriminate against an employee based on their appearance, including wearing traditional native attire or headgear, in others, the law itself can be interpreted to be discriminatory. In 2004, France passed a law banning religious signs in public schools. This included turbans and Muslim headscarves. In 2010, a public debate arose and France passed a law that bans the wearing of full-face covering in public, including but not limited to burqas (enveloping outer garment that covers the body and the face) and niqabs (garment of clothing that covers the face). The law was constitutionally cleared and came into force in April, 2011. Wearing the Muslim headscarf or veil - known as a hijab - is banned in French public schools, and for public servants at their place of work. In public spaces, however, headgear including turbans are permitted with only burqas being banned for security reasons.

A Carnegie Mellon study found that Muslim job candidates experienced more discrimination than Christian job candidates during the hiring process. For Muslim job candidates, there was a 13% lower call back rate compared to Christian job candidates.[400] Research shows that there is evidence for formal discrimination in job call backs and permission to complete applications; interpersonal discrimination through perceived negativity; and low expectations to receive job offers in the workplace for those wearing a hijab. This is sometimes referred to as hijabophobia, or discrimination against women wearing Islamic veils - the hijab, chador, niqab and burqa. Furthermore, the research also found that those wearing a hijab were less likely to receive call backs when there was low employee diversity as compared to when there was higher employee diversity.[401] Similarly, such incidents have been experienced by those wearing a turban.

Indian women who wear a bindi on their forehead, Sikhs who wear a turban, Jews who wear a kippah or Muslim women who wear a hijab often face the question "Why do you wear that"? There is certainly nothing wrong with the question itself. In fact, it demonstrates curiosity and a sincerity to understand more about another person's culture and beliefs. Having said that, if it forms one of the first questions asked in a workplace or social interaction when meeting someone for the first time or first few times, it certainly serves to highlight that the person is indeed different from the rest.

We need to keep in mind that someone wearing a hijab or turban or bindi has likely been asked that question numerous times. It is possible they may be emotionally exhausted from repeatedly having to explain their beliefs and practices. Being inclusive means respecting these choices and not making it a factor that differentiates. Yes, we are all curious to understand more about why someone chooses to hold a particular belief or engage in a practice that seems very different from our own. The good thing is that we

**I can only see your difference**

live in a time where such information is readily available at our fingertips, within a few clicks on our phones. This way we can satisfy our curiosity without making someone feel like we are highlighting the difference between us and them.

Companies do pay a price for religious biases and discrimination. In a highly publicized case, Abercrombie & Fitch was found to be liable for religious discrimination after firing a Muslim employee for wearing her hijab.[402] In a separate case, a Muslim job applicant who refused to shake the hand of a male boss won a discrimination case in Sweden; the job applicant won on religious grounds and a court ordered the company to compensate her.[403] In the EEOC versus AutoZone, Inc. case, a Sikh employee was harassed by co-workers, who often referred to him as "Bin Laden," and made other inflammatory jokes about him. The case was settled for $75,000, AutoZone had to adopt a new policy that specifically addressed religious discrimination; and human resource employees and managers had to be retrained.[404]

## What I Eat & Drink Somehow Matters?

Beliefs can also have an influence on people's food habits. Some of these food practices are based in religion, others are not and could be based on people's beliefs on sustainability, animal rights, or even their own health. Hindus do not eat beef; Muslims do not eat pork, eat halal meat and observe the fasting month of Ramadan; some Jews eat food that is Kosher; and colleagues may be vegetarian, vegan, plant-based or pescatarian. Sometimes it is not beliefs that influence our food choices. With allergies and intolerances on the rise,[405] we are increasingly likely to have colleagues who are making conscious food choices. Whatever the reasons may be, the talent in our workplaces have a range of food practices. Is your workplace inclusive to these practices?

For those who are vegetarian or vegan or plant-based, office cafeterias can be challenging to find substantial and delicious options at lunch times, forcing employees to bring food from home to eat at their desk. While this may not seem like a big deal, it takes away from the important social interactions that happen during lunch time, and a good break away from the office desk. Food choices seem to be a hot topic. Colleagues adopting food practices different from the norm are forced to continuously justify themselves because they are unable to find options at lunch or during workplace social events. I have heard leaders of SMEs (small and medium enterprises) in the pork-loving Nordics jokingly share that the real reason that they do not want to hire more diverse talent is because they may need to alter the menu at the annual Christmas lunches to accommodate dietary beliefs. These 'jokes' reflect underlying biases and have a profound impact on organisational decisions.

As a Hindu who has always been vegetarian, and who in the past decade has moved to a plant-based diet due to severe intolerances and for sustainability reasons, I have lived and continue to live through many of the non-inclusive practices and micro-aggressive behaviours that come from practising my beliefs. I have lost count of the number of times I have had to explain my dietary choices, or been made to feel like I was causing an inconvenience by requesting a special meal option at workplace social events. While these microaggressions can seem less severe than others that we have looked at up until now, they certainly contribute to how someone feels within their teams and at work. They add to the mental strain of having to leave these aspects of themselves outside of work or to make efforts to "hide" or make them less obvious at the workplace. They contribute to the feeling of not being respected or valued for one's own beliefs and practices. On many occasions, I have not told organisers that I follow a plant-based diet because of wanting to avoid the feeling of not being like everyone else. I have stayed hungry through those meals and gone home and eaten by myself.

Awareness is key. With Netflix documentaries like *Forks over Knives*, *Cowspiracy*, and *Game Changers*, there is also awareness about why people - like me - have certain beliefs about our dietary practices. Awareness helps reduce biases and given that there are a growing number of people around the world who are adopting a flexitarian and plant-based diet – for sustainability reasons, this awareness is welcome. I have to admit that it is a relief that the incessant questioning about my food habits is reducing. Did you know that the Millennials are currently the most meat free generation, with projections that in 2021, 35% of Gen Z will ditch meat?[406] These trends are forcing companies to be more inclusive towards people's dietary practices; making food choice diversity normalised in our workplaces.

When it comes to food, there is a fine line between appreciation and appropriation, respect and mockery, celebration and exploitation. For many - particularly those from ethnic minority backgrounds - food helps make up for a sense of loss that ethnic minorities feel when they have to adapt their dressing to the West and their language to English or the majority language. Food is the part of their culture that they can and want to hold onto. It is worth it then for organisations to think about the role that food in their lunch offerings can play in being more inclusive to the different ethnic groups in the workplace.

**Hungry again**

Let us for a moment look at an organisation that is well-known for its mind-blowing variety of food options - Google. Google's food perks do not stop at providing three free meals a day for their talent. What is astonishing is the sheer range of food options available on "campus", as their office spaces are known. In their HQ - Mountain View campus - it is estimated that there are 30 different places for employees to dine at, catering to the range of food practices, choices, and preferences of their employees.

Has that got you hungry and wondering why Google invests so much in food? Here is something interesting: it is not just for keeping employees satisfied and happy - though that is certainly the case – its actual purpose is to inspire innovative thinking. Really? How?

Laszlo Bock, the Senior Vice President of People Operations explains - in his book *Work Rules: Insights from Inside Google That Will Transform How You Live and Lead* - that the purpose of the cafes and micro-kitchens (smaller areas stocked with food and drink closer to workstations) is to create a place for employees to leave their desk and interact with other people whose desks are not near their own. Bock reveals that most of these food sources are strategically placed between two separate work teams, and the goal of that placement is to draw these different folks together and nudge them to interact and collaborate. "At minimum, they might have a great conversation. And maybe they'll hit on an idea for our users that hasn't been thought of yet." So, it seems like there is more to the free food at Google. The wide variety is a smart move to make sure everyone feels included in their efforts to ignite innovation.

Closely related to food habits are choices surrounding alcohol consumption. Whether for religious, health or personal reasons, employees may choose not to consume alcohol or to consume it in limited quantities. Yet, many workplace social events often centre around the consumption of alcohol. An after-work drink at the local pub or bar is often the default means to socialise and network with others. Though these efforts to socialise with colleagues are usually well-intentioned, they may leave employees who don't drink feeling excluded, or worse, feeling forced to attend to avoid missing out on valuable team building or networking opportunities. Even when they do attend, these colleagues are often battered with micro-aggressive questions about why they do not drink. Men who don't drink have told me the assumption is that they "must be driving", while women who don't consume alcohol often face questions and assumptions regarding pregnancy. Those employees who choose not to attend social events because of the emphasis on alcohol may feel left out of the "morning after" banter. It doesn't seem fair, does it? Perhaps it is time to explore alternative ways to make your next social event inclusive for all, regardless of choices surrounding alcohol.

Active allyship in this dimension involves having a real respect for others' beliefs and practices, and in this dimension the phrase "to each his own" may be the best way towards inclusion. In inclusive workplaces, employees feel like they can bring their whole selves to work, including their beliefs and practices, without the fear of discrimination and isolation because of their religious beliefs, what they wear, eat or drink.

☞ To find out how to be an active ally as an individual, team, and organisation, turn to the chapter titled 'Active Allyship in Action'.

# Marital & Parenthood Choices

*"Sometimes, the smallest things take up the most room in your heart."*

WINNIE THE POOH, fictional anthropomorphic teddy bear created by English author A. A. MILNE and English illustrator E. H. SHEPARD

People make a variety of choices when it comes to relationships, marriage and parenthood. As we look around our workplaces, we are likely to have colleagues who are married, others who are divorced, some who are in partnerships and yet others who are single out of choice or circumstance. We are likely to have colleagues who are in heterosexual and homosexual partnerships - married or unmarried. We are likely to have colleagues who have children with a partner or spouse - or on their own. We are likely to have colleagues who don't have or want children. We are likely to have colleagues who have their own biological children - and those who have adopted or are planning to adopt a child. All of these are deeply personal choices that people make. Yet some of these choices - if not all - form the basis of biases and discrimination in our workplaces.

## The Maternal Wall

One of the greatest challenges for women is that career progression seems to coincide with the female biological clock. Sociologists have shown that women have had to contend with the patriarchal nature of workplace environments, which reinforce the perception that being an 'ideal worker' is incompatible with being a 'good mother'.[407] Women are confronted with the motherhood penalty - arising from *maternal wall bias.* Maternal wall bias occurs when decision makers and colleagues view mothers or pregnant women as being less competent and less committed to their jobs. Women of childbearing age who do not have children - some of whom may never want or be able to - also face this bias. The widespread presence of this bias acts as a major barrier for women and has an impact on everything from whether they are hired in the first place to how they are appraised and the opportunities available to them for career advancement.

Let me ask you this - who do you think is considered to be an ideal employee? Is it someone who is deeply committed? By committed, you may be thinking of someone who sacrifices personal priorities and family responsibilities to further one's career. This likely involves working late nights and weekends or attending to work demands as and when the need arises, even dropping personal commitments to make that happen. This ideal seems to be in direct conflict to what is seen as a 'good parent'. Good parent? Or good mother? That really depends where you are in the world. Even today, in most societies the primary caregiver is likely to be the mother.

Even in more gender equal societies like the Nordic region of Denmark, Finland, Norway, Sweden and Iceland where we do find relatively more fathers actively involved in the early years of a child's life, mothers still do more of the childcare work. More than half of fathers (55%), and almost two thirds of all mothers (62%)[408] say that it makes more sense for women than for men to take longer leave because a child needs the mother more than the father. Coming back to what it means to be a 'good parent', if the ideal parent is seen as one who puts their children at the centre of their lives, and points their physical, mental, and emotional energy towards their children - then this appears to be in direct conflict with a woman being perceived as being an ideal employee.

These stereotypes affect hiring and promotion decisions, and decision makers prefer men to women. In a field experiment conducted in the two large Spanish cities of Barcelona and Madrid, two pairs of fictitious résumés (a man and a woman) were sent to 1,372 job offers from a broad selection of occupations.[409] In one pair, candidates had equivalent curriculum vitae (CVs) except for their sex and their qualifications (either meeting standards or higher). In the second pair, candidates differed by sex and parenthood status (either with or without children). The researchers concluded that the observed differences in favour of men signalled gender bias in recruitment. This bias is reduced when women have higher qualifications and increased when they have children.

## Support for Mothers

To support mothers - and to some extent fathers – legislation has forced companies to make efforts to provide leave benefits. Some form of parental leave exists in most countries as maternity, paternity and adoption leave, childcare leave, and in some countries, there is a provision to enable employees to care for loved ones. Some countries have marriage leave, but this may only be available for heterosexual marriages if the country has not legalised gay/lesbian marriages; others have IVF leave. In some companies, onsite childcare facilities are provided to make it more convenient for parents to be near to their very young children while working.

Often, these parental policies provide greater support for mothers instead of fathers, with maternity leave options usually longer than paternity leave options. While this may be justified given the physical and health demands on a woman during pregnancy and childbirth, there seems to be a lack of provision for the range of parenthood choices in our societies.

What about a single Dad or the gay or lesbian parents or the adoptive parents, or any combination of these? What about the heterosexual family man who wants to attend every ballet recital of his son, every soccer game of his daughter or every guitar concert of his non-binary child? If you had to read that sentence again because you thought it did not seem right, what does that say about your own biases? In the public sector, collecting information about families through the use of categories like "mother" and "father" leave out a variety of family configurations, including same-sex parents, foster parents, guardians, and single parents. Thankfully, many have now switched to more inclusive categories like "Parent/Guardian 1" and "Parent/Guardian 2.".

The maternal wall bias is very real and must be broken. Alongside, there is a more general and deeply embedded *parenthood bias* that we need to address. Our workplaces expect talent to be either committed to their work or to their families. We have an implicit assumption that our talent cannot do both. The reason for the struggle does not lie in the employees' capabilities, but rather with the inherent systemic biases and requirement of talent to conform to a prototype of what is expected. Some aspects of this prototype are rooted in the early industrial era, when employees were seen as a resource - and hence the term human resources. They would come into factories, punch their timecard in, perform their duties as per their role, take breaks only when allowed, and leave at the end of the day, punching their timecard on the way out.

Our organisations have since evolved but there are still some lingering aspects of distrust and bias in the way they function, which makes me wonder if we have changed fast enough at all. We do not trust parents to work from home because we expect them to be distracted with childcare and housework; we do not expect women to be committed or be as competent because we assume that women will not give their everything to the job; we do not expect fathers to be involved in their children's lives the way mothers are; and we do not expect members of the LGBTQ+ community to have children, biologically their own or adoptive. These biases - so deeply embedded in people's minds - are holding us back from true inclusion in our workplaces.

Closely related to the maternal wall bias are the expectations placed on women to bear the load of the unpaid work of the household. These expectations include taking care of children, cooking, cleaning, laundry, scheduling, maintaining social engagements and family relationships - the list goes on. This expectation, though changing, has roots in history and how labour was defined in 16th and 17th century Europe. At that time unions defined paid labour as being a man's job and unpaid labour being a woman's. This notion propagated through colonialism to other parts of the world.[410] Patriarchal culture, parenting styles and educational systems all add to these biases in defining the role of women - for women - both in societies and households. Even in the world's most egalitarian countries, women still perform a larger proportion of unpaid housework. Sweden ranks top in the EU's Gender Equality Index,[411] with almost 80% of women in employment, but 74% of women do housework or cook for at least one hour every day, compared to 56% of men.[412] In Denmark, the figures are slightly worse: 81% of women do the cooking or housework, while 55% of men pitch in.[413] Of course, relative to other countries, the Nordic countries fare better. The EU average of men doing the household work stands at 34%.[414]

We can look to the Nordics to draw inspiration for what more can be done beyond the parental policies we have to date. Nordic countries are certainly known for being leaders in gender-equality mindsets in society and in workplaces, where three in four working-age women are in paid employment.[415] These countries are known for their gender-equal, paid, shared parental schemes. Sweden gives 480 days at 80% pay and in Denmark, by law the government covers 52 weeks of leave, though not always at full pay. In Norway, the leave is both flexible and generous with mothers able to take 35 weeks at full pay or 45 weeks at 80% pay. Fathers can take between zero and ten weeks depending on their partners' income. Together, parents can receive an additional 46 weeks at full pay or 56 weeks at 80% of their income.

Companies based in this region even go beyond what is mandated by law to support their employees' marital and parenthood choices, and some broaden the scope of 'loved ones' to include partners, spouses and parents. In 2020, LEGO announced that - in an effort to create a family-friendly workplace for all - by 2022 all LEGO employees, regardless of where they live in the world, will have 26 weeks paid childcare leave for primary caregivers and 8 week paid childcare leave for secondary caregivers. LEGO has gone one step further by introducing four weeks of caregiver leave for employees to take care of loved ones, and a global safety net to ensure financial safety for colleagues and their families in the event of death or disability.[416]

While Nordic dads take more parental leave than the international average,[417] the rates vary across the Nordic countries. Iceland leads the pack with fathers taking 30% of the parental leave available to them, while in Finland and Denmark that number is just 8.3% and 8.6% respectively. It is important to keep in mind that according to the OECD,[418] family-friendly policies have resulted in large improvements in gender equality in the labour market in the 25-year period between the mid-1960s and 1990s. This has contributed to the economic growth in the region. It also helps that in the Nordic region, governments provide universal, high quality and highly subsidised childcare.

## Breaking Down the Wall

Existing policies and supporting infrastructure are good steps; but they are clearly not enough. The parenthood wall bias, and in particular, the maternal wall bias, are real and thriving and desperately need to be addressed. We need companies to be bold and rethink the way they view talent who are parents. We need to move beyond putting a band-aid on the issue. We need to address the cause of the wound – the bias itself.

Instead of writing off a potential hire because of the parenthood gap in their resume, why not ask them what they learnt in their time away from the working world? Parenthood teaches many life skills: multitasking, patience, empathy, resilience to perform with less sleep, and flexibility; after all, life with babies and young children does not go a pre-prescribed way. These are all skills which are vital to a changing, dynamic business world.

Our workplaces should be ones that support our talent's choices in their personal life. To some degree, the COVID-19 pandemic highlighted individual circumstances; and humanised our employees. We became aware of colleagues who were single, those who were single-parents, or those with young children. We saw babies in parents laps as they were on Zoom calls, or had children running through rooms as a parent was participating in a Teams meeting. The people in our workplaces face challenges and have priorities. They are human, not machinery. *We* are human.

Why do we need to address this dimension? Because it is mentally and emotionally exhausting for employees to not bring their whole selves to work. It is exhausting for women to keep proving themselves as competent and capable as their male colleagues in an effort to overcome the biases against them. It is exhausting for the father who wants to be a devoted parent to keep up with the unreasonable expectations of commitment to work rather than a balance with his commitment to his family. It is exhausting for the gay or lesbian family who may not have come out about their sexual orientation for fear of bias at work. It is exhausting for all of them - and for the many other people who make personal marital and parenthood choices. This exhaustion weighs heavily on the mental, emotional, and physical health of employees, and can result in lowered productivity, job satisfaction and even turnover. Having children is not the cause of these outcomes. The problem lies in the systemic biases that exist, the preference we have for a certain protype who is committed only to their work, and the lack of adequate support for something that is an essential part of human existence.

To find out how to be an active ally as an individual, team, and organisation, turn to the chapter titled 'Active Allyship in Action'.

**The coexistence of parenthood and work**

# Kromann Reumert

## Balance and Flexibility - the Keys to a Secure Talent Base

Kromann Reumert is the leading law firm in Denmark with offices in Copenhagen, Aarhus and London, employing a team of almost 500 dedicated people covering 30+ practice areas. Kromann Reumert takes pride in providing their clients with value-added solutions that are based on a thorough knowledge of their business. Their cooperation with clients is characterized by commitment and attentiveness, and they continually strive to remain a reliable and responsible partner in all respects. The vision at Kromann Reumert is to set the standard together while their mission is to deliver value-adding solutions. More than half - 51% to be exact - of their employees are women, and among their senior attorneys and directors, the share of women is 50%.

Birgitte Brix Bendtsen, Head of People & Development at Kromann Reumert explains the efforts made in Kromann Reumert in the area of D&I.

"At the Danish law firm Kromann Reumert, we want talent to thrive, develop and stay in our organisation. As a knowledge-based organisation, our primary service to clients are the bright minds of our employees. Career development and job satisfaction are key strategic priorities for Kromann Reumert that we continuously develop and deliver on in a competitive market for talent. We recognize and address the continuously changing needs and preferences of our employees. These changes are due to both generational differences as well as an employees' personal situation and motivation as they progress through different life stages.

"Parenthood is a key life stage and motivational change driver. At Kromann Reumert most of our attorneys begin their career as law students. Parenthood is therefore a natural and common life stage to experience at our company. Over time, we have developed both company-wide and departmental expertise to address the changes surrounding the individual employee, the impact on the employee's team and the impact on the company in terms of continuously having a group of employees on parental leave.

"At Kromann Reumert, we have a range of company-wide initiatives that address our employees' changing preferences due to parenthood. We want to increase employee retention of new parents. Our experience shows us that employee turnover of our female attorneys who return from their first parental leave is very high and much higher than that of our male attorneys. This poses a challenge to us, as we work towards having more women in top management.

"To address this and stop the negative attrition trend, we formed a top management committee led by People & Development. The committee's focus was to identify the key initiatives that would increase retention among young parents. One of the main things we did in the committee was to facilitate numerous workshops with both male and female attorneys to investigate what could be done to improve attrition among young parents as well as increase job satisfaction. The results were clear: our talent wanted individual flexibility, flexibility, flexibility. This was key to most of the young or aspiring parents as opposed to just offering more opportunities for working part-time.

"In response, we expanded our internal flexibility program called EXPECT Balance to include several initiatives targeting first-time parents. It is not enough just to talk about the importance of balance and flexibility. You need to live it and make it easily available. That is the reason why we have formalized the various possibilities in our internal flexibility program and policy. The main aim of EXPECT Balance is to give our employees the opportunity to create the necessary balance and flexibility in their daily life that they need, while at the same time delivering on responsibilities at work. Our thought behind this is that balance and flexibility are pivotal to ensuring that our employees can be the best version of themselves towards both clients, colleagues, and family. The initiatives in EXPECT Balance are available to all employees and include the opportunity to:

- **Work from other locations than the office.** For example, working from home or a holiday cabin.
- **Work flexible hours at times that suit you best.** For example, leaving work after lunch to pick up children or go for a run and then work again in the evening. Or working a four-day work week by delivering on all your work hours over the course of four intense days and then taking a day off

(with full pay). A four-day work week can be implemented for shorter or longer periods of time (for example for just one week or over the course of six months).

- **Work part-time.** We currently have 25 female and male employees who work part-time.
- **Have parenthood conversations to align expectations that naturally arise and change following family expansion.** Topics include needs, expectations, roles, motivation, ambitions etc., that sometimes change over the course of family expansion. The following parenthood conversations take place: #1: Approximately three months before childbirth, #2: Four months into parental leave for mothers and 1.5 months for fathers, #3: Three months before mothers return to work, #4: One week before returning to work, #5: One month after returning to work and #6: Three months after returning to work.
- **Return to work flexibly following parental leave.**
- **Participate in Kromann Reumert's mentorship program for our young attorneys, where they choose a mentor within our organisation.** Our mentors are partners or directors who have volunteered to be part of the mentorship program. Over the course of nine months, they support the mentee on the subject of their choice, which typically centers around career development and/or parenthood.

"One of the reasons why we estimate that most of our fathers take both paternal leave and parental leave in connection with childbirth is because there is a natural acceptance in our organisation towards taking parental leave for about three months. The period is short enough for it to be a manageable workload for the remaining employees as well as short enough for the attorney to still feel included in the department.

"One of the key milestones in parental leave occurred a few years ago when a senior, well-respected male attorney and role model went on parental leave. It sparked the interest and intrinsic acceptance among other male employees to such a great extent that it is now common for a male attorney to take parental leave.

"It is not easy to create balance and flexibility in the daily life of talent, while at the same time allowing for them to follow their career dreams and deliver on their responsibilities at work. At Kromann Reumert, this is of utmost importance as a means to secure the talent base of high performers."

## Key Takeaways:

- Involve and listen to your employees to learn more about their needs and dreams.
- Develop effective initiatives that strengthen career development.
- Create an attractive working environment by making balance and flexibility a vital part of the firm's organisational life and brand.
- Involve top management as active participants to ensure commitment to the initiatives.
- Identify role models in the organisation to enable positive shifts in mindset and action.

Explore more about Kromann Reumert at https://www.kromannreumert.com

# Socio-economic Background

*"Classism and greed are making insignificant all the other kinds of isms."*

Ruby Dee, American actress, poet, playwright, screenwriter, journalist, and civil rights activist

## The Ubiquity of Classism

Classism is widespread. Our societies have classism; our workplaces have classism; even our educational systems have classism. Municipalities enact zoning rules for the purpose of excluding low income residents. Employers screen applicants by residential address and weed out people who live in notoriously poor neighbourhoods. Schools place wealthier students in more advanced classes with more experienced teachers. Countries require voters to show identification documents that poor people have more difficulty obtaining.

*Classism* or class discrimination are the prejudices we hold and the discriminatory behaviour we display based on social class - a hierarchy based on wealth, income, education, occupation, and social networks. This prejudice and discrimination seep their way into individual attitudes, behaviours, systems of policies and practices that are set up to benefit the upper class at the expense of the lower class. People who are from lower classes, and often seen as poor, face constant stigmatization. Employees make efforts to hide where they live, or change their accent, to avoid being seen as being from a lower class.

Classism is very much present in most societies and workplaces and can exist at the individual, collective, and even the institutional level. Classism goes beyond racism, though they both certainly fuel each other's growth. The existence of upper and lower classes seem to be endemic to human existence with classism being in existence since medieval times, when peasants were part of the lower classes; and knights, nobles and monarchs formed the upper classes. At that time, and maybe even true in certain societies today, people from upper classes did not mix with people from lower classes.

One of the key vehicles propagating classism in society has been the media. Portraying people of lower classes as poor, less educated, dirty, and homeless has a deep impact on how people from lower classes are perceived in real life as well. As a contrast, those from upper classes are portrayed as wealthy, well-dressed, highly educated and having material comforts. Media, including social media, is used by people to learn more about different social classes, and it has an influence on what others believe. Lower classes who are portrayed negatively can experience discrimination in school and social life. Teenagers who grew up in poverty report higher levels of discrimination, and the poorer the teens were, the more discrimination they experienced.[419]

When we think of classism, many of us think of the caste system and we may automatically think of India. In her book *Caste: The Origins of Our Discontents*,[420] Isabel Wilkerson describes caste as a man-made social order developed to rank the value of certain groups of people. This order is based on the assumed supremacy of one group and assumed inferiority of others according to heritage, personal characteristics, religious preferences, or economic status. The superior group uses these characteristics to segregate people and assign parameters for the appropriate behaviours of each group.

The caste system in India is one of the oldest known caste systems, dating back to about 1000 B.C., and was created as a means of categorising people into different professions: The Brahmins were the priests; Kshatriyas were the warriors; Vaishyas were the merchants, farmers, tradesmen; the Shudras were the labourers; and the Dalits (also referred to as scheduled castes and includes tribes) were the untouchables who did work that no one else would do. The caste system was created as a means of organising society, but was misinterpreted and misused during the Moghul and British occupation of India giving it its negative name. India's caste system was abolished in 1950, and as part of the efforts to right the historical injustices, quotas were set for the lowest caste, known as the Dalits, in government jobs and educational institutions. These quotas were extended in 1989 to include Other Backward Classes (OBC) which included people belonging between the upper classes and lowest classes.

The topic of the caste system is hugely contentious amongst the Indian diaspora around the world. The mere mention of it often generates very polarised views, with some defending the very basis upon which it first came into existence and others supporting the need for quotas for those who are disadvantaged. Either way - if you do engage in this topic with an Indian - you are in for a long, and perhaps heated, discussion. The reality, however, is that the caste system, though slowly eroding, is still a part of societal practices like marriage, with families discriminating against marrying outside one's own caste.

If you are thinking that the caste system only exists outside the walls of the office, you may be surprised to know that you are sadly mistaken. In Silicon Valley - yes, that is right - California regulators sued Cisco Systems in 2020, stating that an engineer faced discrimination at the company's headquarters because he was a

Dalit Indian.[421] With 90% of Indians in the Tech industry in the US coming from the upper castes of Indian society, cases like these are surprisingly common. In this case, the lawsuit alleges that two upper caste supervisors ridiculed their employee in front of all the other higher caste Indian employees at Cisco, saying that he was a Dalit and only got into the engineering school because of affirmative action. All three men were from the same prestigious engineering school, Indian Institutes of Technology (IITs). It is hard to imagine that a centuries-old social stratification system continues to have such an influence on how people are treated thousands of miles away from its country-of-origin, but it appears it does.

Classism and some form of the caste system exists everywhere - even in more egalitarian countries in the world like Denmark. Classism manifests between those who live in neighbourhoods with higher real estate prices, those who can afford expensive cars in a country that is well-known for its bicycles and elevated car prices, those who send their children to private school in a county with free and high-quality public-school options - and those who don't. What is different in Denmark is that the expression of these socio-economic differences in society is less overt, with its citizens making conscious efforts to try not to "seem too different from everyone else". That is thanks to Janteloven (or Jante's Law) being deeply rooted in Scandanavian culture.

Jante's Law are ten rules of how to live life that were outlined in the Danish- Norwegian author Axel Sandemose's 1933 novel, *A Fugitive Crosses his Tracks*. The first law states that (translated) 'You are not to think you are anything special'. While the emergence of Jante's Law is relatively recent in the region's history, the ten laws reinforce the region's socialist principles, and are imbibed in children in the very early stages of education, with toddlers being taught these laws of not being different from their friends.

While you may be hard-pressed to find the Dane who flaunts their wealth, it does make me wonder that if classism exists even in the most egalitarian societies of the world, could it just be a natural part of human society? After all, caste systems date back to over 3000 years.

To help those from lower classes and provide opportunities for social mobility, legislation has been put into effect in many parts of the world like India to protect those from poorer socio-economic backgrounds through quotas and reservation systems. One could argue that these efforts may actually contribute to the widening income and wealth disparity in these societies, but what are the alternatives? While it may continue to prevail in societies, the influence of caste systems in our workplaces needs an expiry date. The fact that biases and discrimination based on a person's socio-economic background impact hiring and promotion decisions is deeply concerning.

## Classism at Work

Classism in our workplaces is embedded into who we socialise with at work, who we hire and who we promote. It is perhaps more subtle in workplace situations, and the biases more implicit. We see evidence of it though. Employers who screen out applicants because of the residential neighbourhood that they live in; interviewers making hiring decisions based on the class of society a potential candidate is from; talent who is overlooked for a promotion because of the caste they belong to. Imagine that you are a hiring manager and a potential candidate had a good university degree, but lived in low-income public housing. Would you hire this person? If the person has the requisite skills and capabilities to perform the job, not hiring her/him/them simply on the basis of where they live is biased and unfair.

It has been shown that one's socio-economic background influences a young person's choice of study and therefore the work they get into. In a study done in the UK, students from poorer families are less likely to take science subjects in grades 11 and 12, and those who do are then less likely to obtain grades high enough to encourage further study of the subject.[422] The reasons for this are not clear, with possible explanations including fewer opportunities and lack of role models at home and in workplaces. What is clear, however, is that as we think about how to ensure a diverse future talent pipeline for companies in the STEM industries, this is a concern we must address. The report, *Working with class: The state of social immobility in graduate recruitment*,[423] which surveyed 2000 graduates in the UK, found that almost two-thirds of respondents (61%) did not think businesses are doing enough to hire people from diverse backgrounds.

A report from the Social Mobility Commission in the UK[424] found that those from more affluent backgrounds are 80% more likely to be in a professional job than their working-class peers. In the UK, poor social mobility and workplace discrimination is estimated to cost the economy £270 billion each year.[425] With a growing middle-class around the world with substantial spending power, the ability to understand the socio-economic diversity of customers becomes even more relevant. Companies in the Fintech industry are eager to reach customers from disadvantaged backgrounds with their online financial tools in developing and under-developed markets. With even some of the poorest people in the world having access to a mobile device, this is a lucrative customer group for the Fintech industry. Yet, the majority of employees within this industry come from middle-class communities and cannot fully empathise and understand the ways of thinking about money, expenses, and savings of their customers. Having talent from diverse socio-economic backgrounds gives companies the advantage of being able to better understand the needs of customers, and in turn be able to create marketing campaigns that appeal to a wider group of customers across socio-economic boundaries.

While evidence of concrete efforts to address this dimension of diversity in our workplaces is limited, we are beginning to see some very positive steps, particularly in the UK. Deloitte[426] and PwC UK. [427]In February 2021, Freshfields Bruckhaus Deringer ('Freshfields'), one of the largest multinational law firms in the world, launched the Freshfields Aspiring Professionals Programme in the UK,[428] in partnership with the Social Mobility Foundation, to promote social mobility and racial equality in professional careers. The three-year programme will welcome a cohort of 100 students each year from lower socio-economic and racially diverse backgrounds across the UK, helping those from social mobility 'cold spots' gain access to professional careers.

Socio-economic diversity enables organisations to employ talent from a range of backgrounds, with different knowledge, ideas, and experiences to bring to the table, but hinges on the organisation being a fair employer and treating all employees equitably in a fair workplace environment. To be able to achieve this requires each employee to be an ally of all socio-economic backgrounds – to eliminate classism from our workplaces. Am I being too idealistic? I think not.

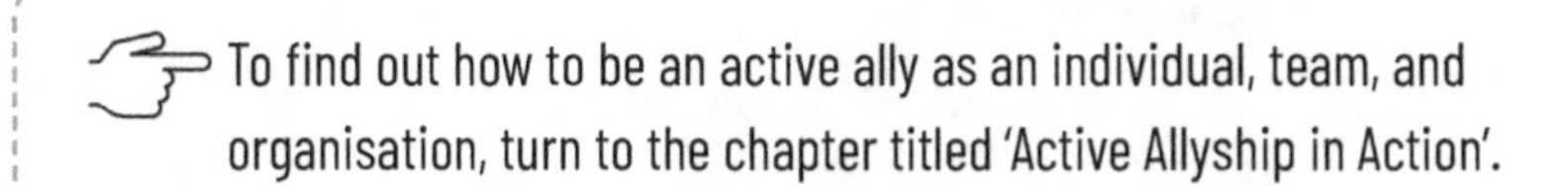

To find out how to be an active ally as an individual, team, and organisation, turn to the chapter titled 'Active Allyship in Action'.

# Active Allyship in Action

*"When the whole world is silent,
even one voice becomes powerful."*

Malala Yousafzai, Pakistani activist for female education and the youngest Nobel Prize laureate

In this section, tools and suggestions for being an active ally are provided for the twelve dimensions of diversity that have been looked at in this book. This is to serve as a guide to help all of us become more active in our efforts as allies of inclusion to co-create inclusive workplaces – where all employees can bring their whole diverse selves to work. The suggestions follow from the Active Ally of Inclusion (AAI) Model that was explained earlier in the book. Suggestions for developing our Knowledge, Attitude and Behaviours are presented in this section.

Having read the book so far, you would have already addressed the 'Knowledge' aspect of the AAI model, having developed a solid understanding and knowledge of each of twelve dimensions of diversity. You would have also had a chance to reflect upon where you might be along the model: in *denial* or *passive* or already an *active* ally.

As you think about the next steps for yourself, your team, and your organisation, it may be helpful to keep the following in mind:

- Conduct a *D&I audit* of yourself, your team, and your organisation.

  This involves collecting data through personal reflections, interviews, and surveys on the state of D&I at present. This would act as a canvas upon which the next steps are taken. Ensure that everyone in the organisation - regardless of hierarchical position - undergoes effective unconscious bias training.

- Cultivate a *psychologically safe environment*.

  In inclusive workplaces, employees both feel comfortable to call out the biases and microaggressions of others, and at the same time feel confident that they will not be shamed and judged when their biases and microaggressions have been called out. Underpinning this is the widespread understanding that we are all biased.

Could some diversity dimensions be more crucial to address at a particular point in time depending on the circumstances? Absolutely. For every organisation and society, some of these dimensions may warrant greater emphasis as the biases and microaggressions in those dimensions are more prevalent at a point in time. The good news is that inclusion efforts in one area do have ripple benefits to others. However, this does not mean that we emphasize only those and not the others. That would be regressing back to the ways that things have been done up until now. We must *diversify diversity* and ensure that our D&I strategy focuses on all the dimensions of diversity so that we truly create an inclusive environment for all.

While this next section will provide you with suggestions on becoming an active ally of inclusion, the suggestions here are certainly not exhaustive. The hope is that it will give you a set of next steps that you can take for yourself, your team, and your organisation; while also inspiring you to think about further steps that you can take for yourself and your own workplaces.

---

**Active Ally of Inclusion (AAI) Model**

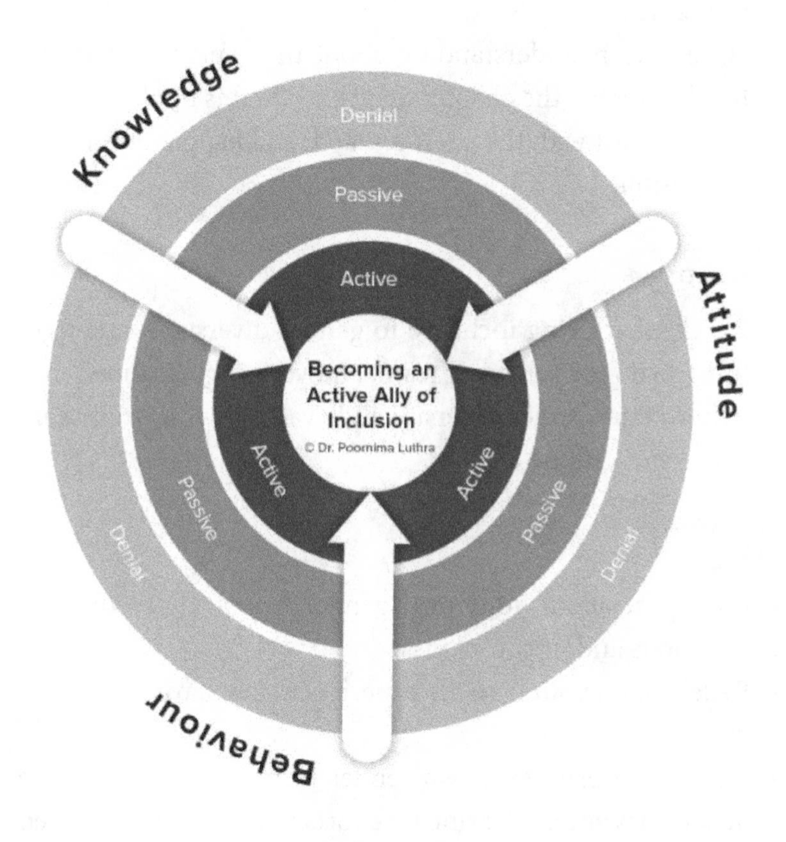


---

# Active Ally of All Genders

***How can I be an active ally of all genders?***

KNOWLEDGE

→ Know what biases and microaggressions look like from the gender lens.
→ Have a keen understanding about the gender dimension. Read or reread the chapter on gender in this book.
→ Keep abreast with the latest research and happenings in this dimension.

ATTITUDE

→ Believe that being inclusive to gender diversity is the right thing to do for you, your team, and your organisation.
→ Believe that gender diversity adds value to you, your team and organisation.

BEHAVIOURS

→ Introspect about your own gender biases, those that are conscious and unconscious.
→ Reflect upon your own life experiences that have led to your gender biases.
→ Actively observe your own gender-related micro-aggressive behaviours and make sincere efforts to reduce them. When unsure, go to your *bias compass circle* to learn more and check your biases.

- → Be open to feedback about your own micro-aggressive behaviours.
- → Call out gender related microaggressions and biased behaviours in your workplace by respectfully asking the right questions and engaging in honest and open conversations.
- → Report observed sexual harassment to the relevant authorities.
- → Engage in inclusive communication.
- → Make conscious efforts to ensure gender representation in various groups and meetings.
- → Make active efforts to sponsor and mentor marginalised gender groups. This could involve providing leadership training opportunities, suggesting their name for roles and positions that are open, and providing advice, guidance, and support to keep them motivated.
- → Actively support gender inclusive initiatives in your workplace. This could involve engaging in conversations on Yammer or during meetings; or attending events, talks, workshops; or helping to set up, support and participate in Employee Resource Groups (ERGs).

**Reflections and notes:**

..........................................................................................

..........................................................................................

..........................................................................................

..........................................................................................

..........................................................................................

..........................................................................................

## *How can we, as a team and an organisation, be an active ally of all genders?*

### Knowledge

→ Have a collective understanding of what gender biases and microaggressions look like within teams.

→ Make consistent efforts to further your team's understanding about gender biases. This could include periodically reading and discussing an article about the issue.

→ Create a strong business case. Understand why gender diversity is good for your business; not just from a financial point of view.

→ Know where you are as an organisation now, and where you want to be in terms of gender representation. Be authentic and honest.

### Attitude

→ Have a collective belief that being inclusive to gender diversity is the right thing to do.

→ Have a collective belief that every single employee across all gender identifications should feel respected and valued.

→ Have a collective belief of the benefits to gain from gender diversity.

### Behaviours

→ Acknowledge and communicate openly where you are as an organisation at present when it comes to gender diversity, and that greater efforts need to be made.

- → Communicate your company's stand on non-tolerance for sexual harassment and sexism - actively and authentically.
- → Ensure that your team is inclusive to those from minority gender identifications.
- → Identify gender biases in your team's processes, policies and practices and make efforts to correct them.
- → Embed embracing gender diversity in all aspects of the work your team does, including ensuring that all groups have adequate gender representations.
- → Be on a look out for gender biased conversations and decision making. Call them out.
- → Evaluate gender representation at all levels of the organisation. Make efforts to correct gender imbalances being mindful to avoid tokenism and quota fulfilment.
- → Be very aware of gender biases in marketing campaigns and ensure adequate gender representation.
- → Enable the setup of Employee Resource Groups (ERGs) to provide support to marginalised gender groups. Encourage participation from all, not just from those marginalised groups. Resource them well.
- → Actively hire for gender diversity, while being conscious not to engage in tokenism.
- → Address gender related systemic biases in talent management. More specific steps in this area could include:
    - → Ensure that all corporate communications are gender inclusive.
    - → Gender-neutralise all job advertisements.
    - → Overhaul the hiring and recruitment process to reduce systemic biases. This can include:
        - → Having "blind" CVs where gender cues are removed.

  - → Ensuring that all resume reviewers have been adequately trained in being aware of their biases.
  - → Having a structured interview protocol with consistent questions for all prospective candidates.
  - → Having equal gender representation on interview panels.
  - → Having clear and objective selection criteria based on the job criteria.
- → Conduct an internal audit of gender pay gaps and make efforts to close the gap.
- → Work in partnership with educational institutions where your company's talent from an underrepresented gender serve as role models for children and students.
- → Be conscious to avoid efforts being seen as tokenism. Focus on the person's competencies and work towards achieving critical mass and push through the initial discomfort and unease.
- → Assess workplace inclusion through employee engagement surveys and track progress.

**Reflections and notes:**

..........................................................................................

..........................................................................................

..........................................................................................

..........................................................................................

..........................................................................................

..........................................................................................

# Active Ally of All Sexual Orientations

***How can I be an active ally of all sexual orientations?***

KNOWLEDGE

→ Identify the kind of ally you are:
  → A straight ally is a heterosexual person who supports equal civil rights, gender equality and LGBT social movements, challenging homophobia, biphobia, and transphobia.
  → A gay ally is a LGBTQ+ person who supports equal civil rights, gender equality and LGBTQ+ social movements, challenging homophobia, biphobia, and transphobia.

→ Ensure that you know what biases and microaggressions look like from the sexual orientation lens. Learn about these and familiarise yourself with the vocabulary and what is considered inappropriate and insensitive.

ATTITUDE

→ Believe that being inclusive to the range of sexual orientations is the right thing to do for you, your team, and your organisation.

BEHAVIOURS

→ Introspect about your own sexual-orientation biases - conscious and unconscious. Notice any awkwardness around LGBTQ+ colleagues. Reflect on where these biases may have stemmed from - your own family and educational background, social and cultural environment, along with media, religious, and government influences.

→ Actively observe your own sexual orientation related micro-aggressive behaviours and make sincere efforts to reduce them. When unsure, go to your *bias compass circle* to learn more and check your biases.

→ Be open to feedback about your own micro-aggressive behaviours.

→ Make active efforts to sponsor and mentor LGBTQ+ talent to enable them to progress through the organisation. This could involve providing them with leadership training opportunities, suggesting their name for roles and positions that are open, and providing advice, guidance, and support to keep them motivated.

→ Help set up, support, and participate in Employee Resource Groups (ERGs).

**Reflections and notes:**

..............................................................................................

..............................................................................................

..............................................................................................

..............................................................................................

..............................................................................................

..............................................................................................

### *How can we, as a team and an organisation, be an active ally of all sexual orientations?*

#### Knowledge

→ Provide training to all employees on how to manage and interact appropriately with members from the LGBTQ+ community. Address unconscious biases and microaggressions during the training and provide common language to normalise sexual orientation choices.

#### Attitude

→ Have a collective belief that being inclusive to the range of sexual orientations is the right thing to do for your team, and your organisation.

→ Have a collective belief that being inclusive adds value to your team and organisation, reduces stress and anxiety by enabling all employees to be open with their sexual orientation choices, and bring their whole diverse selves to work.

#### Behaviours

→ Call out sexual-orientation microaggressions and biases in teams and individual interactions by asking the right questions and engaging in honest and open conversations.

→ Make a conscious effort with colleagues from the LGBTQ+ community to make them feel included without drawing undue attention to their sexual orientation.

→ Set up employee networks and support groups for the LGBTQ+ community within the organisation to provide socialization and mutual help, act as a consultative body for management, provide advice on marketing and advertising and support the implementation of D&I policies.

→ Have clear and consistent non-discriminatory LGBTQ+ D&I policies and employee codes of conduct implemented globally with local adaptation where necessary. These should provide clear guidelines on appropriate behaviour that is non-discriminatory and lay out the consequences for discriminatory behaviours.

→ Evaluate and redesign talent management practices and processes to be non-discriminatory to sexual orientation differences within hiring practices, same-sex partner benefits and shared parental leave.

→ Conduct and monitor employee engagement surveys for LGBTQ+ discriminatory behaviours and practices.

→ Create an inclusive marketing policy that goes beyond gay vague. Ensure products and services, and the marketing of them, is inclusive to the LGBTQ+ community globally, while being sensitive to local culture and meeting local legislative requirements. Seek advice and insights from LGBTQ+ colleagues.

→ Organise and actively support inclusive initiatives for the LGBTQ+ community in your workplace. Enable the setup of Employee Resource Groups (ERGs) to provide support to LGBTQ+ talent. Encourage participation from all, not just from those marginalised groups. Resource them well.

→ Support and participate actively in public events supporting LGBTQ+ rights like Pride events, conferences, and career fairs.

→ Engage with external stakeholders, including clients and suppliers, on anti-discriminatory practices and policies.

# Active Ally of All Generations

*How can I be an active ally of all generations?*

### Knowledge

→ Know which generation you are from. Read or reread the chapter on age in this book.

→ Ensure that you know what biases and microaggressions look like from the generational lens.

→ Increase your Generational Intelligence (GQ): Have a keen curiosity to understand the different generations in your team and organisation, particularly about how each generation communicates, how they receive and provide feedback, what motivates them, their preferences for teamwork and their attitudes towards technology.

→ Be aware of the intersectionality between the generational dimension of diversity and other dimensions like gender and ethnicity.

### Attitude

→ Believe that being inclusive to generations is the right thing to do for you, your team, and your organisation.

→ Develop generational empathy towards those from other generations.

### Behaviours

→ Introspect about your own age-related biases - conscious and unconscious.

→ Actively observe your own age-related micro-aggressive behaviours and make sincere efforts to reduce them.
→ Be open to feedback about your own micro-aggressive behaviours.
→ Call out age-related microaggressions and biased behaviours in your team and workplace by asking the right questions and engaging in honest and open conversations. Engage in respectful but tough conversations by the coffee machine, over lunch and in meetings to get fellow colleagues to think about micro-generational differences and microaggressions.
→ Use mindful communication and customised feedback, as well as targeted motivation for each generation.

**Reflections and notes:**

........................................................................................

........................................................................................

........................................................................................

........................................................................................

........................................................................................

........................................................................................

## *How can we, as a team and an organisation, be an active ally of all generations?*

### Knowledge

→ Know which generation your colleagues are from.
→ Ensure that your teams, and organisation know what biases and microaggressions look like from the generational lens.
→ Map the generations and micro-generations in your team and organisation.

### Attitude

→ Have a collective belief that being inclusive to generations is the right thing to do for your team, and your organisation.
→ Have a collective belief that every generation adds value to your team and organisation.

### Behaviours

→ Create psychologically safe environments where talent feel comfortable to call out age-related microaggressions and biased behaviours with teams and your workplace.
→ Use mindful communication and customised feedback, as well as targeted motivation for each generation.
→ Address generational biases in hiring/promotion practices.
→ Ensure products and services, and marketing campaigns consider the age diversity of customers.
→ Redesign organisational processes or equipment to make them generationally suitable.
→ Organise and actively support generationally inclusive initiatives in your workplace. Ensure that activities and Employee Resource Groups (ERGs) are inclusive to all group groups and are not biased.

# Active Ally of All Physical Abilities and Appearances

***How can I be an active ally of all physical abilities and appearances?***

## Knowledge

→ Make an effort to know what biases and microaggressions look like from the physical abilities and appearance lens.
→ Have a keen understanding about what is happening in the field of disability and appearance in terms of diversity and inclusion.

## Attitude

→ Believe that being inclusive to those with physical disabilities is the right thing to do for you, your team, and your organisation.
→ Believe that people with physical disabilities and diverse appearances add value to your team and organisation.

## Behaviours

→ Introspect about your own biases - conscious and unconscious - towards those with physical disabilities and others' appearances. Be very aware of feelings and behaviours of pity or "looking down upon" the other person because of their physical disabilities and appearances. When unsure, go to your bias compass circle to learn more and check your biases.

→ Actively observe your own micro-aggressive behaviours and make sincere efforts to reduce them, including "sizing someone else up" based on their physical disabilities and/or appearances.
→ Be open to feedback about your own micro-aggressive behaviours.
→ Call out disability and appearance related microaggressions and biased behaviours in your teams and workplace by asking the right questions and engaging in honest and open conversations.
→ Support hiring and promotion of people with physical disabilities and diverse appearances, making special effort to avoid it seeming tokenistic or "pity-hiring". Actively communicate the competencies the person brings to the team.
→ Support talent with disabilities and diverse appearances by ensuring that their voice is heard, respected, and valued.
→ Make active efforts to sponsor and mentor those with disabilities to enable them to progress through the organisation. This could involve providing them with leadership training opportunities, suggesting their name for roles and positions that are open, and providing advice, guidance, and support to keep them motivated.
→ Actively support disability inclusive initiatives in your workplace. This could involve engaging in conversations on Yammer or during meetings; or attending events, talks, workshops on this. It could also include helping to set up, support and participate in Employee Resource Groups (ERGs).

### *How can we, as a team and as an organisation, be an active ally of all physical abilities and appearances?*

#### Knowledge

- → Build awareness on working with colleagues with disabilities through training on avoiding stereotyping and developing disability etiquette.
- → Build understanding amongst managers and leaders of physical appearance biases: lookism, weightism, heightism and hairism.

#### Attitude

- → Have a collective belief that being inclusive to physical abilities and appearances is the right thing to do for your team, and your organisation.
- → Have a collective belief that people with physical disabilities and who look different add value to your team and organisation.
- → Develop empathy towards those with physical disabilities and those to experience physical appearance biases.

#### Behaviours

Ensure reasonable adjustments are put in place to ensure disabled talent can overcome any substantial disadvantages they may have within the recruitment process, doing their job and progressing in work.

→ Redesign recruitment and career progressions processes:
  → Avoid using generic requirements in job descriptions like driving, typing, lifting or the ability to sit for a long period of time unless actually required by the job.
  → Conduct "blind" interviews or phone interviews to assess candidates before face-to-face interviews so that anyone who can get the job done is shortlisted.
  → Conduct inclusive panel interviews by interviewing with 2 to 4 team members who can increase diversity of thought during the interviewing process.
  → Have a flexible but structured interview process. Use structured interview questions to avoid asking biased questions towards those with disabilities or those who do not conform to expected physical appearance standards. Be willing to provide accommodations to give those with physical disabilities a fair chance.
  → Use interview case studies to focus on the applicants' value systems and skills needed for the job.
  → Make space for physically diverse talent to hold roles at all levels but be very conscious to avoid tokenism or "pity-hiring". Be clear to communicate that someone has been hired because of their competencies and what they bring to the team.
  → Have mentorship programs for physically disabled employees.
  → Provide opportunities for growth and learning. This may include skill-building programs for those with physical disabilities.

- → Nurture an inclusive workplace for those with physical disabilities and diverse appearances:
  - → Support talent with disabilities and diverse appearances by ensuring that their voice is heard, respected, and valued.
  - → Support a culture where biases and microaggressions are called out.
  - → Have open, honest and proactive communication between managers, employees with disabilities, and other interested groups like human resources or legal.
- → Create accessible workplaces. Make accommodations:
  - → Adjust the workplace through renovations or simple furniture adjustments to make it easier for someone with a physical disability to work. It can be as easy as moving a few chairs, lowering a light switch or making a plug more accessible. It is really about productivity and less about the cost.
  - → Involve IT to explore if technology could help with the accommodation needed.
  - → Provide flexible scheduling and telecommuting opportunities.
- → Build partnerships:
  - → Enlist the support of senior management for disability initiatives, forming partnerships with outside disability organizations.
  - → Enable the setup of Employee Resource Groups (ERGs) to provide support to disabled talent. Encourage participation from all, not just from those marginalised groups. Resource them well.

- → Embrace the physically disabled customer segment:
    - → Engage with physically disabled talent within the organisation and with external organisations to develop greater insight into the needs of this customer group and actively involve them in the design of products and services.
    - → Ask customers for their input on having someone with a disability work with them or for you. Collate feedback and make adjustments.
    - → Engage with customers through focus groups or marketing campaigns to help them address their own physical abilities and appearance biases. This may make your company even more favourable in your customer's eyes.

**Reflections and notes:**

.......................................................................................

.......................................................................................

.......................................................................................

.......................................................................................

.......................................................................................

.......................................................................................

# Active Ally of Cognitive Diversity

## *How can I be an active ally of cognitive diversity?*

### Knowledge

→ Understand what biases and microaggressions look like from the cognitive category of dimensions across education, experiences and skills, personality, and ways of working, as well as ways of thinking and learning.

→ Have a keen understanding about what is happening in the field of cognitive diversity and inclusion.

### Attitude

→ Believe that being inclusive to cognitive diversity is the right thing to do for you, your team, and your organisation.

→ Believe that people with cognitive diversity add value to your team and organisation.

### Behaviours

→ Introspect about your own biases - conscious and unconscious - towards cognitive diversity.

→ Actively observe your own micro-aggressive behaviours related to other people's education, experiences and skills, personality, and ways of working, as well as ways of thinking and learning and make sincere efforts to reduce them.

→ Be open to feedback about your own micro-aggressive behaviours.

- → Call out cognitive diversity related microaggressions and biased behaviours in your workplace by asking the right questions and engaging in honest and open conversations.
- → Support hiring and promotion of talent with cognitive diversity, making special effort to avoid it seeming tokenistic. Actively communicate the competencies the person brings to the team.
- → Support talent who are cognitively diverse by ensuring that their voice is heard, respected, and valued.
- → Actively support cognitive diversity initiatives in your workplace. This could involve engaging in conversations on Yammer or during meetings, or attending events, talks, workshops on this.

**Reflections and notes:**

..........................................................................................

..........................................................................................

..........................................................................................

..........................................................................................

..........................................................................................

..........................................................................................

***How can we, as a team, and as an organisation, be an active ally of cognitive diversity?***

### Knowledge

→ Understand what cognitive diversity means and how it can add value to your team and organisation. Build understanding around the different dimensions within cognitive diversity: education, experiences and skills, personality, as well as ways of working, and ways of thinking and learning.

→ Build awareness on working with cognitively diverse colleagues through training on avoiding stereotyping and developing supportive etiquette, particularly with diverse personality types and neurodiverse talent.

→ Debunk myths and stereotypes about cognitive diversity, especially in the area of personality types and neurodiverse talent.

### Attitude

→ Have a collective belief that being inclusive to cognitive diversity is the right thing to do for your team, and your organisation.

→ Have a collective belief that people with cognitive diversity add value to your team and organisation.

→ Develop empathy towards those who are cognitively diverse.

### Behaviours

Ensure reasonable adjustments are put in place to ensure cognitively diverse talent can overcome any substantial disadvantages they may have within the recruitment process, doing their job and progressing in work.

- → Redesign recruitment and career progressions processes:
  - → Overcome university bias:
    - → Be aware of university bias, affinity bias and halo and horn effects when hiring new hires.
    - → Consciously cast a wider net to reach candidates beyond the universities from which talent have previously been hired from.
    - → Look beyond universities when hiring talent.
  - → Embrace a range of experiences and skills, personalities and ways of working, and ways of thinking and learning.
  - → Re-evaluate the use of personality tests in hiring and promotion decisions. Think about alternative and additional ways of assessing potential hires. Once hired, use personality tests for adjusting training, coaching, and mentoring to individual talent's personality to help benefit them the most.
  - → Make accommodations for neurodiverse talent:
    - → Job descriptions: Use structured, clear, and concise language; avoid complicated, metaphorical language; split the descriptions into 'essential' and 'desirable' skills.
    - → Interview process: Have more informal "hangout" sessions rather than a formal interview process. Use short project-based tasks to assess the candidates capabilities.

→ Workplace accommodations:
    → Flexible working hours/ timings.
    → Workplace arrangements:
        → Provide individual offices for neurodiverse talent.
        → Provide noise-cancelling headsets and blue light glasses to reduce auditory and visual stimulation.
→ Have mentors and clear points of contact for assistance and support.

**Reflections and notes:**

................................................................................

................................................................................

................................................................................

................................................................................

................................................................................

................................................................................

# Active Ally of All Ethnicities and Cultures

## *How can I be an active ally of all ethnicities and cultures?*

### Knowledge

- → Cultivate a curiosity about the world and its ethnicities. Cultivate knowledge regarding diverse ethnicities, cultures and countries.
- → Appreciate that the world is experienced differently by different ethnicities.
- → Introspect about your own ethnic biases, conscious and unconscious.
- → Undergo effective cross-cultural training.
- → Articulate your own current mindset by building your own Cultural Thumbprint™. Ask colleagues to provide their cultural thumbprints of you. Compare and reflect.

### Attitude

- → Believe that being inclusive to ethnic diversity is the right thing to do for you, your team, and your organisation.
- → Believe that ethnic diversity adds value to you, your team and organisation.
- → Have a positive attitude when interacting with different ethnicities.

### Behaviours

- → Make efforts to cultivate global mindset, global dexterity, and cultural empathy:
  - → Show a real interest in another person's background and culture without making them feel like they are different or do not belong.
  - → Read up and avoid asking about people's life choices, especially in the early stages of interaction.
  - → Do not judge or stare in a way that makes others feel uncomfortable.
  - → Treat those who are different like everyone else.
  - → Avoid code switching or expecting others to code switch.
  - → Avoid cultural appropriation. Ensure that when adopting or speaking about other cultures, you are being respectful about the culture of that ethnic group and showing cultural appreciation that is authentic.
- → Use cross-culturally effective communication.
- → Make genuine efforts to pronounce another person's name the way they would pronounce it.
- → Give those with a different name a fair chance: The next time you meet someone new or when you look at that job application of a person with a different sounding name, keep in mind that it is your first chance at being an active ally – one who is respectful and genuinely open-minded.
- → Actively observe your own micro-aggressive behaviours and make sincere efforts to reduce them. When unsure, go to your *bias compass circle* to learn more and check your biases. Be open to feedback about your own micro-aggressive behaviours.

- → Call out ethnic/culture related microaggressions and biased behaviours in your workplace by asking the right questions and engaging in honest and open conversations.
- → Report observed racism to the relevant authorities.
- → Make active efforts to sponsor and mentor marginalised ethnic groups to enable them to progress through the organisation. This could involve providing them with leadership training opportunities, suggesting their name for roles and positions that are open, and providing advice, guidance, and support to keep them motivated.
- → Actively support ethnicity inclusive initiatives in your workplace. This could involve engaging in conversations on Yammer or during meetings, or attending events, talks, workshops on this. It could also include helping to set up, support and participate in Employee Resource Groups (ERGs).

**Reflections and notes:**

.........................................................................................

.........................................................................................

.........................................................................................

.........................................................................................

.........................................................................................

.........................................................................................

## *How can we, as a team and as an organisation, be an active ally of all ethnicities and cultures?*

### Knowledge

→ Have a collective understanding of what ethnic biases and microaggressions look like within teams.
→ Make consistent efforts to further your team's understanding about ethnic biases. This could involve periodically reading and discussing an article about the issue.
→ Ensure everyone in the team and organisation goes through cultural competency training.
→ Understand deeply why ethnic diversity is good for your business, not just from a financial point of view. Create a strong business case.
→ Know where you are as an organisation now, and where you want to be in terms of ethnic representation.
→ Set up best practice forums, knowledge networks, international task forces, project teams, steering boards and other cross-border coordination mechanisms.

### Attitude

→ Have a collective belief that being inclusive to ethnic diversity is the right thing to do.
→ Have a collective belief that every single employee across all ethnic identifications should feel respected and valued.
→ Have a collective belief of the benefits to gain from ethnic diversity.

### Behaviours

- → Ensure that your team is inclusive to those from minority ethnic identifications.
- → Identify ethnic biases in your team's processes, policies and practices and make efforts to correct them.
- → During meetings, be on a look out for ethnic biased conversations, microaggressions and biased decision making. Call them out.
- → Actively hire for ethnic diversity while being conscious not to engage in tokenism. This will involve ensuring that ethnic diversity is a dimension that is embedded into recruitment and promotion processes. Be clear to communicate that someone has been hired because of their competencies and what they bring to the team.
- → Be explicitly clear on your company's stand on non-tolerance for racism. Have this communicated actively and authentically by leadership and reinforced by management.
- → Acknowledge openly where you are as an organisation now when it comes to ethnic diversity, and that greater efforts need to be made.
- → Evaluate ethnic representation at all levels of the organisation. Make efforts to correct ethnic imbalances being mindful to avoid tokenism and quota fulfilment. This may take time, but it is important to communicate and demonstrate that ensuring equal ethnic representation at all levels is high on the priority of the organisation.
- → International Mobility/ Cross-border Mobility (long-term or short-term) opportunities for employees. These can be demand-driven and learning-driven international assignments.

- → Adopt global performance management, appraisal and rewards, as well as recruitment and selection practices.
- → Define how to make your organisation inclusive for ethnic diversity. This will involve embedding ethnic diversity as a dimension into practices and processes, alongside addressing ethnic related systemic biases across recruitment and selection, talent management, products and services and marketing.
- → Involve and engage with members of cultural and ethnic groups to avoid cultural appropriation.
- → Enable the setup of Employee Resource Groups (ERGs) to provide support to marginalised gender groups. Encourage participation from all, not just from those marginalised groups. Resource them well.

**Reflections and notes:**

................................................................................

................................................................................

................................................................................

................................................................................

................................................................................

................................................................................

# Active Ally of Beliefs and Practices

***How can I be an active ally of beliefs and practices?***

KNOWLEDGE

→ Understand that everyone has a set of beliefs and practices that they come to the workplace with.
→ Read up on beliefs that you may be unfamiliar with. For example, why someone wears a turban or hijab; why someone does not eat beef; why someone fasts during Ramadan; why someone chooses to adopt a plant-based diet; why someone does not drink alcohol. There is a wealth of information out there to help us understand why people believe the things they do and why they choose to engage in certain practices.
→ Be curious and find out more about different beliefs and practices of the people that you work with including festivals and traditions.
→ Introspect about your own biases, conscious and unconscious about other people's beliefs and practices.

ATTITUDE

→ Believe that being inclusive to people's beliefs and practices is the right thing to do.
→ Believe that every single employee, regardless of their beliefs and practices, should feel respected and valued.

### Behaviours

→ Observe your own micro-aggressive behaviours about other people's beliefs and practices and make sincere efforts to reduce them. Educate yourself about why people make such choices to satisfy any curiosity and reduce the incessant questioning about someone's beliefs and values.
→ Be open to feedback about your own micro-aggressive behaviours.
→ Call out belief-related microaggressions and biased behaviours in your workplace by asking the right questions and engaging in honest and open conversations.

**Reflections and notes:**

.................................................................................

.................................................................................

.................................................................................

.................................................................................

.................................................................................

.................................................................................

## *How can we, as a team and as an organisation, be an active ally of beliefs and practices?*

### Knowledge

→ Understand that everyone has a set of beliefs and practices that they come to the workplace with.
→ Unpack your team's collective biases, conscious and unconscious about other people's beliefs and practices. This will require some time to reflect as a team about where these biases may lie.
→ Increase awareness about beliefs that the talent in your team and organisation may be unfamiliar with.

### Attitude

→ Have a collective belief that being inclusive to people's beliefs and practices is the right thing to do as a team and organisation.
→ Have a collective belief that every single employee, regardless of their beliefs and practices, should feel respected and valued.

### Behaviours

→ Create psychologically safe environments where talent feel comfortable to call out belief-related microaggressions and biased behaviours.
→ Identify belief-based biases in your team's processes, policies and practices and make efforts to correct them. Be

aware not to discriminate against someone based on their religious beliefs.

→ During meetings, be on a look out for belief biased conversations, microaggressions and biased decision making. Call them out.

→ Be explicitly clear on your company's stand on non-tolerance for religious discrimination.

→ Celebrate a set of main festivals of all the religious/ traditions in your team and organisation to increase awareness and show respect for beliefs and traditions of talent.

→ Cater to the diversity of food choices at workplace cafeterias and during social events without making it feel like an inconvenience.

→ Organise social and networking events that do not centre around the consumption of alcohol.

→ Support, facilitate and create opportunities for talent to engage in health or interest practices that are important to them.

**Reflections and notes:**

.........................................................................................

.........................................................................................

.........................................................................................

.........................................................................................

.........................................................................................

.........................................................................................

# Active Ally of Marital and Parenthood Choices

## *How can I be an active ally of people's marital and parenthood choices?*

### Knowledge

→ Understand that there is a range of personal choices when it comes to marriage/ partnerships and parenthood.
→ Introspect about your own biases, conscious and unconscious about other people's marriage/ partnerships and parenthood choices.

### Attitude

→ Believe that being inclusive to people's marriage/ partnerships and parenthood choices is the right thing to do.
→ Believe that every single employee, regardless of their marriage/ partnerships and parenthood choices, should feel respected and valued.

### Behaviours

→ Observe your own micro-aggressive behaviours about other people's marriage/ partnerships and parenthood choices and make sincere efforts to reduce them. Educate yourself about why people make such choices to satisfy any curiosity and increase understanding about someone's marriage/ partnerships and parenthood choices.

→ Be open to feedback about your own micro-aggressive behaviours.
→ Call out marriage or parenthood related microaggressions and biased behaviours in your workplace by asking the right questions and engaging in honest and open conversations.

**Reflections and notes:**

..........................................................................................

..........................................................................................

..........................................................................................

..........................................................................................

..........................................................................................

..........................................................................................

### *How can we, as a team and as an organisation, be an active ally of people's marital and parenthood choices?*

#### Knowledge

→ Recognise the range of personal choices when it comes to marriage/ partnerships and parenthood.
→ Train managers and leaders on being empathetic and understanding towards the personal choices and commitments that their talent makes.
→ Introspect about your collective biases, conscious and unconscious about other people's marriage/ partnerships and parenthood choices.

#### Attitude

→ Have a collective belief that being inclusive to people's marriage/ partnerships and parenthood choices is the right thing to do for your team and organisation.
→ Have a collective belief that every single employee, regardless of their marriage/ partnerships and parenthood choices, should feel respected and valued.

#### Behaviours

→ During meetings, be on a look out for marriage or parenthood biased conversations, microaggressions and biased decision making. Call them out.
→ Identify marriage or parenthood biases in your team's and organisation's processes, policies and practices and make

efforts to correct them. Be aware to not discriminate against someone based on their parenthood choices.

→ Revise your company's marriage and parenthood policies and benefits to embrace the diversity of options in society.
→ Make conscious efforts to limit the biases against parents of children, both women and men, by having "blind" recruitment practices and structured interview processes by a diverse panel.
→ Explore and implement ways to make it easier for parents to manage their work commitments with their family commitments. This could involve widely accepted work-from-home options, flexible working hours, and onsite childcare facilities.
→ Redefine notions of productivity and commitment to the organisation to be inclusive to family commitment.

**Reflections and notes:**

........................................................................................

........................................................................................

........................................................................................

........................................................................................

........................................................................................

........................................................................................

# Active Ally of Socio-Economic Backgrounds

***How can I be an active ally of people's socio-economic backgrounds?***

### Knowledge

→ Understand and respect the diversity in people's socio-economic backgrounds.
→ Introspect about your own biases, conscious and unconscious about other people's socio-economic backgrounds.

### Attitude

→ Believe that being inclusive to diverse socio-economic backgrounds is the right thing to do.
→ Believe that every single employee, regardless of their socio-economic background, should feel respected and valued.

### Behaviours

→ Observe your own micro-aggressive behaviours about other people's socio-economic backgrounds and make sincere efforts to reduce them.
→ Be open to feedback about your own micro-aggressive behaviours.
→ Call out socio-economic background related microaggressions and biased behaviours in your workplace by asking

the right questions and engaging in honest and open conversations.

→ Be a mentor or coach to young talent from disadvantaged socio-economic backgrounds.

**Reflections and notes:**

............................................................................................

............................................................................................

............................................................................................

............................................................................................

............................................................................................

............................................................................................

***How can we, as a team and as an organisation, be an active ally of people's socio-economic backgrounds?***

**KNOWLEDGE**

→ Understand and respect the diversity in people's socio-economic backgrounds.
→ Introspect about your collective biases, conscious and unconscious about other people's socio-economic backgrounds.

**ATTITUDE**

→ Have a collective belief that being inclusive to diverse socio-economic backgrounds is the right thing to do for your team and organisation.
→ Have a collective belief that every single employee, regardless of their socio-economic background, should feel respected and valued.

**BEHAVIOURS**

→ Create psychologically safe environments where talent feels comfortable to call out socio-economic background related microaggressions and biased behaviours in your workplace.
→ During meetings, be on a look out for socio-economic background biases, microaggressions and biased decision making. Call them out.
→ Identify socio-economic background biases in your team's processes, policies and practices and make efforts to correct

them. Be aware to not discriminate against someone based on their socio-economic background.

→ Create outreach programs, in partnership with relevant organisations, to reach out to talent from disadvantaged backgrounds. Gain strong and active internal support for these programs.
→ Make conscious efforts to limit the biases against socio-economic background during recruitment and selection:
  → Have "blind" recruitment practices with residential and educational institution information removed.
  → Implement structured interview processes conducted by a diverse interview panel.

**Reflections and notes:**

............................................................................

............................................................................

............................................................................

............................................................................

............................................................................

............................................................................

# Final Thoughts

*"If you want to improve the organisation, you have to improve yourself and the organisation gets pulled up with you."*

Indra Nooyi, Indian-American business executive and former chairperson and Chief Executive Officer of PepsiCo

As I sit and write this final chapter, Kamala Harris has become the first female Vice-President and the first woman of colour of African and Indian descent to occupy one of the highest positions in the American government. This gives us all a renewed hope and energy that the world of the future will indeed be a more inclusive one. In the words of Kamala Harris: "While I may be the first woman in this office, I will not be the last". We stand at a crucial point in human history; we have the opportunity to create the workplaces of the future – workplaces that embrace diversity fully and are inclusive - for all. For this to happen - we need to *diversify diversity.*

I have found myself being asked why I wrote this book. A great question for any author. For many reasons actually. Some are deeply personal - my own life episodes of discrimination and my desperate hope for the world to be different - better - for my children, nieces, and nephews. Professionally, I have always had a burning desire to help companies embrace and benefit from the true diversity that is represented in our talent.

I may be an idealist and naive in believing in the inherent goodness of people. I do believe that the majority of us want to do better to create workplaces free from as much bias and discrimination as possible. We have simply lacked the *why* and the *how* – until now. Too often, I keep hearing "I want to be less biased; I want my workplace to be less biased but what can I do?"; or "I don't fully understand why there is such a focus on D&I? Isn't D&I just about skin colour and gender?"; or "My workplace already has diversity, so I don't need to do much"; or "D&I seems to be a problem in the US and UK, we do not have a problem here". I wrote this book to help us build a rich understanding of the various dimensions of diversity, looking at them through more of a global lens, and to provide us with a set of strategies on how to be an active ally.

The twelve dimensions are by no means exhaustive. There may be other dimensions of diversity that you - or those with whom you work - identify, which have not been covered in this book. I look forward to writing about these in a future edition.

Join me on this journey to make our workplaces truly inclusive for all; let us embrace the diversity of all our talent; those already in our organisations and those who are yet to join us. My hopes are many. Having read this book, I hope that you are feeling confident to be an active ally equipped with a solid understanding of the dimensions of diversity and their associated biases, along with a set of tools to demonstrate active allyship. My hope is that you use this book for your own individual journey towards active allyship at work, maybe even at home and within your communities.

I hope that you will use this book as a means of building inclusive teams and workplaces. I hope that this book will encourage discussion and action; we must have courageous conversations and sometimes those conversations may be uncomfortable. I hope that you are now comfortable with being uncomfortable; and above all else, I hope this book has inspired you to do more.

I often end my D&I training sessions saying this:

*In order for us to walk in someone else's shoes,*
*we must first take off our own.*

Welcome. Take off your shoes and take the first step on your path as an active ally of inclusion…

*Poornima*

# Thank You

I believe that people come into your life for a reason and that everyone we meet enriches our lives in some way. I have been blessed to have many such people in my life who have enabled me to grow into the person I am today, and who have been the catalyst and strength behind this book. Tanuj, my darling partner in life, you have been my rock all these years – thank you for your faith in me and for supporting my pursuits wholeheartedly. To my babies, Rohan and Tejas, thank you for choosing me to be your Mama and being the real driver behind why I wrote this book. My dream for you and for my nieces is for a world that is free from discrimination and truly inclusive for all.

I am deeply grateful to my parents for many things in my life, but most importantly for nurturing in me a strong sense of identity and purpose, along with a thirst to constantly keep learning. I am also very thankful to have parents in-law who have been such an integral part of my life. I will always treasure their steady love and support.

To all my fellow active allies, thank you for engaging in many deep and powerful conversations. To all the leaders, trainees, and students I have had the pleasure of interacting with, thank you for the rich discussions and for providing me with the motivation to write this book. To the companies who shared their authentic and inspiring efforts, thank you. This book would not have been possible without these wonderful, precious, and diverse people in my life. I am grateful.

# About the Author

Dr. Poornima Luthra is the founder and CEO of TalentED Consultancy ApS and an external Faculty at the Copenhagen Business School. Poornima is a TEDx speaker, and contributor to the World Economic Forum, UNESCO courier and The Economist Intelligence Unit. She has spent the last fifteen years researching and teaching university courses in the field of talent management, with a focus on diversity and inclusion. Since 2019, Poornima has taken her years of academic experience into the corporate world with the vision of making workplaces more inclusive for all. Poornima focuses on inspiring inclusive mindsets and expanding the areas of diversity we look at through strategic consulting, corporate training, keynote sessions, talks, articles, blog posts and podcasts.

For more information, visit www.talented.dk.

# Endnotes


1. Criado Perez, Caroline. *Invisible Women: Data Bias in A World Designed for Men*. Harry N. Abrams, 2019
2. https://www.glassdoor.com/about-us/diversity-inclusion-2019/
3. https://business.linkedin.com/talent-solutions/blog/diversity/2020/why-the-head-of-diversity-is-the-job-of-the-moment
4. Sundiatu Dixon-Fyle, Kevin Dolan, Vivian Hunt, and Sara Prince, *Diversity Wins: How Inclusion Matters* (McKinsey & Company, May 19, 2020).
5. https://www.bcg.com/en-us/publications/2018/how-diverse-leadership-teams-boost-innovation.aspx
6. Richard Kersley, Eugene Klerk, Anais Boussie, Bahar Sezer Longworth, Joelle Anamootoo Natzkoff, and Darshana Ramji, *The CS Gender 3000 in 2019: The Changing Face of Companies* (Credit Suisse Research Institute, October 10, 2019): p. 22-23
7. https://www.bloomberg.com/news/articles/2020-07-27/u-k-firms-with-more-women-on-exec-boards-outperform-on-profits
8. https://www.catalyst.org/research/why-diversity-and-inclusion-matter-financial-performance/

9 Juan M. Madera, Linnea Ng, Jane M. Sundermann, and Mikki Hebl, Top Management Gender Diversity and Organizational Attraction: When and Why It Matters, *Archives of Scientific Psychology*, vol. 7, no. 1 (2019): p. 90-101.

10 Cara C. Maurer and Israr Qureshi, Not Just Good for Her: A Temporal Analysis of the Dynamic Relationship Between Representation of Women and Collective Employee Turnover, *Organization Studies* (2019).

11 https://www.webershandwick.com/news/millennials-at-work-perspectives-on-diversity-inclusion/

12 https://www2.deloitte.com/global/en/pages/about-deloitte/articles/millennialsurvey.htmlDeloitte Millennial Survey 2020:

file:///C:/Users/User/Downloads/deloitte-2020-millennial-survey.pdf

13 Deloitte Millennial Survey 2018: https://www2.deloitte.com/content/dam/Deloitte/global/Documents/About-Deloitte/gx-2018-millennial-survey-report.pdf

14 Sean McCallaghan, Leon T.B. Jackson, and Marita M. Heyns, Examining the Mediating Effect of Diversity Climate on the Relationship Between Destructive Leadership and Employee Attitudes, *Journal of Psychology in Africa*, vol. 29, no. 6 (2019): p. 563-569; Elissa L. Perry and Aitong Li, Diversity Climate in Organizations, in *Oxford Research Encyclopedia of Business and Management* (Oxford University Press, 2020).

15 Luu Trong Tuan, Chris Rowley, and Vo Thanh Thao, Addressing Employee Diversity to Foster Their Work Engagement, *Journal of Business Research*, vol. 95 (2019): p. 303-315.

16 Dnika J. Travis, Emily Shaffer, and Jennifer Thorpe-Moscon, *Getting Real About Inclusive Leadership: Why Change Starts With You* (Catalyst, 2019).

17 Elissa L. Perry and Aitong Li, Diversity Climate in Organizations, in *Oxford Research Encyclopedia of Business and Management* (Oxford University Press, 2020).

18 Helen H. Yu and David Lee, Gender and Public Organization: A Quasi-Experimental Examination of Inclusion on Experiencing

and Reporting Wrongful Behavior in the Workplace, *Public Personnel Management*, vol. 49, no. 1 (2020): p. 3-28.

19 Juliet Bourke and Andrea Espedido, Why Inclusive Leaders Are Good for Organizations, and How to Become One, *Harvard Business Review*, March 29, 2019.

20 Rocío Lorenzo, Nicole Voigt, Karin Schetelig, Annika Zawadzki, Isabell M. Welpe, and Prisca Brosi, *The Mix That Matters: Innovation Through Diversity* (The Boston Consulting Group, 2017).

21 Sarah E. Gaither, Evan P. Apfelbaum, Hannah J. Birnbaum, Laura G. Babbitt, and Samuel R. Sommers, Mere Membership in Racially Diverse Groups Reduces Conformity, *Social Psychology and Personality Science*, vol. 9, no. 4 (2018): p. 402-410.

22 American Psychological Association, Groupthink, *APA Dictionary of Psychology* (2020).

23 Astrid C. Homan, Dealing with Diversity in Workgroups: Preventing Problems and Promoting Potential, *Social and Personality Psychology Compass*, vol. 13, no. 5 (2019).

24 Alison Reynolds and David Lewis, Teams Solve Problems Faster When They're More Cognitively Diverse, *Harvard Business Review* (March 30, 2017).

25 Matthew Corritore, Amir Goldberg, and Sameer B. Srivastava, The New Analytics of Culture, *Harvard Business Review* (January-February 2020).

26 Dnika J. Travis, Emily Shaffer, and Jennifer Thorpe-Moscon, *Getting Real About Inclusive Leadership: Why Change Starts With You* (Catalyst, 2019).

27 International Labour Organization, *Women in Business and Management: The Business Case for Change* (2019): p. 21.

28 McKay, P. F., Avery, D. R., Liao, H., & Morris, M. A. (2011). Does diversity climate lead to customer satisfaction? It depends on the service climate and business unit demography. *Organization Science, 22*(3), 788–803.

29 http://womeninfintech.co.uk/wp-content/uploads/2017/11/wif_2017_powerlist.pdf

30 https://www2.deloitte.com/uk/en/pages/financial-services/articles/fintech-has-bigger-gender-problem-than-it-realises.html

31 https://www2.deloitte.com/uk/en/pages/financial-services/articles/fintech-has-bigger-gender-problem-than-it-realises.html

32 https://www2.deloitte.com/uk/en/pages/financial-services/articles/fintech-has-bigger-gender-problem-than-it-realises.html

33 Lassébie, J., et al. (2019), Levelling the playing field: Dissecting the gender gap in the funding of start-ups, *OECD Science, Technology and Industry Policy Papers,* No. 73, OECD Publishing, Paris.

34 https://www.bcg.com/publications/2020/managing-next-decade-women-wealth

35 Female Invest: https://www.femaleinvest.com/

36 https://www.theguardian.com/world/2018/jul/04/london-clubs-and-racism-the-west-end-is-a-hostile-environment; Talbot, D., & Böse, M. (2007). Racism, criminalization and the development of night-time economies: Two case studies in London and Manchester. *Ethnic & Racial Studies, 30*(1), 95–118; https://www.independent.co.uk/voices/comment/oh-yes-its-ladies-night-and-the-feelings-wrong-8381432.html; https://nypost.com/2019/10/14/man-sues-manhattan-bar-for-discrimination-over-ladies-night-entry-fee/

37 https://www.hcn.org/issues/51.3/race-and-racism-racist-policing-plagues-portlands-nightclubs

38 May, R. A. B. (2018). Velvet Rope Racism, Racial Paranoia, and Cultural Scripts: Alleged Dress Code Discrimination in Urban Nightlife, 2000–2014. *City & Community, 17*(1), 44–64.

39 Søgaard, T. F. (2017). Ethnicity and the Policing of Nightclub Accessibility in the Danish Night-time Economy. *Drugs: Education, Prevention & Policy, 24*(3), 256–264.

40 https://www.forbes.com/sites/soniathompson/2020/02/05/data-shows-consumers-want-diversity-in-marketing-why-many-brands-struggle-to-get-it-right-and-how-to-fix/#22de6bed32f5

41 Shelley Zalis, Inclusive Ads Are Affecting Consumer Behavior, According to New Research, *Think with Google,* November 2019.

42 https://www2.deloitte.com/us/en/insights/industry/retail-distribution/the-consumer-is-changing.html

43 https://www.marketingweek.com/career-salary-survey-2020-marketing-diversity-crisis/

44 Paula Loop and Paul DeNicola, You've Committed to Increasing Gender Diversity on Your Board. Here's How to Make It Happen, *Harvard Business Review*, February 18, 2019.

45 Steven A. Creek, Kristine M. Kuhn, and Arvin Sahaym, Board Diversity and Employee Satisfaction: The Mediating Role of Progressive Programs, *Group & Organization Management* (2017).

46 Steven A. Creek, Kristine M. Kuhn, and Arvin Sahaym, Board Diversity and Employee Satisfaction: The Mediating Role of Progressive Programs, *Group & Organization Management* (2017).

47 Jie Chen, Woon Sau Leung, Wei Song, and Marc Georgen, Research: When Women Are on Boards, Male CEOs Are Less Overconfident, *Harvard Business Review*, September 12, 2019; Jie Chen, Woon Sau Leung, Wei Song, and Marc Georgen, Why Female Board Representation Matters: The Role of Female Directors in Reducing Male CEO Overconfidence, *Journal of Empirical Finance*, vol. 52 (2019): p. 70-90.

48 Jie Chen, Woon Sau Leung, Wei Song, and Marc Georgen, Research: When Women Are on Boards, Male CEOs Are Less Overconfident, *Harvard Business Review*, September 12, 2019; Jie Chen, Woon Sau Leung, Wei Song, and Marc Georgen, Why Female Board Representation Matters: The Role of Female Directors in Reducing Male CEO Overconfidence, *Journal of Empirical Finance*, vol. 52 (2019): p. 70-90.

49 Yaoyao Fan, Yuxiang Jiang, Xuezhi Zhang, and Yue Zhou, Women on Boards and Bank Earnings Management: From Zero to Hero, *Journal of Banking & Finance*, vol. 107 (2019).

50 Binay K. Adhikari, Anup Agrawal, and James Malm, Do Women Managers Keep Firms Out of Trouble? Evidence from Corporate Litigation and Policies, *Journal of Accounting and Economics*, vol. 67, no. 1 (2019): p. 202-225.

51 Dnika J. Travis, Emily Shaffer, and Jennifer Thorpe-Moscon, *Getting Real About Inclusive Leadership: Why Change Starts With You* (Catalyst, 2019).

52 https://www.mckinsey.com/featured-insights/diversity-and-inclusion/diversity-wins-how-inclusion-matters

53 https://www2.deloitte.com/us/en/pages/about-deloitte/articles/inclusion-insights.html

54 https://www.forbes.com/sites/daviddisalvo/2013/06/22/your-brain-sees-even-when-you-dont/#3eb381a8116a

55 Libet, B. (1985). Unconscious Cerebral Initiative and the Role of Conscious Will in Voluntary Action. *Behavioral and Brain Sciences*, *8*(4), 529–566

56 Kahneman D, Frederick S (2002). Representativeness Revisited: Attribute Substitution in Intuitive Judgment. In Gilovich T, Griffin DW, Kahneman D (eds.). Heuristics and Biases: The Psychology of Intuitive Judgment. Cambridge: Cambridge University Press. pp. 51–52. ISBN 978-0-521-79679-8.

57 European Institute for Gender Equality: https://eige.europa.eu/

58 https://edition.cnn.com/2020/11/23/business/germany-quotas-women-boards/index.html

59 https://www.gov.uk/discrimination-your-rights

60 McIntosh, P. (2003). *White privilege: Unpacking the invisible knapsack.* In S. Plous (Ed.), *Understanding prejudice and discrimination* (p. 191–196). McGraw-Hill.

61 https://metro-co-uk.cdn.ampproject.org/c/s/metro.co.uk/2020/09/25/black-and-ethnic-minority-employees-need-more-mental-health-support-in-the-workplace-13325119/amp/

62 Criado Perez, Caroline. *Invisible Women: Data Bias in A World Designed for Men.* Harry N. Abrams, 2019.

63 Schrader, P.G. & Lawless, Kimberly. (2004). The Knowledge, Attitudes, & Behaviors Approach How to Evaluate Performance and Learning in Complex Environments. *Performance Improvement. 43.* 8 - 15. 10.1002/pfi.4140430905.

64 https://hbr-org.cdn.ampproject.org/c/s/hbr.org/amp/2020/11/what-inclusive-leaders-sounds-like

65 https://www.un.org/sustainabledevelopment/gender-equality/

66 Englad, P. (2010). The Gender Revolution: Uneven and Stalled. *Gender and Society, 24*(2), 149-166.

67 Roy,S. (2019). Discriminatory Laws Against Women : A Survey of the Literature (English). Policy Research working paper;no. WPS 8719 Washington, D.C.: World Bank Group. http://documents.worldbank.org/curated/en/393191548685944435/Discriminatory-Laws-Against-Women-A-Survey-of-the-Literature

68 https://blogs.worldbank.org/voices/sexual-harassment-where-do-we-stand-legal-protection-women

69 https://www.weforum.org/agenda/2015/11/18-countries-where-women-need-their-husbands-permission-to-get-a-job/

70 https://wbl.worldbank.org/en/data/exploretopics/wbl_sj

71 https://www.un.org/en/un75/women_girls_closing_gender_gap

72 https://www.un.org/en/un75/women_girls_closing_gender_gap

73 http://www.unesco.org/new/en/media-services/single-view/news/closing_gender_gap_in_education/

74 http://www3.weforum.org/docs/WEF_GGGR_2020.pdf

75 Council on foreign relations: https://www.cfr.org/

76 McKinsey & Company report Women in the Workplace 2020: https://www.mckinsey.com/featured-insights/diversity-and-inclusion/women-in-the-workplace

77 https://www.statista.com/statistics/685208/number-of-female-ceo-positions-in-ftse-companies-uk/

78 https://www.accountancydaily.co/ftse-350-companies-female-execs-increase-profits

79 https://www.oecd.org/els/emp/last-mile-longest-gender-nordic-countries-brief.pdf

80 https://www.cato.org/sites/cato.org/files/pubs/pdf/pa-835.pdf

81 https://www.cato.org/sites/cato.org/files/pubs/pdf/pa-835.pdf

82 Grant Thornton, Women in Business: Building a Blueprint for Action(2019): p. 5

83 2018 McKinsey report "Why diversity matters": https://www.mckinsey.com/business-functions/organization/our-insights/why-diversity-matters

84 2017 PWC report: https://www.pwc.com/gx/en/about/diversity/iwd/iwd-female-talent-report-web.pdf

85 McKinsey & Company report 'Women in the Workplace 2020': https://www.mckinsey.com/featured-insights/diversity-and-inclusion/women-in-the-workplace

86 https://hbr.org/2017/10/a-study-used-sensors-to-show-that-men-and-women-are-treated-differently-at-work

87 https://www.cato.org/sites/cato.org/files/pubs/pdf/pa-835.pdf

88 https://en.natmus.dk/historical-knowledge/denmark/prehistoric-period-until-1050-ad/the-viking-age/the-people/women/

89 Barker, M.-J. (2020). *Gender: a Graphic Guide*. Icon Books, Limited.

90 https://www.weforum.org/agenda/2018/03/kids-aren't-biased-at-6-and-then-this-happens/

91 https://youtu.be/qv8VZVP5csA

92 https://youtu.be/LSpuEg4DIm8

93 Boys and Girls on stereotypes: https://youtu.be/aTvGSstKd5Y

94 Koh, Eunkang. (2008). Gender Issues and Confucian Scriptures: Is Confucianism Incompatible with Gender Equality in South Korea?. *Bulletin of the School of Oriental and African Studies*. 71. 345 - 362.

95 Adeyinka Abideen Aderinto (2001) Patriarchy and Culture: The Position of Women in a Rural Yoruba Community, Nigeria, *The Anthropologist*, 3:4, 225-230,

96 Sathiparsad, R., Taylor, M., & Dlamini, S. (2008). Patriarchy and Family Life: Alternative Views of Male Youth in Rural South Africa. *Agenda: Empowering Women for Gender Equity*, (76), 4-16.

97 Adisa, Toyin & Cooke, Fang & Iwowo, Vanessa. (2019). Mind Your Attitude: The Impact of Patriarchy on Women's Workplace Behaviour. *Career Development International.*

98 https://ceoworld.biz/2020/06/21/ranked-worlds-best-countries-for-women-2020/

99 Felmlee, Diane & Inara Rodis, Paulina & Zhang, Amy. (2019). Sexist Slurs: Reinforcing Feminine Stereotypes Online. *Sex Roles.* 10.1007/s11199-019-01095-z.

100 2014 study by George Washington University: https://www.researchgate.net/publication/275005639_Influence_of_Communication_Partner's_Gender_on_Language

101 Storage, Daniel & Charlesworth, Tessa & Banaji, Mahzarin & Cimpian, Andrei. (2020). Adults and Children Implicitly Associate Brilliance with Men More Than Women. *Journal of Experimental Social Psychology.* 10.1016/j.jesp.2020.104020.

102 Bian, L., Leslie, S.-J., & Cimpian, A. (2018). Evidence of Bias Against Girls and Women in Contexts that Emphasize Intellectual Ability. *American Psychologist, 73*(9), 1139–1153.

103 Jaxon, Jilana & Lei, Ryan & Shachnai, Reut & Chestnut, Eleanor & Cimpian, Andrei. (2019). The Acquisition of Gender Stereotypes about Intellectual Ability: Intersections with Race. *Journal of Social Issues.* 10.1111/josi.12352.

104 https://unesdoc.unesco.org/ark:/48223/pf0000253479

105 PwC's Women in Technology study: https://www.pwc.co.uk/who-we-are/women-in-technology/time-to-close-the-gender-gap.html

106 https://www.pwc.co.uk/women-in-technology/women-in-tech-report.pdf

107 https://www.svb.com/globalassets/library/uploadedfiles/content/trends_and_insights/reports/women_in_technology_leadership/svb-suo-women-in-tech-report-2019.pdf

108 https://www.ncwit.org/sites/default/files/resources/womenintech_facts_fullreport_05132016.pdf

109 https://hbr.org/2015/03/the-5-biases-pushing-women-out-of-stem

110 https://www.pwc.co.uk/women-in-technology/women-in-tech-report-infographic.pdf

111 https://www.frontiersin.org/articles/10.3389/fpsyg.2018.01866/full

112 Anderson RC, Klofstad CA (2012) Preference for Leaders with Masculine Voices Holds in the Case of Feminine Leadership Roles. *PLOS ONE* 7(12): e51216.

113 https://www.americanscientist.org/article/how-voice-pitch-influences-our-choice-of-leaders

114 UK Department of Education: https://www.besa.org.uk/key-uk-education-statistics/

115 U.S. Department of Education: https://nces.ed.gov/programs/coe/indicator_clr.asp#:~:text=See%20Digest%20of%20Education%20Statistics,school%20level%20(36%20percent).

116 https://data.oecd.org/teachers/women-teachers.htm#indicator-chart

117 Klecker, Beverly M., & Loadman, William E. (1999). Male elementary school teachers ' ratings of job satisfaction by years of teaching experience. *Education*. 1 19. 131 504-513.

118 Barnard, Cynthia & Hovingh, Lori & Nezwek, Michele & Pryor-Bayard, Deborah & Schmoldt, Jill & Stevens, James & Sturrus, Wendy & Wabeke, Susan & Weaver, Lorie. (2000). Recommendations for Improving the Recruitment of Male Early Childhood Education Professionals: The Female Viewpoint.

119 Rochlen, Aaron & McKelley, Ryan & Whittaker, Tiffany. (2010). Stay-at-Home Fathers' Reasons for Entering the Role and Stigma Experiences: A Preliminary Report. *Psychology of Men & Masculinity*, 11, 279-285.

120 https://abcnews.go.com/blogs/headlines/2014/02/heres-a-list-of-58-gender-options-for-facebook-users

121 https://genhq.com/gen-z-generation-no-longer-easily-defined-gender/

122 https://www.pewsocialtrends.org/2019/01/17/generation-z-looks-a-lot-like-millennials-on-key-social-and-political-issues/

123 Gaucher D, Friesen J, Kay AC. Evidence that gendered wording in job advertisements exists and sustains gender inequality. *J Pers Soc Psychol.* 2011 Jul;101(1):109-28.

124 https://hbr.org/2019/04/one-way-to-reduce-gender-bias-in-performance-reviews

125 https://fortune.com/2014/08/26/performance-review-gender-bias/

126 https://hbr.org/2018/03/is-the-confidence-gap-between-men-and-women-a-myth

127 https://www.theatlantic.com/magazine/archive/2014/05/the-confidence-gap/359815/

128 https://hbr.org/2018/03/is-the-confidence-gap-between-men-and-women-a-myth

129 https://youtu.be/zeAEFEXvcBg

130 https://hbr.org/2013/08/why-do-so-many-incompetent-men

131 https://hbr.org/2013/08/why-do-so-many-incompetent-men

132 https://youtu.be/zeAEFEXvcBg

133 Goldin, C., & Rouse, C. (2000). Orchestrating Impartiality: The Impact of "Blind" Auditions on Female Musicians. *The American Economic Review*, *90*(4), 715-741.

134 Goldin, C., & Rouse, C. (2000). Orchestrating Impartiality: The Impact of "Blind" Auditions on Female Musicians. *The American Economic Review*, *90*(4), 715-741.

135 Bertrand, M., Black, S. E., Jensen, S., & Lleras-Muney, A. (2014). Breaking the glass ceiling? The effect of board quotas on female labor market outcomes in Norway (No. w20256). National Bureau of Economic Research.

136 https://www.bbc.com/news/entertainment-arts-41497265

137 https://www.payscale.com/data/gender-pay-gap#section03

138 https://ec.europa.eu/info/sites/info/files/factsheet-gender_pay_gap-2019.pdf

139 https://ec.europa.eu/info/sites/info/files/factsheet-gender_pay_gap-2019.pdf

140 https://www.theguardian.com/society/2020/jun/18/gender-pay-gap-begins-students-straight-after-university-graduate-data-report-uk

141 Chi, Wei & Li, Bo. (2014). Trends in China's gender employment and pay gap: Estimating gender pay gaps with employment selection. *Journal of Comparative Economics.* 42. 708–725.

142 Zhipin.com

143 https://www.payscale.com/data/gender-pay-gap

144 https://ec.europa.eu/info/policies/justice-and-fundamental-rights/gender-equality/equal-pay/gender-pay-gap-situation-eu_en#why-do-women-earn-less

145 6th European Working Conditions Survey, Eurofound, 2015

146 Correll, S. J., Benard, S., & Paik, I. (2007). Getting a Job: Is There a Motherhood Penalty? 1. *American journal of sociology*, 112(5), 1297-1339.

147 http://www.oecd.org/social/over-the-rainbow-the-road-to-lgbti-inclusion-8d2fd1a8-en.htm

148 https://www.pewforum.org/fact-sheet/gay-marriage-around-the-world/

149 https://www.forbes.com/sites/frederickallen/2013/03/22/howard-schultz-to-anti-gay-marriage-starbucks-shareholder-you-can-sell-your-shares/?sh=6e4c575843fa

150 https://www.nbcnews.com/feature/nbc-out/companies-lgbtq-inclusive-ads-weren-t-always-risk-free-n1024971

151 Eisend, Martin & Hermann, Erik. (2019). Consumer Response to Homosexual Imagery in Advertising: A Meta-Analysis. *Journal of Advertising.*

152 https://www.nbcnews.com/feature/nbc-out/companies-lgbtq-inclusive-ads-weren-t-always-risk-free-n1024971

153 Out Now (2015) 'LGBTI Diversity: Show Me the Business Case.', LGBTI 2020 Study, pp. 49. Utrecht, Netherlands: Out Now

154 Wang, P. & Schwarz, J. (2010). Stock Price Reactions to GLBT Non-discrimination Policies. *Human Resource Management, 49*

(2), 195– 216.

155 Johnston, D & Malina, M. (2008). Managing Sexual Orientation Diversity. The Impact on Firm Value. *Group Organization Management, 33* (5).

156 Credit Suisse (2016). Credit Suisse ESG Research. https://plus.credit-suisse.com/rpc4/ravDocView?docid=QYuHK2

157 Open for business: The economic and business case for LGB&T inclusion : https://www.wko.at/site/Charta-der-Vielfalt/Service/studien/Brunswick_Open_for_Business.pdf; The Business Case for Diversity in the Workplace: sexual orientation and gender identity Report on good practices, European Commission: https://www.raznolikost.hr/admin/uploads/trainers/report_companies_final_en.pdf

158 The Business Case for Diversity in the Workplace: sexual orientation and gender identity Report on good practices, European Commission: https://www.raznolikost.hr/admin/uploads/trainers/report_companies_final_en.pdf

159 https://www.ibm.com/employment/inclusion/downloads/IBM_Gender_Transition_in_the_global_workplace.pdf

160 Open for business: The economic and business case for LGB&T inclusion : https://www.wko.at/site/Charta-der-Vielfalt/Service/studien/Brunswick_Open_for_Business.pdf

161 Badgett, M., Durso, L., Kastanis, A & Mallory, C. (2013). The Business Impact of LGBT Supportive Workplace Policies. Los Angeles: The Williams Institute.

162 https://image-src.bcg.com/Images/BCG-A-New-LGBTQ-Workforce-Has-Arrived-Inclusive-Cultures-Must-Follow-Jun-2020_tcm9-251548.pdf

163 https://www.hrc.org/resources/corporate-equality-index

164 https://www.weforum.org/agenda/2017/01/why-so-many-businesses-support-lgbt-rights/

165 https://www.outnowconsulting.com/market-reports/lgbt-diversity-show-me-the-business-case-report.aspx

166 https://www.marketingmag.com.au/hubs-c/gay-lesbian-marketing-lgbtiqa/

167 GLAAD is an American non-governmental media monitoring organization founded by LGBT people in the media: https://www.glaad.org/

168 Bearman, P. S., & Bruckner, H. (2002). Opposite-sex twins and adolescent same-sex attraction. *American Journal of Sociology*,107, 1179–1205; Greenberg, D. F. (1988). *The construction of homosexuality*. Chicago, IL: University of Chicago Press; Terry, J. (1999). *An American obsession: Science, medicine, and homosexuality in modern society*. Chicago, IL: University of Chicago Press.

169 Nadal, Kevin & Wong, Yinglee & Issa, Marie-ANNE & Meterko, Vanessa & Leon, Jayleen & Wideman, Michelle. (2011). Sexual Orientation Microaggressions: Processes and Coping Mechanisms for Lesbian, Gay, and Bisexual Individuals. *Journal of LGBT Issues in Counseling*. 5. 21-46.

170 Adamczyk, Amy & Pitt, Cassady. (2009). Shaping Attitudes About Homosexuality: The Role of Religion and Cultural Context. Social science research. 38. 338-51; Herek, Gregory & McLemore, Kevin. (2012). Sexual Prejudice. *Annual Review of Psychology*. 64. 10.1146/annurev-psych-113011-143826.

171 https://www.theguardian.com/society/2015/apr/05/10-per-cent-population-gay-alfred-kinsey-statistics

172 Rivera D.P. (2011) Sexual Prejudice. In: Goldstein S., Naglieri J.A. (eds) Encyclopedia of Child Behavior and Development. Springer, Boston, MA.

173 Herek, G. M. (2000). The psychology of sexual prejudice. *Current Directions in Psychological Science*, 9, 19-22.

174 Weinberg, G.H. (1972). *Society and the healthy homosexual*. New York: St. Martin's

175 Hudson, W. W., & Ricketts, W. A. (1980). A strategy for the measurement of homophobia. *Journal of Homosexuality*, 5(4), 357–372.

176 Simon, A. (1998). The relationship between stereotypes of and attitudes toward lesbians and gays. In G.M. Herek (Ed.), Stigma and

sexual orientation (pp. 62–81). Thousand Oaks, CA: Sage.

177 Elze, D. (1992). "It has nothing to do with me." In W.J. Blumenfeld (Ed.), *Homophobia: How we all pay the price* (pp. 95–113). Boston: Beacon Press; Ryan, C., & Futterman, D. (1998). *Lesbian & gay youth: Care & counseling.* New York: Columbia University Press.

178 Kanbur N. (2020). Internalized Homophobia in Adolescents: Is it really about Culture or Religion?. *Journal of the Canadian Academy of Child and Adolescent Psychiatry,* 29(2), 124–126.

179 Kanbur N. (2020). Internalized Homophobia in Adolescents: Is it really about Culture or Religion?. *Journal of the Canadian Academy of Child and Adolescent Psychiatry,* 29(2), 124–126.

180 Morin, S. F. (1977). Heterosexual bias in psychological research on lesbianism and male homosexuality. *American Psychologist, 32*(8), 629–637

181 Herek, G. M. (1990). The context of anti-gay violence: Notes on cultural and psychological heterosexism. *Journal of Interpersonal Violence*, 5, 316-333.

182 https://psychology.ucdavis.edu/rainbow/html/prej_defn.html

183 https://www.glassdoor.com/about-us/diversity-inclusion-2019/

184 Ozeren, Emir. (2014). Sexual Orientation Discrimination in the Workplace: A Systematic Review of Literature. Procedia - *Social and Behavioral Sciences*. 109.

185 M.V. L. Badgett, Brad Sears, Holning Lau & Deborah Ho (2009), Bias in the Workplace: Consistent Evidence of Sexual Orientation and Gender Identity Discrimination 1998–2008, 84 Chi.-*Kent L. Rev*. 559.

186 Klawitter, Marieka. (2015). Meta-Analysis of the Effects of Sexual Orientation on Earnings. Industrial Relations: A Journal of Economy and Society. 54.

187 Drydakis, N. (2019) Sexual orientation and labor market outcomes. IZA World of Labor, 111

188 https://www.bcg.com/publications/2020/inclusive-cultures-must-follow-new-lgbtq-workforce

189 Nadal, K. L., Wong, Y., Issa, M., Meterko, V., Leon, J., & Wideman, M. (2011). Sexual orientation microaggressions: Processes and coping mechanisms for lesbian, gay, and bisexual individuals. *Journal of LGBT Issues in Counseling, 5(*1), 21-46.

190 Nadal, Kevin & Wong, Yinglee & Issa, Marie-ANNE & Meterko, Vanessa & Leon, Jayleen & Wideman, Michelle. (2011). Sexual Orientation Microaggressions: Processes and Coping Mechanisms for Lesbian, Gay, and Bisexual Individuals. *Journal of LGBT Issues in Counseling*. 5. 21-46.

191 Nadal, Kevin & Wong, Yinglee & Issa, Marie-ANNE & Meterko, Vanessa & Leon, Jayleen & Wideman, Michelle. (2011). Sexual Orientation Microaggressions: Processes and Coping Mechanisms for Lesbian, Gay, and Bisexual Individuals. *Journal of LGBT Issues in Counseling*. 5. 21-46.

192 https://www.bcg.com/publications/2020/inclusive-cultures-must-follow-new-lgbtq-workforce

193 https://today.yougov.com/topics/lifestyle/articles-reports/2020/06/01/sexuality-spectrum-pride-lgbtq-poll

194 https://www.ipsos.com/sites/default/files/ct/publication/documents/2017-11/ipsos-mori-almanac-2017.pdf

195 United Nations, "Percentage of Total Population by Broad Age Group, Both Sexes (Per 100 Total Population)," *World Population Prospects 2019* (2019).

196 https://www.statista.com/statistics/265759/world-population-by-age-and-region/

197 https://www.statista.com/statistics/829705/global-employment-by-generation/

198 Basu, Kaushik (25 July 2007). "India's demographic dividend". BBC News.

199 https://www.statista.com/statistics/265759/world-population-by-age-and-region/

200 Richard Fry, "Millennials Are the Largest Generation in the U.S. Labor Force," *Pew Research Center Fact Tank* (April 11, 2018).

201 https://www.cnbc.com/2019/11/12/baby-boomers-will-be-work-forces-fastest-growing-generation-in-2020.html

202 https://www.cnet.com/news/say-what-young-people-are-just-smarter/

203 https://www.nbcnews.com/better/lifestyle/ok-boomer-diving-generation-what-does-it-mean-ncna1077261; https://www.nytimes.com/2019/10/29/style/ok-boomer.html

204 https://www.nytimes.com/2019/10/29/style/ok-boomer.html

205 https://www.dol.gov/general/topic/discrimination/agedisc

206 https://www2.deloitte.com/content/dam/Deloitte/us/Documents/about-deloitte/us-inclusion-survey-research-the-bias-barrier.pdf

207 https://www2.deloitte.com/content/dam/Deloitte/us/Documents/about-deloitte/us-inclusion-survey-research-the-bias-barrier.pdf

208 https://www.glassdoor.com/about-us/diversity-inclusion-2019/

209 https://www.pwc.com/gx/en/ceo-survey/2015/assets/pwc-18th-annual-global-ceo-survey-jan-2015.pdf

210 https://hbr.org/2009/02/the-four-biggest-reasons-for-i

211 https://genhq.com/

212 https://www.statista.com/statistics/265759/world-population-by-age-and-region/

213 https://www.bbc.com/news/business-21535772

214 Centre for Generational Kinetics: https://genhq.com/

215 https://en.unesco.org/covid19/educationresponse

216 https://data.unicef.org/topic/early-childhood-development/covid-19/

217 https://www.who.int/en/news-room/fact-sheets/detail/disability-and-health

218 https://www.un.org/development/desa/disabilities/resources/factsheet-on-persons-with-disabilities/disability-and-employment.html#:~:text=There%20are%20370%20million%20persons,high%20as%2080%25%20or%20more.

219 Pfeifer, Christian (2012). "Physical attractiveness, employment and earnings". *Applied Economics Letters. 19* (6): 505–510.

220 Remove labels this Ramadan: https://youtu.be/84OT0NLlqfM

221 https://www.forbes.com/sites/serenitygibbons/2018/06/19/you-have-7-seconds-to-make-a-first-impression-heres-how-to-succeed/#4c7216ef56c2

222 Stone, Christopher & Stone, Dianna. (2014). Stone, C., & Stone, D. L. (2014). Factors affecting hiring decisions about veterans. Human Resource Management Review.. *Human Resource Management Review.*

223 https://www.disabled-world.com/

224 https://www.un.org/development/desa/disabilities/disability-laws-and-acts-by-country-area.html

225 https://www.accenture.com/t20181108T081959Z__w__/us-en/_acnmedia/PDF-89/Accenture-Disability-Inclusion-Research-Report.pdf#zoom=50

226 Office of National Statistic: https://www.ons.gov.uk/

227 https://risepeople.com/blog/why-dont-employers-hire-people-with-disabilities/

228 Boni-Saenz, Alexander & Heinemann, Allen & Crown, Deborah & Emanuel, Linda. (2006). The Business of Employing People with Disabilities: Four Case Studies.

229 Bonaccio, S., Connelly, C.E., Gellatly, I.R. et al. (2020), The Participation of People with Disabilities in the Workplace Across the Employment Cycle: Employer Concerns and Research Evidence. *J Bus Psychol* 35, 135–158.

230 https://www.pwc.com/gx/en/ceo-survey/2015/assets/pwc-18th-annual-global-ceo-survey-jan-2015.pdf

231 Harder, Jenna & Keller, Victor & Chopik, William. (2019). Demographic, Experiential, and Temporal Variation in Ableism.

232 Disability: A Research Study on Unconscious Bias. ENEI 2014, www.enei.org

233 Disability: A Research Study on Unconscious Bias. ENEI 2014,

www.enei.org

234 Kulkarni, Mukta & Valk, Reimara. (2010). Don't ask, don't tell: Two views on human resource practices for people with disabilities. *Journal of Hepatology* - J HEPATOL. 22. 134-134.

235 https://www.badenochandclark.com/

236 https://www.marvel.com/tv-shows/marvel-s-hero-project/1

237 https://www.ilo.org/global/lang--en/index.htm

238 https://www.accenture.com/t20181108T081959Z__w__/us-en/_acnmedia/PDF-89/Accenture-Disability-Inclusion-Research-Report.pdf

239 https://www.dol.gov/

240 https://www.business.com/articles/hire-disabled-people/

241 https://economictimes.indiatimes.com/news/company/corporate-trends/what-companies-and-government-are-doing-to-empower-persons-with-disabilities/articleshow/65254315.cms?from=mdr

242 www.nike.com

243 https://ankhgear.com/collections/apparel

244 https://www.accenture.com/t20181108T081959Z__w__/us-en/_acnmedia/PDF-89/Accenture-Disability-Inclusion-Research-Report.pdf#zoom=50

245 https://www.ibm.com/blogs/think/2020/07/ada-at-30-colleagues-with-diverse-abilities-make-us-all-stronger/

246 https://economictimes.indiatimes.com/news/company/corporate-trends/what-companies-and-government-are-doing-to-empower-persons-with-disabilities/articleshow/65254315.cms?from=mdr

247 https://economictimes.indiatimes.com/news/company/corporate-trends/what-companies-and-government-are-doing-to-empower-persons-with-disabilities/articleshow/65254315.cms?utm_source=contentofinterest&utm_medium=text&utm_campaign=cppst

248 http://news.bbc.co.uk/2/hi/asia-pacific/4762803.stm

249 https://www.salon.com/2006/01/24/jeffries/; https://www.huffpost.com/entry/abercrombie-fitch-hot_n_7135880

250 https://en.paperblog.com/a-juice-bar-that-only-hires-attractive-guys-opens-tomorrow-in-chicago-1804263/

251 Cialdini, R. B. (1993). *Influence: Science and practice* (3rd ed.). HarperCollins College Publishers.

252 Dion, K.; Berscheid, E.; Walster, E. (1972). "What is beautiful is good". *Journal of Personality and Social Psychology*. 24 (3): 285–290; Miller, Arthur G. (1970). "Role of physical attractiveness in impression formation". *Psychonomic Science*. 19 (4): 241–243.

253 Dion, K.; Berscheid, E.; Walster, E. (1972). What is beautiful is good. *Journal of Personality and Social Psychology. 24* (3): 285–290.

254 Wheeler, Ladd; Kim, Youngmee (1997). What is Beautiful is Culturally Good: The Physical Attractiveness Stereotype has Different Content in Collectivistic Cultures. *Personality and Social Psychology Bulletin. 23* (8): 795–800.

255 Hamermesh, Daniel S.; Biddle, Jeff E. (1994). Beauty and the Labor Market. *The American Economic Review*. 84 (5): 1174–1194.

256 Berscheid, E.; Walster, E. (1969). *Interpersonal Attraction*, Reading, MA: Addison-Wesley.

257 Timothy A. Judge, Charlice Hurst, and Lauren S. Simon.(2009). Does It Pay to Be Smart, Attractive, or Confident (or All Three)? Relationships Among General Mental Ability, Physical Attractiveness, Core Self-Evaluations, and Income. *Journal of Applied Psychology,* Vol. 94, No. 3; American Psychological Association, May 16.

258 Kanazawa, S., Still, M.C. Is There Really a Beauty Premium or an Ugliness Penalty on Earnings?. *J Bus Psychol, 33*, 249–262 (2018).

259 https://edition.cnn.com/2017/07/28/opinions/ugliness-premium-opinion-drexler/index.html

260 Lee M, Pitesa M, Pillutla MM, Thau S. (2018), Perceived entitlement causes discrimination against attractive job candidates in the

domain of relatively less desirable jobs. *Journal of Personality and Social Psychology. 114*(3):422-442.

261 Stefanie K. Johnson, Kenneth E. Podratz, Robert L. Dipboye & Ellie Gibbons (2010) Physical Attractiveness Biases in Ratings of Employment Suitability: Tracking Down the "Beauty is Beastly" Effect, *The Journal of Social Psychology, 150:*3, 301-318,

262 https://qz.com/work/1115220/are-attractive-people-more-likely-to-get-hired-not-always-says-new-london-school-of-business-study/

263 Stefanie K. Johnson, Kenneth E. Podratz, Robert L. Dipboye & Ellie Gibbons (2010) Physical Attractiveness Biases in Ratings of Employment Suitability: Tracking Down the "Beauty is Beastly" Effect, *The Journal of Social Psychology, 150:*3, 301-318.

264 Lennon, Sharron. (2009). Effects of Clothing Attractiveness on Perceptions. *Home Economics Research Journal.* 18. 303 - 310.

265 Centers for Disease Control and Prevention: https://www.cdc.gov/nchs/fastats/obesity-overweight.htm

266 National Health Service: https://www.nhs.uk/conditions/obesity/

267 https://www.economist.com/graphic-detail/2019/10/28/china-worries-about-its-bulging-waistlines

268 Ahirwar, Rajeev & Mondal, Prakash. (2018). Prevalence of obesity in India: A systematic review. Diabetes & Metabolic Syndrome: *Clinical Research & Reviews.* 13.

269 Ahirwar, Rajeev & Mondal, Prakash. (2018). Prevalence of obesity in India: A systematic review. Diabetes & Metabolic Syndrome: *Clinical Research & Reviews.* 13.

270 M.V. Roehling, "Weight-Based Discrimination in Employment: Psychological and Legal Aspects," *Personnel Psychology 52*, no. 4 (December 1999): 969-1016

271 https://sloanreview.mit.edu/article/the-opportunity-costs-of-weight-bias-at-work/

272 Nowrouzi-Kia, Behdin & Mcdougall, Alicia & Gohar, Basem & Nowrouz-Kia, B & Casole, Jennifer. (2015). Weight Bias in the

Workplace: A Literature Review. Occup Med Health Aff. 3. 2.

273 Giel KE, Thiel A, Teufel M, Mayer J, Zipfel S. (2010) Weight bias in work settings - a qualitative review. Obesity Facts. Feb;3(1):33-40

274 E.N. Ruggs, M.R. Hebl, and A. Williams (2015), Weight Isn't Selling: The Insidious Effects of Weight Stigmatization in Retail Settings, *Journal of Applied Psychology 100,* no. 5 (September): 1483-1496

275 J.R. Shapiro, E.B. King, and M.A. Quinones, Expectations of Obese Trainees: How Stigmatized Trainee Characteristics Influence Training Effectiveness, *Journal of Applied Psychology, 92,* no. 1 (January 2007): 239-249

276 T.A. Judge and D.M. Cable (2011), When It Comes to Pay, Do the Thin Win? The Effect of Weight on Pay for Men and Women, *Journal of Applied Psychology ,96,* no. 1 (January): 95-112.

277 E.B. King, S.G. Rogelberg, M.R. Hebl, et al. (2916), "Waistlines and Ratings of Executives: Does Executive Status Overcome Obesity Stigma?" *Human Resource Management* 55, no. 2 (March-April): 283-300

278 Judge, T. A., & Cable, D. M. (2004). The Effect of Physical Height on Workplace Success and Income: Preliminary Test of a Theoretical Model. *Journal of Applied Psychology, 89*(3), 428–441

279 https://timiacobb.home.blog/2019/02/17/lets-talk-hairism/

280 Koval CZ, Rosette AS. The Natural Hair Bias in Job Recruitment. *Social Psychological and Personality Science.* August 2020

281 https://perception.org/goodhair/results/

282 United Nations Educational, Scientific and Cultural Organization, https://en.unesco.org/

283 http://uis.unesco.org/sites/default/files/documents/new-methodology-shows-258-million-children-adolescents-and-youth-are-out-school.pdf

284 https://www.independent.co.uk/news/education/education-news/school-students-uk-social-mobility-oecd-andreas-schleicher-study-gcse-a8597951.html

285 https://www.theatlantic.com/business/archive/2016/08/property-taxes-and-unequal-schools/497333/

286 https://hechingerreport.org/a-decade-of-research-on-the-rich-poor-divide-in-education/

287 https://www.americanprogress.org/issues/education-postsecondary/reports/2018/05/23/451186/neglected-college-race-gap-racial-disparities-among-college-completers/

288 Courtice, A.J. (2016), "Education: The American Caste System Edition II", Sbpra.

289 https://hbr.org/2020/09/graduates-of-elite-universities-get-paid-more-do-they-perform-better

290 https://www.payscale.com/college-salary-report/bachelors

291 https://www.usnews.com/best-colleges

292 https://www.forbes.com/sites/paologaudiano/2018/03/19/recruiting-talent-from-top-schools-is-a-terrible-idea/?sh=2a19a1ed271c

293 https://www.emolument.com/career_advice/uk_university_salary_2017#gsc.tab=0

294 https://www.gov.uk/government/news/graduates-continue-to-benefit-with-higher-earnings

295 https://www.forbes.com/sites/paologaudiano/2018/03/19/recruiting-talent-from-top-schools-is-a-terrible-idea/?sh=2a19a1ed271c

296 https://hbr.org/2020/09/graduates-of-elite-universities-get-paid-more-do-they-perform-better

297 https://www.businessinsider.com/apple-google-hire-jobs-without-degree-experts-say-college-important-2020-10

298 https://www.cnbc.com/2018/08/16/15-companies-that-no-longer-require-employees-to-have-a-college-degree.html

299 https://hbr.org/2020/09/graduates-of-elite-universities-get-paid-more-do-they-perform-better

300 Mansharamani, V. (2020). Think for yourself: Restoring common sense in an age of experts and artificial intelligence.

301 https://www.cnbc.com/2020/06/15/harvard-yale-researcher-fu-

ture-success-is-not-a-specific-skill-its-a-type-of-thinking.html

302 https://www.london.edu/think/so-hire-me-how-diverse-experiences-increase-professional-value

303 Banerjee, Sourindra & Prabhu, Jaideep & Chandy, Rajesh. (2015). Indirect Learning: How Emerging-Market Firms Grow in Developed Markets. *Journal of Marketing*. 79. 10-28. 10.1509/jm.12.0328.

304 https://www.pwc.com/gx/en/ceo-survey/2015/assets/pwc-18th-annual-global-ceo-survey-jan-2015.pdf

305 https://www.london.edu/think/so-hire-me-how-diverse-experiences-increase-professional-value

306 https://www.forbes.com/sites/forbestechcouncil/2018/06/15/hiring-in-tech-potential-over-experience/?sh=7af9d9974754; https://hbr.org/2014/06/21st-century-talent-spotting

307 https://www.prisonpolicy.org/reports/outofwork.html

308 https://www.gov.uk/government/publications/unlock-opportunity-employer-information-pack-and-case-studies/employing-prisoners-and-ex-offenders

309 https://www.cnbc.com/2018/09/18/why-companies-are-turning-to-ex-cons-to-fill-slots-for-workers.html

310 https://www.gov.uk/government/publications/unlock-opportunity-employer-information-pack-and-case-studies/employing-prisoners-and-ex-offenders

311 https://www.ft.com/content/7c41944e-7e3d-11e8-bc55-50daf11b720d

312 https://www.greyston.org/the-case-for-open-hiring

313 https://www.greyston.org/the-case-for-open-hiring

314 https://www.businessinsider.com.au/benefits-of-hiring-ex-convicts-for-small-business-owners-2012-1

315 https://www.businessinsider.com.au/benefits-of-hiring-ex-convicts-for-small-business-owners-2012-1

316 https://www.gov.uk/government/publications/unlock-opportuni-

ty-employer-information-pack-and-case-studies/employing-prisoners-and-ex-offenders

317 https://www.discovermagazine.com/the-sciences/how-identical-twins-develop-different-personalities

318 Kristof-Brown, A. L., Zimmerman, R. D., & Johnson, E. C. (2005). Consequences of individual's fit at work: A meta-analysis of person-job, person-organization, person-group, and person-supervisor fit. *Personnel Psychology*, *58*(2), 281–342.

319 https://ise.org.uk/default.aspx

320 https://www.psychologicalscience.org/news/are-workplace-personality-tests-fair.html

321 https://www.newyorker.com/magazine/2018/09/10/what-personality-tests-really-deliver

322 https://www.wsj.com/articles/are-workplace-personality-tests-fair-1412044257

323 https://www.truity.com/sites/default/files/PersonalityType-Career-AchievementStudy.pdf

324 https://www.ted.com/talks/susan_cain_the_power_of_introverts?language=en#t-172027

325 https://www.workdesign.com/2019/12/designing-for-neurodiversity-and-inclusion/

326 https://autisticuk.org/neurodiversity/

327 https://dyslexiaida.org/

328 Sprenger-Charolles., L., L., S. and Siegel., B. (2016) Prevalence and Reliability of Phonological, Surface, and Mixed Profiles in Dyslexia: A Review of Studies Conducted in Languages Varying in Orthographic Depth, *Scientific Studies of Reading, 15*(6): 498-521.

329 https://www.who.int/news-room/fact-sheets/detail/autism-spectrum-disorders

330 https://www.cdc.gov/media/releases/2014/p0327-autism-spectrum-disorder.html

331 https://archive.acas.org.uk/neurodiversity

332 https://www.bbc.com/worklife/article/20190719-neurodiversity

333 https://hbr.org/2017/05/neurodiversity-as-a-competitive-advantage

334 https://go.manpowergroup.com/talent-shortage-2018

335 www.sap.com/

336 https://stackrecruitment.org/2020/05/12/7-benefits-of-employing-autistic-individuals/

337 https://hbr.org/2017/05/neurodiversity-as-a-competitive-advantage

338 https://stackrecruitment.org/2020/05/12/7-benefits-of-employing-autistic-individuals/

339 https://www.forbes.com/sites/cognitiveworld/2019/12/27/neurodiversity-in-artificial-intelligence/?sh=46bd38c5470f

340 https://hbr.org/2017/05/neurodiversity-as-a-competitive-advantage

341 https://www.thetimes.co.uk/article/secret-of-the-super-successful-theyre-dyslexic-dhjsfhztm2d

342 https://dk.specialisterne.com/

343 https://www.forbes.com/sites/cognitiveworld/2019/12/27/neurodiversity-in-artificial-intelligence/?sh=46bd38c5470f

344 Schein, E. H. (2004). *Organizational culture and leadership*. San Francisco: Jossey-Bass.

345 https://today.appstate.edu/2016/04/13/jablonski

346 https://lup.lub.lu.se/luur/download?func=downloadFile&recordOId=8949314&fileOId=8949318

347 https://thepractice.law.harvard.edu/article/the-model-minority-myth/

348 https://www.pewresearch.org/fact-tank/2020/05/07/asian-americans-are-the-fastest-growing-racial-or-ethnic-group-in-the-u-s-electorate/

349 https://www.pewsocialtrends.org/2018/07/12/income-inequality-in-the-u-s-is-rising-most-rapidly-among-asians/

350 https://nymag.com/intelligencer/2017/04/why-do-democrats-feel-sorry-for-hillary-clinton.html

351 European network against racism (ENAR) Report "Racism & Discrimination in Employment in Europe 2013-2017"

352 https://www.mckinsey.com/business-functions/organization/our-insights/why-diversity-matters

353 Sundiatu Dixon-Fyle, Kevin Dolan, Vivian Hunt, and Sara Prince, Diversity Wins: How Inclusion Matters (McKinsey & Company, May 19, 2020).

354 Paul Gompers and Silpa Kovvali, The Other Diversity Dividend, *Harvard Business Review*, July/August 2018.

355 https://www.bls.gov/opub/reports/race-and-ethnicity/2018/home.htm

356 https://www.ethnicity-facts-figures.service.gov.uk/uk-population-by-ethnicity/demographics/working-age-population/latest

357 European network against racism (ENAR) Report "Racism & Discrimination in Employment in Europe 2013-2017"

358 European network against racism (ENAR) Report "Racism & Discrimination in Employment in Europe 2013-2017"

359 https://www.nytimes.com/interactive/2018/03/19/upshot/race-class-white-and-black-men.html

360 National Centre for Education Statistics: https://nces.ed.gov/

361 https://www.ethnicity-facts-figures.service.gov.uk/

362 https://www.thegraidenetwork.com/blog-all/2018/8/1/teacher-bias-the-elephant-in-the-classroom

363 https://www.thegraidenetwork.com/blog-all/2018/8/1/teacher-bias-the-elephant-in-the-classroom

364 Bonefeld, M., & Dickhäuser, O. (2018). (Biased) Grading of Students' performance: Students' names, performance level, and implicit attitudes. *Frontiers in Psychology*, 9(MAY).

365 Seth Gershenson, Cassandra Hart, Constance Lindsay, and Nicholas Papageorge, "The Long-Run Impacts of Same-Race Teachers",

IZA discussion paper 10630, 2017.

366 https://sites.nationalacademies.org/cs/groups/pgasite/documents/webpage/pga_178246.pdf

367 https://www.raeng.org.uk/diversity-in-engineering/diversity-and-inclusion-at-the-academy/celebrating-leading-ethnic-minorities-in-engineer

368 https://royalsociety.org/

369 Gaddis, S.M.. (2017). How Black Are Lakisha and Jamal? Racial Perceptions from Names Used in Correspondence Audit Studies. *Sociological Science. 4.* 469-489. 10.15195/v4.a19.

370 Bertrand, M. & Sendhil M. "Are Emily And Greg More Employable Than Lakisha And Jamal? A Field Experiment On Labor Market Discrimination," *American Economic Review*, 2004, v94(4,Sep), 991-1013.

371 https://politiken.dk/debat/art5731006/Danske-arbejdsgivere-v%C3%A6lger-%E2%80%99Mads%E2%80%99-frem-for-%E2%80%99Muhammed%E2%80%99

372 European network against racism (ENAR) Report "Racism & Discrimination in Employment in Europe 2013-2017"

373 Kang, Sonia & Decelles, Katy & Tilcsik, András & Jun, Sora. (2016). Whitened Resumes: Race and Self-Presentation in the Labor Market. *Administrative Science Quarterly.* 61. 10.1177/0001839216639577.

374 https://www.eeoc.gov/

375 https://www.gsb.stanford.edu/sites/gsb/files/fortune-100-c-suite-organizational-charts-feb-2020.pdf

376 https://thecolourofpower.com/

377 Wilson, J. P., Hugenberg, K., & Rule, N. O. (2017). Racial bias in judgments of physical size and formidability: From size to threat. *Journal of Personality and Social Psychology, 113*(1), 59–80

378 https://www.weforum.org/agenda/2020/08/cognitive-bias-unconscious-racism-moral-licensing/

379 https://perception.org/goodhair/results/

380 https://www.forbes.com/sites/pragyaagarwaleurope/2018/12/30/bias-is-your-accent-holding-you-back/?sh=1534c95c1b5a

381 http://www.bbc.co.uk/newsbeat/article/28225710/accentism-similar-to-racism-suggests-new-research

382 http://jimflege.com/files/Flege_French_accent_JASA_1984.pdf

383 https://hbr.org/2019/11/the-costs-of-codeswitching

384 https://www.pewresearch.org/politics/2019/06/19/the-personal-side-of-speech-and-expression/

385 https://hbr.org/2019/11/the-costs-of-codeswitching

386 https://trends.google.com/trends/explore?date=all&q=cultural%20 appropriation

387 https://www.insider.com/difference-between-cultural-appropriation-and-appreciation-2020-9

388 https://amp-theguardian-com.cdn.ampproject.org/c/s/amp.theguardian.com/food/2020/sep/20/asma-khan-restaurants-ranked-on-how-they-treat-people-chefs-table-netflix-darjeeling-express

389 https://www.businessinsider.com/kurl-on-indian-mattress-ad-uses-malala-cartoon-2014-5

390 https://time.com/101035/mattress-ad-malala-yousafzai/

391 https://www.reuters.com/article/us-usa-crime-face-idUSKBN1YN2V1; https://www.bbc.com/news/technology-52978191

392 Hofstede, Geert. "Motivation, Leadership, and Organization: Do American Theories Apply Abroad?" *Organizational Dynamics* 9.1 (1980b): 42–63

393 Hall, E. T. (1959). *The silent language*. Garden City, N.Y: Doubleday; Hall, E. T. (1966). *The hidden dimension*. Garden City, N.Y: Doubleday.

394 Meyer, E. (2014). *The culture map: breaking through the invisible boundaries of global business.* First edition. New York: PublicAffairs.

395 https://www.bbc.com/news/world-36139904

396 Pollock, D. C., & Van, R. R. E. (2009). *Third culture kids: Growing up among worlds.* Boston: Nicholas Brealey Publ.

397 https://www.pewsocialtrends.org/2019/01/17/generation-z-looks-a-lot-like-millennials-on-key-social-and-political-issues/

398 https://www.forbes.com/sites/daviddisalvo/2013/06/22/your-brain-sees-even-when-you-dont/#3eb381a8116a

399 https://www.eeoc.gov/wysk/what-you-should-know-about-eeoc-and-religious-and-national-origin-discrimination-involving

400 Acquisti, Alessandro & Fong, Christina. (2012). An Experiment in Hiring Discrimination Via Online Social Networks. *SSRN Electronic Journal.*

401 Ghumman, Sonia & Ryan, Ann. (2013). Not welcome here: Discrimination towards women who wear the Muslim headscarf. *Human Relations.* 66. 671-698.

402 https://www.eeoc.gov/newsroom/abercrombie-fitch-liable-religious-discrimination-eeoc-suit-court-says

403 https://www.nytimes.com/2018/08/16/world/europe/sweden-muslim-handshake.html

404 https://www.eeoc.gov/fact-sheet-recent-eeoc-religious-discrimination-litigation

405 https://www.bbc.com/future/article/20201023-food-allergies-why-nut-dairy-and-food-allergy-are-rising

406 https://plantbasednews.org/culture/-35-generation-z-want-meat-free-2021/

407 Fuegen K., Biernat M., Haines E., Deaux K. (2004). Mothers and fathers in the workplace: how gender and parental status influence judgments of job-related competence. *Journal of Social Issues*, 60, 737–7; Byron R. A., Roscigno V. J. (2014). Relational power, legitimation, and pregnancy discrimination. *Gender & Society*, 28, 435–462; Benard S., Correll S. J. (2010). Normative discrimination and the motherhood penalty. *Gender & Society*, 24, 616–646; Ridgeway C. L., Correll S. J. (2004). Motherhood as a status characteristic. *Journal of Social Issues*, 60, 683–700.

408 https://norden.diva-portal.org/smash/get/diva2:1367228/FULLTEXT01.pdf

409 M José González, Clara Cortina, Jorge Rodríguez, The Role of Gender Stereotypes in Hiring: A Field Experiment, *European Sociological Review*, Volume 35, Issue 2, April 2019, Pages 187–204,

410 Barker, M.-J. (2020). *Gender: a Graphic Guide.* Icon Books, Limited.

411 https://eige.europa.eu/publications/gender-equality-index-2019-sweden

412 https://www.statista.com/chart/15880/housework-europe-gender-split/

413 https://www.statista.com/chart/15880/housework-europe-gender-split/

414 https://www.statista.com/chart/15880/housework-europe-gender-split/

415 https://www.oecd.org/els/emp/last-mile-longest-gender-nordic-countries-brief.pdf

416 https://www.lego.com/da-dk/aboutus/careers/stories/a-family-friendly-workplace-for-all?_lrsc=4a3aa61e-9a22-4f1c-a13b-36b3f-7cc88cb

417 https://nikk.no/wp-content/uploads/2019/11/2016-why-dads-take-parental-leave.pdf

418 https://www.oecd.org/els/emp/last-mile-longest-gender-nordic-countries-brief.pdf

419 https://www.med.wisc.edu/news-and-events/2012/june/social-class-discrimination-poorer-health/

420 Wilkerson, I. (2020). *Caste: The origins of our discontents.*

421 https://www.latimes.com/business/story/2020-07-02/california-sues-cisco-bias-indian-caste-system

422 Gorard, Stephen & See, Beng. (2009). The impact of socio-economic status on participation and attainment in science. *Studies in Science Education.* 45 (10).

423 https://employers.debut.careers/report-the-state-of-social-immobility-in-graduate-recruitment/

424 https://www.hrmagazine.co.uk/content/news/state-of-the-nation-report-employers-must-do-more-on-social-mobility

425 https://www.hrmagazine.co.uk/content/news/businesses-must-do-more-on-social-mobility

426 https://www2.deloitte.com/uk/en/pages/about-deloitte-uk/articles/social-mobility.html

427 https://www.pwc.co.uk/who-we-are/our-purpose/empowered-people-communities/social-mobility.html

428 http://news.freshfields.com/en/Global/r/6025/freshfields_launches_new_social_mobility_outreach

CPSIA information can be obtained
at www.ICGtesting.com
Printed in the USA
LVHW111040190521
687865LV00012B/122/J

9 788797 290309